ton
rt

OHIO
SCIENCE
Fusion

fusion [FYOO • zhuhn] a combination of two
or more things that releases energy

This Write-In Student Edition belongs to

Mohammed Bnfaja

Teacher/Room

Consulting Authors

Michael A. DiSpezio
Global Educator
North Falmouth, Massachusetts

Marjorie Frank
*Science Writer and Content-Area Reading
  Specialist*
Brooklyn, New York

Michael Heithaus
*Executive Director, School of Environment, Arts,
  and Society*
*Associate Professor, Department of Biological
  Sciences*
Florida International University
North Miami, Florida

Donna Ogle
Professor of Reading and Language
National-Louis University
Chicago, Illinois

Front Cover: *crab* ©Mark Webb/Alamy; *geyser* ©Frans Lanting/Corbis; *frog* ©DLILLC/Corbis; *flask* ©Gregor Schuster/Getty Images; *rowers* ©Stockbyte/Getty Images.

Back Cover: *gecko* ©Pete Orelup/Getty Images; *bike* ©Jerome Prevost/TempSport/Corbis; *computer* ©Michael Melford/Getty Images; *landscape* ©Rod McLean/Alamy.

Printed in the U.S.A.

ISBN 978-0-544-31784-0

15 0928 19

4500785583   ABCDEFG

Program Advisors

Paul D. Asimow
Professor of Geology and Geochemistry
California Institute of Technology
Pasadena, California

Bobby Jeanpierre
Associate Professor of Science
Education
University of Central Florida
Orlando, Florida

Gerald H. Krockover
Professor Emeritus of Earth,
Atmospheric, and Planetary Science
Education
Purdue University
West Lafayette, Indiana

Rose Pringle
Associate Professor
School of Teaching and Learning
College of Education
University of Florida
Gainesville, Florida

Carolyn Staudt
Curriculum Designer for Technology
KidSolve, Inc.
The Concord Consortium
Concord, Massachusetts

Larry Stookey
Science Department
Antigo High School
Antigo, Wisconsin

Carol J. Valenta
Associate Director of the Museum and
Senior Vice President
Saint Louis Science Center
St. Louis, Missouri

Barry A. Van Deman
President and CEO
Museum of Life and Science
Durham, North Carolina

Ohio Reviewers

Brian Geniusz, MEd.
Science Curriculum Leader
Worthington Schools
Worthington, Ohio

Richard J. Johnson Jr., MEd.
Science Department Chair
Eastlake Middle School
Eastlake, Ohio

Robert Mendenhall
Curriculum Director
Toledo Public Schools
Toledo, Ohio

iii

Power Up with Ohio Science Fusion!

Grade 5

Your program fuses . . .

e-Learning & Virtual Labs

Labs & Explorations

Write-In Student Edition

. . . to generate new energy for today's science learner— you.

Write-In Student Edition

Be an active reader and make this book your own!

Adaptati...

Living things have many similaritie...
have many interesting differences.

Active Reading As you read this page, underline the definition of *adaptation*.

eserts are home to many kinds of snakes. This is because snakes have characteristics that help them survive in a ... For example, snakes have tough, scaly skin that keeps ...rom drying out.

...acteristic that helps a living thin... ...re is called an **adaptation.** Suppos... ...imal is born with a new character... ...s characte... helps the an... ...is likely to repro... ...vive, the a... characteristic to it... ...d pass o... animal's habitat does... ...As lon... ...e this characteristic a... ...ge, it... duce. Over time, the a... ...lik... ...in the population. In... ...ions of ...al animals become adap... ...eir habitats.

These hares live in ve... ...ferent habitats. Because of th... ...have different adaptatio...

Write your ideas, answer questions, make notes, and record activity results right on these pages.

...tic hare lives in a cold
ha... .... It has thick fur to keep
it w... ...and small ears that
prev... ...eat from being lost.

A jackrabbit lives i...
habitat. Jacl...
larg...

Learn science concepts and skills by interacting with every page.

e-Learning & Virtual Labs

Digital lessons and virtual labs provide e-learning options for every lesson of *ScienceFusion*.

Do it!

Load (kg)

0.1   0.2

Set the truck's mass.

Set the truck's mass.

7 of 13

What Objects are Part of the Solar System?

Saturn is most famous for its rings.

Jupiter   Uranus and Neptune

Saturn

Saturn has a gaseous surface with an icy, rocky core.

4 of 10

On your own or with a group, explore science concepts in a digital world.

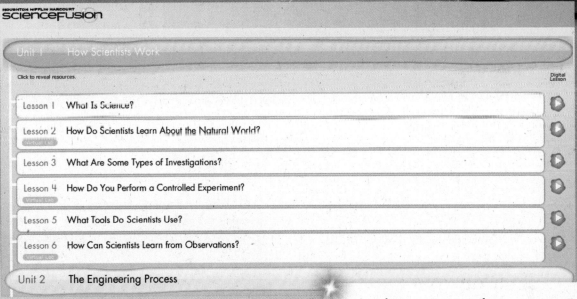

HOUGHTON MIFFLIN HARCOURT
sciencefusion

Unit 1	How Scientists Work

Click to reveal resources.

Digital Lesson

Lesson 1	What Is Science?
Lesson 2 Virtual Lab	How Do Scientists Learn About the Natural World?
Lesson 3	What Are Some Types of Investigations?
Lesson 4 Virtual Lab	How Do You Perform a Controlled Experiment?
Lesson 5	What Tools Do Scientists Use?
Lesson 6 Virtual Lab	How Can Scientists Learn from Observations?
Unit 2	The Engineering Process

Investigate every science concept with multiple virtual labs in every unit.

Continue your science explorations with these online tools:

→ ScienceSaurus   → People in Science

→ NSTA SciLinks   → Media Gallery

→ Video-based Projects → Vocabulary Cards

→ **Science and Engineering Leveled Readers with complete AUDIO!**

What Do Scientists Do?

What Do Scientists Do?

Into the Ocean Depths

Labs & Explorations

Science is all about doing.

Ask questions and test your ideas.

Draw conclusions and share what you learn.

What Makes Up a Land Ecosystem?

If you were asked to list the living things around you, what would you list? You would probably list shrubs and trees, cats and dogs, birds, and maybe garden snakes. But what about those things living beneath your feet? Would you also list them?

Materials
meterstick
4 stakes
string
gloves
magnifying glass or box
collecting jars
field guides

Go out into the schoolyard, a nearby park, or a nature preserve. Select a study site where there is a variety of plants and soil coverings.

In your study site, measure a 1 meter by 1 meter square area. Use the stakes and string to mark this sample area.

Count and identify the producers and consumers you observe within your sample area. Record your observations.

Caution! Make su to wear gloves wh doing this step. Carefully turn over rocks, leaves, or tw your sample area.

Use the collecting ja a magnifying glass o box, and field guides observe, identify, and classify any organism that you may find.

Exciting investigations for every lesson.

The Design Process (Part 1)

Technology is all over—video games, 3D TVs, microwaves. But technology doesn't just happen. It comes about through a step-by-step process.

Active Reading As you read these pages, bracket sentences that describe a problem. Write *P* in the margin. Underline sentences that describe a solution. Write *S* by them.

When engineers design new technologies, they follow a *design process*. The process includes several steps. Here's how the process starts.

1. Find a Problem Engineers must first identify a need, or a problem to be solved. They brainstorm possible solutions. There may be more than one good solution.

2. Plan and Build Engineers choose the solution they think is most practical.

They build a working model, or **prototype**, to test.

Throughout the design process, engineers keep careful records. Good records include detailed notes and drawings. Records help them remember what they have done and provide information to others working on similar problems. If the prototype doesn't work, the records can provide clues to a solution that *might* work next time.

Engineers make detailed drawings for their prototypes, as well as notes about the materials they plan to use. The notes and drawings are a record that they can study as they build and make changes to the prototype.

Engineers use their notes and drawings to build the first prototype. This prototype is a skate that is designed to work on rough surfaces.

Problem Solved!

The first step in the design process is identifying a problem and thinking up solutions.

The design process begins

70

...t can spark new and improved designs of

...ur favorite sport or activity. Draw each
...t material makes up each piece. Label the
...perties made it a good design choice.

List three features of this bicycle helmet. Draw arrows to the feature(s) that are for safety. Circle the feature(s) that are for comfort.

...challenge—complete **Design It: Balloon Racer** in

71

OHIO **5.SIA.4** Analyze and interpret data. **5.SIA.6** Think critically and logically to connect evidence and explanations.

S.T.E.M.
Engineering & Technology

Football Safety Gear

Football is a rough sport. In order to protect players from injury, designers have developed protective gear.

The first helmets were custom made out of leather by horse harness makers. Later, ear holes and padding were added. These helmets had little padding and no face guards.

Hard plastic shells, fitted foam linings, and metal facemasks now make helmets more protective. Some helmets even contain sensors that transmit signals to warn if a player's head has been hit hard enough to cause a serious injury.

Critical Thinking

How do modern materials make it possible to build a better helmet than one made of just leather?

271

By asking questions, testing your ideas, organizing and analyzing data, drawing conclusions, and sharing what you learn...

You are the scientist!

Contents

Levels of Inquiry Key ■ DIRECTED ■ GUIDED ■ INDEPENDENT

EARTH SCIENCE

LIFE SCIENCE

PHYSICAL SCIENCE

Safety in Science

Indoors Doing science is a lot of fun. But, a science lab can be a dangerous place. Falls, cuts, and burns can happen easily. When you are doing a science investigation, you need to be safe. Know the safety rules and listen to your teacher.

Adult scientists have to follow lab safety rules, too.

Pay attention to these safety rules.

1 **Think ahead.** Study the investigation steps so you know what to expect. If you have any questions, ask your teacher. Be sure you understand all caution statements and safety reminders.

2 **Be neat and clean.** Keep your work area clean. If you have long hair, pull it back so it doesn't get in the way. Roll or push up long sleeves to keep them away from your activity.

3 **Oops!** If you spill or break something, or get cut, tell your teacher right away.

4 **Watch your eyes.** Wear safety goggles anytime you are directed to do so. If you get anything in your eyes, tell your teacher right away.

5 **Yuck!** Never eat or drink anything during a science activity.

6 **Don't get shocked.** Be careful if an electric appliance is used. Be sure that electric cords are in a safe place where you can't trip over them. Never use the cord to pull a plug from an outlet.

7 **Keep it clean.** Always clean up when you have finished. Put everything away and wipe your work area. Wash your hands.

8 **Play it safe.** Always know where to find safety equipment, such as fire extinguishers. Know how to use the safety equipment around you.

Outdoors

Lots of science research happens outdoors. It's fun to explore the wild! But, you need to be careful. The weather, the land, and the living things can surprise you.

This scientist has to protect his eyes.

Follow these safety rules when you're doing science outdoors.

1 **Think ahead.** Study the investigation steps so you know what to expect. If you have any questions, ask your teacher. Be sure you understand all caution statements and safety reminders.

2 **Dress right.** Wear appropriate clothes and shoes for the outdoors. Cover up and wear sunscreen and sunglasses for sun safety.

3 **Clean up the area.** Follow your teacher's instructions for when and how to throw away waste.

4 **Oops!** Tell your teacher right away if you break something or get hurt.

5 **Watch your eyes.** Wear safety goggles when directed to do so. If you get anything in your eyes, tell your teacher right away.

6 **Yuck!** Never taste anything outdoors.

7 **Stay with your group.** Work in the area as directed by your teacher. Stay on marked trails.

8 **"Wilderness" doesn't mean go wild.** Never engage in horseplay, games, or pranks.

9 **Always walk.** No running!

10 **Play it safe.** Know where safety equipment can be found and how to use it. Know how to get help.

11 **Clean up.** Wash your hands with soap and water when you come back indoors.

© Houghton Mifflin Harcourt Publishing Company (t) ©Carsten Peter/National Geographic Image Collection/Alamy Images; (border) ©PhotoObjects.net/Jupiterimages/Getty Images

UNIT 1
How Scientists Work

Big Idea

Scientists answer questions by careful observations and investigations.

OHIO 5.SIA.1, 5.SIA.2, 5.SIA.3, 5.SIA.4, 5.SIA.5, 5.SIA.6, 5.SIA.7, 5.SIA.8

I Wonder Why

Why do some scientists work outdoors and others work inside a laboratory? Turn the page to find out.

Here's Why Scientists work to answer questions. Some questions can be answered with outdoor investigations. Other questions require tools in a lab.

In this unit, you will explore the Big Idea, the Essential Questions, and the Investigations on the Inquiry Flipchart.

Levels of Inquiry Key ■ DIRECTED ■ GUIDED ■ INDEPENDENT

Big Idea Scientists answer questions by careful observations and investigations.

Essential Questions

Now I Get the Big Idea!

Science Notebook

Before you begin each lesson, be sure to write your thoughts about the Essential Question.

OHIO 5.SIA.1 Identify questions that can be answered through scientific investigations. 5.SIA.2 Design and conduct a scientific investigation. 5.SIA.5 Develop descriptions, models, explanations and predictions. 5.SIA.6 Think critically and logically to connect evidence and explanations. 5.SIA.8 Communicate scientific procedures and explanations.

Lesson 1

Essential Question

What Is Science?

Engage Your Brain!

Find one answer to the following question in this lesson and write it here.

What are some science skills you could use when studying fish in an aquarium?

_____

_____

_____

Active Reading

Lesson Vocabulary

List the terms. As you learn about each one, make notes in the Interactive Glossary.

_____

_____

_____

Use Headings

Active readers preview headings and use them to pose questions that set purposes for reading. Reading with a purpose helps active readers focus on understanding what they read in order to fulfill the purpose.

What All Scientists Do

Digging up fossils. Peering through telescopes. Mixing chemicals in a lab. Using computers to make weather predictions. These are only a few of the things scientists do.

Does solving puzzles and searching for buried treasures sound like fun? If so, you might like being a paleontologist. Paleontologists are scientists who study the history of life on Earth. Like all scientists, they try to explain how and why things in the natural world happen. They answer questions by doing investigations. An **investigation** is a procedure carried out to carefully observe, study, or test something in order to learn more about it.

In addition to knowing a lot about living things of the past, paleontologists have to use many skills. In fact, all scientists use these skills. All scientists **observe**, or use their five senses to collect information. And all scientists **compare**, finding ways objects and events are similar and different.

Observe

Write one observation you could make about the fossil.

_____

_____

Paleontologists use fossils to answer questions such as, "What was Earth's environment like in the past?"

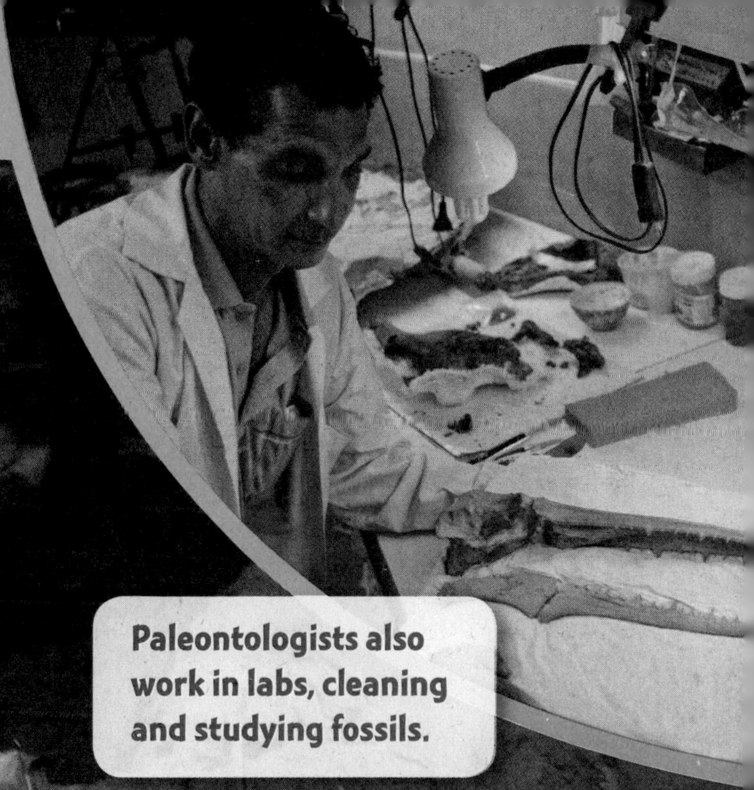

Paleontologists also work in labs, cleaning and studying fossils.

This paleontologist needs to observe the landscape to predict where fossils might be hidden. Once he finds the fossils, he compares them to fossils found in other parts of the world.

Paleontology is just one branch of science. **Science** is the study of the natural world and involves using critical thinking. Scientists use critical thinking when they *evaluate*, or judge, explanations and evidence. They also think critically when they *analyze*, or break down, information.

▶ Observe and compare these two skulls. List two ways they are similar and two ways they are different.

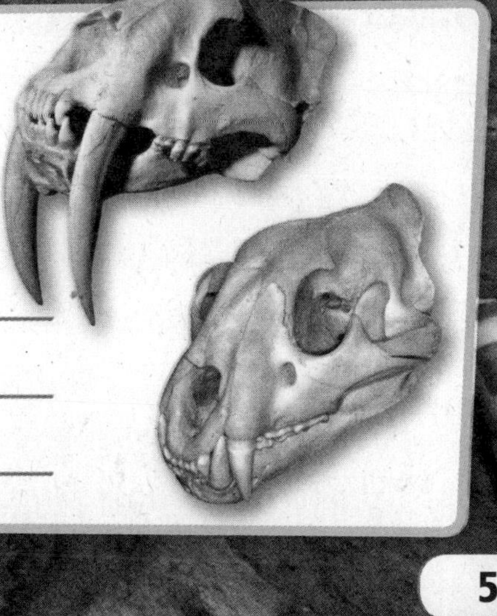

Similarities	Differences
______________________	______________________
______________________	______________________
______________________	______________________

Prove It!

In the 1600s, keeping meat fresh wasn't easy. Meat quickly spoiled and filled with worm-like maggots. Where did they come from?

Active Reading On these pages, circle examples of evidence.

Rotten Meat turns into Maggots!

▶ Draw a large *X* through the explanation that was shown *not* to be true.

Information collected during a scientific investigation is called **evidence**. Evidence helps support conclusions, such as dinosaurs lived on Earth. Some evidence is direct, such as seeing a fossil dinosaur skull. Direct evidence is also called *empirical evidence*. Another kind of evidence is indirect, or inferred evidence, such as finding a dinosaur's fossil footprint.

Travel back in time to the 1660s. Most scientists explain that flies and maggots come from rotting food. As evidence they show how a dead animal's body soon becomes loaded with maggots.

But Dr. Francesco Redi, an Italian scientist, is not convinced. Redi examines all sides of the scientific evidence supporting the current explanation to develop his *critique,* or review of the facts. He then proposes an alternative explanation: Living things must come from other living things. He **plans and conducts investigations** to gather evidence. Redi traps maggots inside jars with pieces of meat. He watches the

The meat in the open jar soon became "wormy," while the meat in the sealed jar did not.

Redi placed fresh meat in two jars. He covered one jar and left the other jar uncovered.

maggots turn into adult flies. He observes adult flies laying eggs and more maggots coming out of these eggs.

Redi then sets up an experiment. He places meat in several jars. Some jars are sealed, others are not. Redi observes that only the meat in jars he left open have maggots.

Redi repeats his experiments many times. He tries dead fish, frogs, and snakes. All the evidence supports his idea: Living insects can only come from other living insects.

▶ Fill in the blanks in this sequence graphic organizer.

| Use critical thinking to develop _____. |
| ↓ |
| Plan and conduct _____. |
| ↓ |
| Use _____ to explain observations. |

Maggots Hatch from eggs that flies lay.

A Sticky Trap

Humans are too big to get stuck in a spider's web. But there are some sticky traps you need to avoid when thinking like a scientist.

Active Reading As you read these two pages, turn the main heading into a question in your mind. Then underline sentences that answer the question.

▶ Look at the words in the spider web below. Star the things you *should* use to draw conclusions properly. Cross out the others.

How to Draw Conclusions

Scientists **draw conclusions** from the results of their investigations. Any conclusion must be backed up with evidence. Other scientists evaluate the conclusion based on how much evidence is given. They also evaluate how well the evidence supports the conclusion.

Don't jump to conclusions too quickly. That's a sticky trap in science! As Dr. Redi did, repeat your investigations. Think about what you can **infer** from your observations. And then—only then—draw your conclusions.

Suppose you spend a week observing spiders. You might conclude that all spiders build webs to catch their food. This may be true of the spiders you observed, but it's not true of all spiders. Some spiders, such as wolf spiders, hunt for their prey instead.

Opinions

Favorites

Observations

Logical reasoning

Inferences

Evidence

Feelings

© Houghton Mifflin Harcourt Publishing Company (bkg) ©Hu Zhao/Alamy

Observation Information collected by using the senses	The insect is stuck in the spider web.
Inference An idea or a conclusion based on an observation	A spider is going to use the bug for food later.
Opinion A personal belief that does not need proof	Spiders are really gross!

Logical Reasoning

Personal feelings and opinions should not affect how you do investigations. Nor should they affect your conclusions. An **opinion** is a belief or judgment. It doesn't have to be backed up with evidence.

Doing science is about using *logical* *reasoning* to evaluate evidence and to draw conclusions. When you reason logically, you use things that you know to be true or false to draw conclusions. For example, knowing that some spiders are venomous justifies concluding that people should be careful when handling spiders.

► Write one observation, one inference, and one opinion about what you see in the photo.

Observation	
Inference	
Opinion	

Knowledge Grows

How is a man investigating electricity and wires more than 350 years ago connected to the latest video game release?

Stephen Gray, a scientist born in 1666, was working at home when he discovered that electrical energy could move along a short metal wire. Gray carried his materials to friends' homes. He showed them how the materials worked and, together, they made the wire longer and longer.

Today there are so many ways for scientists to **communicate**, or share, the results of investigations. When scientists communicate clearly, others can repeat their investigations. They can compare their results with those of others. They can expand on one another's ideas. In these ways, scientific knowledge grows.

energy by living organisms

DATA

Communicate

List several ways you can communicate.

_____

_____

_____

_____

1729 Stephen Gray shows that electrical energy can be carried through a wire.

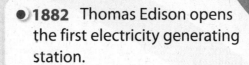

1882 Thomas Edison opens the first electricity generating station.

Knowledge grows when it is communicated. Each science discovery leads to new questions. More is learned and new things are invented.

The first video game was invented in 1958. The inventor was a scientist named William Higinbotham. The reason? To make Visitor's Day at his lab more interesting for the public! Hundreds of people lined up to play the game.

Take a look at the timeline. The science behind Higinbotham's game goes back hundreds of years or more.

1947 The transistor, needed to make radios and computers, is invented.

1953 The first computer is sold.

1958 William Higinbotham invents the first video game.

1967 First handheld calculator invented.

1971 First coin-operated arcade video games in use.

The first arcade games were not very complex.

1972 The first home video game systems are sold.

1977 The first handheld video games are sold.

2009 Scientists use super-fast video game cards inside computers to investigate the structure of molecules.

The video games of today are fast, complex, and interactive.

Meet Scientists

There are more people working as scientists today than ever before in history. Yet, there are plenty of unanswered questions left for you to answer!

Active Reading As you read these two pages, underline what each type of scientist studies.

Astronomer

Astronomers ask questions about how the universe works. Because novas, black holes, and galaxies are so far away, they use time/space relationships to investigate them. For example, astronomers measure space distances in units called light-years. That's how far light can travel in one Earth year.

Do the Math!
Use Fractions

Earth and Mars travel around the sun. Each time Earth makes one complete trip, Mars makes about $\frac{1}{2}$ of its trip.

1. How many trips does Earth make around the sun in the time it takes Mars to make one trip?

_____

2. In the drawing below, put an *X* where Mars will be after Earth completes five trips around the sun.

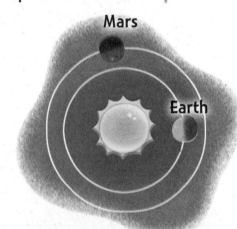

Mars

Earth

You don't have to be a pro to do astronomy. People have discovered many comets and exploding stars using telescopes in their back yards!

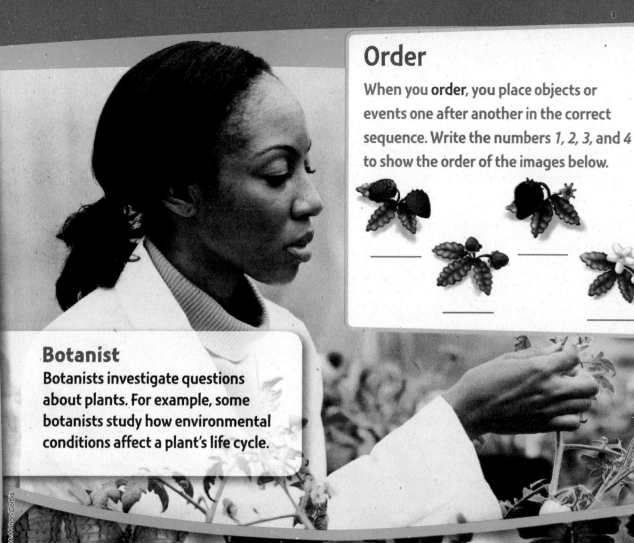

Order

When you **order**, you place objects or events one after another in the correct sequence. Write the numbers *1, 2, 3,* and *4* to show the order of the images below.

_____   _____

_____   _____

Botanist

Botanists investigate questions about plants. For example, some botanists study how environmental conditions affect a plant's life cycle.

Taxonomist

Taxonomists are scientists who identify types of living things and classify them by how they are related. When you classify, you organize objects or events into categories based on specific characteristics.

Classify

Look at the butterflies on this page. What are some ways you could classify them?

_____

_____

_____

Lexias dimalis
Asia

Yon

Agria

rynia smalfildia
Asia

Agri

ona

Prepona dexamenes
America

Doxopoca agathina
America

Marpesia petrous
America

us

Africa

pona emophon
America

Sum It Up!

When you're done, use the answer key to check and revise your work.

Read the summary, and fill in the missing words.

The goal of a scientist is to understand the natural world. To do this, a scientist plans and conducts 1. _____ .

Scientists use the 2. _____ they gather to draw

3. _____ .

A good scientist does not let his or her personal beliefs, or

4. _____, influence their study.

There are many important skills that scientists use. For example, when scientists use 5. _____ , they use things they know to be true and false to draw conclusions.

Read each of the statements below. Write the science skill that each student used.

6. Angela made a list of how the two planets were alike.

_____

7. Krystal sorted the rocks into five groups based on their color.

_____

8. Robbie explained the results of his investigation to his classmates.

_____

9. Dmitri noted how the feathers looked and felt.

_____

10. Juan organized the steps of the process from first to last.

_____

14

Answer Key: 1. investigations 2. evidence 3. conclusions 4. opinions 5. logical reasoning 6. compare 7. classify 8. communicate 9. observe 10. order

Name _____

Word Play

1 Complete the crossword puzzle. If you need help, use the terms in the yellow box.

Across

1. The study of the natural world through investigation
5. Collecting information by using the senses
6. An idea or a conclusion based on an observation
7. Facts and information collected over time
8. To put things into groups
9. A belief or a judgment

Down

2. The sharing of information
3. The observations and information that support a conclusion
4. The process of studying or testing something to learn more about it
5. To arrange things by when they happened or by their size

Apply Concepts

2 Compare these two birds. List how they look similar and different.

Similarities:

_____

_____

Differences:

_____

_____

3 Suppose someone tells you they saw a bird never before seen in your state. What kinds of evidence would you ask for?

_____

_____

_____

4 Many types of germs live in soil. How should this affect the way you conduct a soil sample investigation?

_____

_____

_____

5 One morning you see an outdoor garbage can tipped over. Plastic bags are torn open. What could you infer?

_____

_____

_____

Take It Home!

How can you communicate with people around the world, collect real data, and help answer a question? Research citizen science projects online. Choose an interesting project. Participate with your family.

Ask a Zoologist

Q. Do all zoologists work in a zoo?

A. Some, but not all, zoologists work in zoos. Zoologists are scientists who study animals. The word "zoo" comes from the Latin word for animal.

Q. Do zoologists get to play with animals?

A. No. Most zoologists study wild animals in their habitats. They try to observe animals without disturbing them.

Q. Do zoologists get to have wild animals as pets?

A. Wild animals do not make good pets. Zoologists do not take wild animals home. Pets such as cats and dogs have grown used to living with people. Wild animals have not.

wombat

Now It's Your Turn!

What question would you ask a zoologist?

_____

_____

_____

_____

Wombats live in Tasmania and southeastern Australia.

17

Animals That Start with "K"

Some zoologists study animal behavior, or how animals act. A zoologist spotted some interesting behaviors in Australia and wrote these journal entries. Match the sentences with the pictures by entering the day of the journal entry near the picture it describes.

Day 1 This afternoon we saw an adult koala carrying a young koala on its back.

Day 2 Today our team saw a kangaroo. It had a joey (a young kangaroo) in its pouch.

Day 3 Our team saw a kangaroo hopping quickly. We measured its speed—nearly 24 kilometers per hour!

Day 4 This morning we saw a koala. It was eating leaves from a eucalyptus tree.

Day 5 We saw two kangaroos boxing with each other.

Day _____

Day _____

Day _____

Day _____

Day _____

© Houghton Mifflin Harcourt Publishing Company   (bkgd) ©PhotoDisc; (tl) ©Will & Deni McIntyre/Photo Researchers, Inc.; (tc) ©Peter Skinner/Photo Researchers, Inc.; (tr) ©A. N. T./Photo Researchers, Inc; (bl) ©Theo Allofs/Corbis; (br) ©Wildlight Photo Agency/Alamy

Inquiry Flipchart page 4

OHIO **5.SIA.5** Develop descriptions, models, explanations and predictions. **5.SIA.6** Think critically and logically to connect evidence and explanations. **5.SIA.8** Communicate scientific procedures and explanations.

Name _____

Essential Question

How Do Scientists Learn About the Natural World?

Set a Purpose

What will you learn from this investigation?

_____

_____

_____

_____

_____

Think About the Procedure

How did you choose what predictions to write on your origami predictor?

_____

_____

_____

_____

Record Your Data

In the table below, record your results.

Date	Origami Prediction	Weather Service Prediction	Actual Weather

Draw Conclusions

Use logical reasoning. Of the two kinds of weather predictions, which one was more likely to be correct? Explain.

_____

_____

_____

_____

Analyze and Extend

1. Why was repeating this investigation over several days better than doing it for just one day?

_____

_____

_____

2. How do you think the weather service makes its predictions?

_____

_____

_____

3. Why is it important that scientists make good weather predictions?

_____

_____

_____

_____

4. The line graph shows average October air temperatures in Houston, TX. Can you predict the air temperature in Houston next October? If so, how?

_____

_____

_____

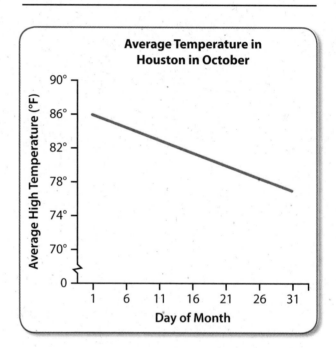

5. What else would you like to find out about how scientists make predictions? Write each idea as a question.

_____

_____

_____

_____

_____

_____

Directions

1. Carefully tear this page out of your book.

2. Cut out the square below. You will use it to make your origami weather predictor.

3. On each set of lines, write a weather prediction.

4. Follow the instructions on the back of this page to fold and use your origami weather predictor.

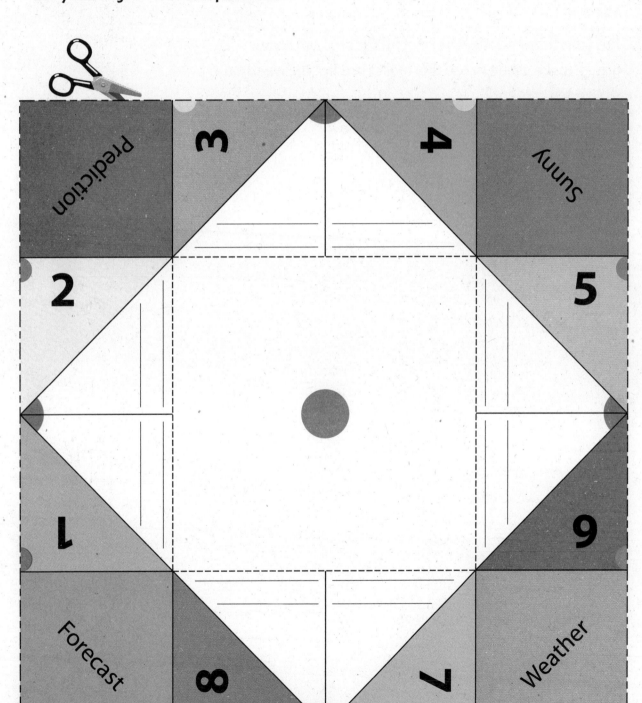

Directions (continued)

5. Fold the blue dots into the blue circle. Turn the paper over, and fold the green dots into the green circle.

6. Fold the paper in half so that the yellow dots touch each other. Make a crease, and unfold the paper. Fold it in half again so that the pink dots touch each other.

7. Put your fingers under the colorful squares. With your group, make a plan to use this tool to predict the weather.

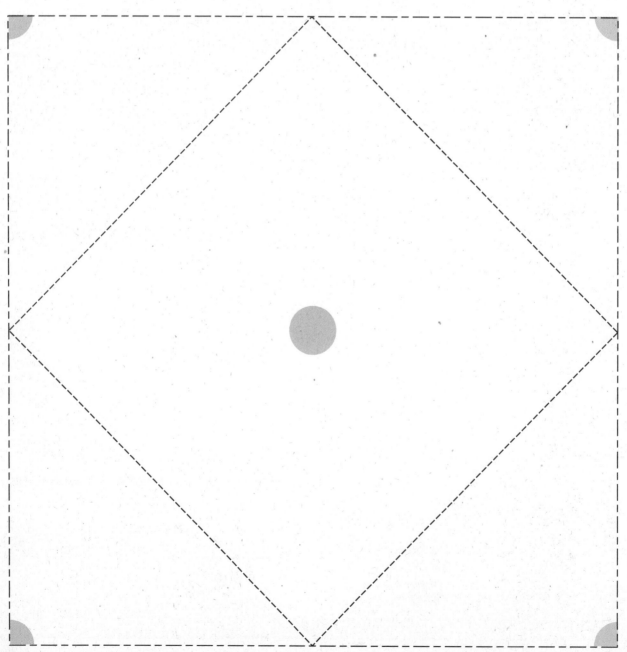

OHIO 5.SIA.1 Identify questions that can be answered through scientific investigations. 5.SIA.2 Design and conduct a scientific investigation. 5.SIA.3 Use appropriate mathematics, tools and techniques to gather data and information. 5.SIA.4 Analyze and interpret data. 5.SIA.5 Develop descriptions, models, explanations and predictions. 5.SIA.6 Think critically and logically to connect evidence and explanations.

Lesson **3**

Essential Question

What Are Some Types of Investigations?

Engage Your Brain!

Find one answer to the following question in this lesson and write it here.

What did this scientist do prior to starting her experiment with plants?

_____

_____

_____

_____

Active Reading

Lesson Vocabulary

List the terms. As you learn about each one, make notes in the Interactive Glossary.

_____

_____

_____

_____

Main Ideas

The main idea of a paragraph is the most important idea. The main idea may be stated in the first sentence, or it may be stated elsewhere. Active readers look for main ideas by asking themselves, What is this paragraph mostly about?

A Process for Science

Testing bridge models, mapping a storm's path, searching the sky for distant planets—each of these investigations uses scientific methods.

Active Reading As you read these two pages, draw a line under each main idea.

How does the shape of the room affect the sound of a voice? **?**

How does having a cold affect a person's singing **?**

Can a human voice shatter glass **?**

How high a note can a singer sing? **?**

Start with a Question

People often ask questions about things they notice. Scientists also ask questions about things they observe. But scientists ask well-defined questions, which are testable questions that can be answered by investigations. A scientific investigation always begins with a question.

Plan an Investigation

Once a scientist has a testable question, it is time to plan an investigation. **Scientific methods** are ways that scientists perform investigations. There are many ways that scientists investigate the world. But all scientific methods use logic and reasoning.

▶ Suppose you've just heard an opera singer warm up her voice. Write your own science question about the sounds a singer makes.

_____

_____

Experimental Testing

In an experiment, scientists control all the conditions of the investigation. They study what happens to a group of samples that differ in only one factor or condition.

Observational Testing

Scientists use observational testing to analyze, evaluate, and critique scientific explanations.

Using Models

Scientists use models when they cannot experiment on the real thing. Models help scientists investigate things that are large (like a planet), expensive (like a bridge), or uncontrollable (like the weather).

Investigations Differ

The method a scientist uses depends on the question he or she is investigating. An **experiment** is an investigation in which all of the conditions are controlled. Models are used to represent real objects or processes. Scientists conduct observational testing to study processes in nature that they can observe but can't control.

Drawing Conclusions

Whatever scientific methods are used, scientists will have results they can use to draw conclusions. The conclusions may answer the question they asked before they began. They may point to other questions and many more ideas for investigations.

▶ Write the type of investigation you should use to answer the following questions.

How do different bridge designs react to strong winds?

_____

How fast does the wind blow where a bridge will be built?

_____

Which type of paint works best to keep a bridge from rusting?

_____

Explosive
Observations

How does a hurricane affect animals? How do whales raise their young? Repeated observations can help answer questions such as these.

As you read these two pages, place a star next to three examples of repeated observation.

Some science questions can only be answered by making repeated observations. This is because some things are just too big, too far away, or too uncontrollable for experiments.

In Yellowstone National Park, for example, heated water shoots out of holes in the ground. This is called a geyser. Old Faithful is a famous geyser that erupts about every hour. Observations of the geyser collected over many years can be used to predict when the next eruption will occur. A prediction is a statement, based on information, about a future event.

Old Faithful

Analyze, Evaluate, and Critique

The time until Old Faithful's next eruption is affected by how long the previous eruption lasted. The data in the table are the result of observational testing. Do the data support the statement above? Explain.

_____

Length of Eruption (min)	1.5	2	2.5	3	3.5	4	4.5
Eruption Interval (min)	50	57	65	71	76	82	89

The first observation of a whale is often its spout.

Scientists have many questions about whales—the largest mammals on Earth. How long do whales live? How do they communicate? How do they care for their young? How far can they travel in a year? These questions can be answered with repeated observation.

For example, the tail flukes of whales are different from one whale to another. Scientists take photos of the flukes and use them to identify individual whales. Once they know which whale is which, they can recognize them each time they are seen in the ocean.

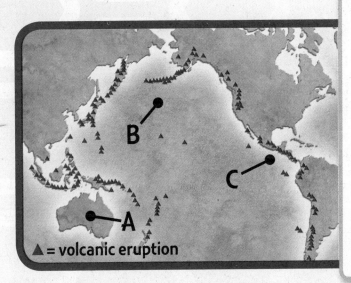

▲ = volcanic eruption

Predict

Scientists have observed and recorded volcanic eruptions for hundreds of years. The map to the left shows that data. Which location—A, B, or C— is most likely to have a volcanic eruption? _____
Why do you think scientists call this region the "Ring of Fire"?

_____

_____

Super Models

How does a bat fly? How might Saturn's rings look close up? How does a heart work? These are some science questions that can be answered with models.

Active Reading Circle different types of models that are described on these two pages.

Complex models can be made on a computer. This model shows where the most damage would occur if an earthquake were to strike.

When Modeling Is Needed

When scientists can't experiment with the real thing, they use models. Models are used to represent how something works or looks that can't be seen. They are also used to investigate things with many hidden parts, such as an ant colony. The closer a model represents the real thing, the more useful it is. Models are changed with new discoveries. Scientists draw conclusions and make predictions by studying their models.

Types of Models

Models are made in different ways. One way is to build a physical model. An earthquake shake table with model buildings on it is a physical model. Another way is to program computer simulation models. Scientists can speed up time in computer models so that they can see what might happen long in the future. Drawing diagrams and flow charts is a third way to make models. These two-dimensional models can be used to show how ideas are related.

Earthquakes are difficult to predict, and they can cause damage. New structures are designed to prevent damage.

28

Scientists build "shake tables" that model the motion of real earthquakes. This photo shows two types of houses being tested. Which house seems to be safer in an earthquake?

Use Models

How is this earthquake model made of gelatin like a real earthquake? How is it unlike a real earthquake?

Alike: _____

_____

Different: _____

_____

You can model the effects of an earthquake, using gelatin for the ground and buildings made of blocks.

How to Excel in Experimentation

You're enjoying a frozen juice pop. The heat of your tongue melts the pop. As you slurp the liquid, you think about how different substances freeze.

Active Reading As you read the next four pages, circle lesson vocabulary each time it is used.

I know that water freezes at 0 degrees Celsius. How does adding other substances to water affect the temperature at which it freezes?

Ask Questions

You know a freezer is cold enough to freeze water. You also know that juice is mostly water. You ask "Does adding substances to water affect its freezing point?"

Many science questions, including this one, can be answered by doing experiments. An **experiment** is a procedure used to test a hypothesis. It's a good idea to make some observations before stating a hypothesis. For example, you might put a small amount of orange juice in a freezer. Then you'd check it every few minutes to look for changes.

Hypothesize

A *hypothesis* is a statement that can be tested and will explain what can happen in an investigation. In the case of the freezing question, you think about what you already know. You can also talk to other people. And you can do research such as asking an expert.

You find out that the freezing point and melting point of a material should be the same temperature. An expert suggests that it is better to measure the melting point than the freezing point.

Design an Experiment

A well-designed experiment has two or more setups. This allows you to compare results among them. For the freezing/melting experiment, each setup will be a cup of liquid.

A **variable** is any condition in an experiment that can be changed. In most experiments, there are many, many variables to consider. The trick is to keep all variables the same in each setup, except one. That one variable is the one you will test.

Among the setups should be one called the control. The **control** is the setup to which you will compare all the others.

You've decided to dissolve different substances in water and freeze them. Then you plan to take them out of the freezer and use a thermometer to check their temperatures as they melt.

Hypothesize

Fill in the blank in the hypothesis. Any substance dissolved in water will _____ the temperature at which the mixture freezes and melts.

Identify and Control Variables

When you identify and control variables, you determine which conditions should stay the same and which one should be changed. Circle the variable that will be tested. Underline the variables that will remain the same.

- the kinds of cups

- the amount of water

- the material that is dissolved in the water

- the temperature of the freezer

- the types of thermometers

- the amount of time you leave the cups in the freezer

© Houghton Mifflin Harcourt Publishing Company

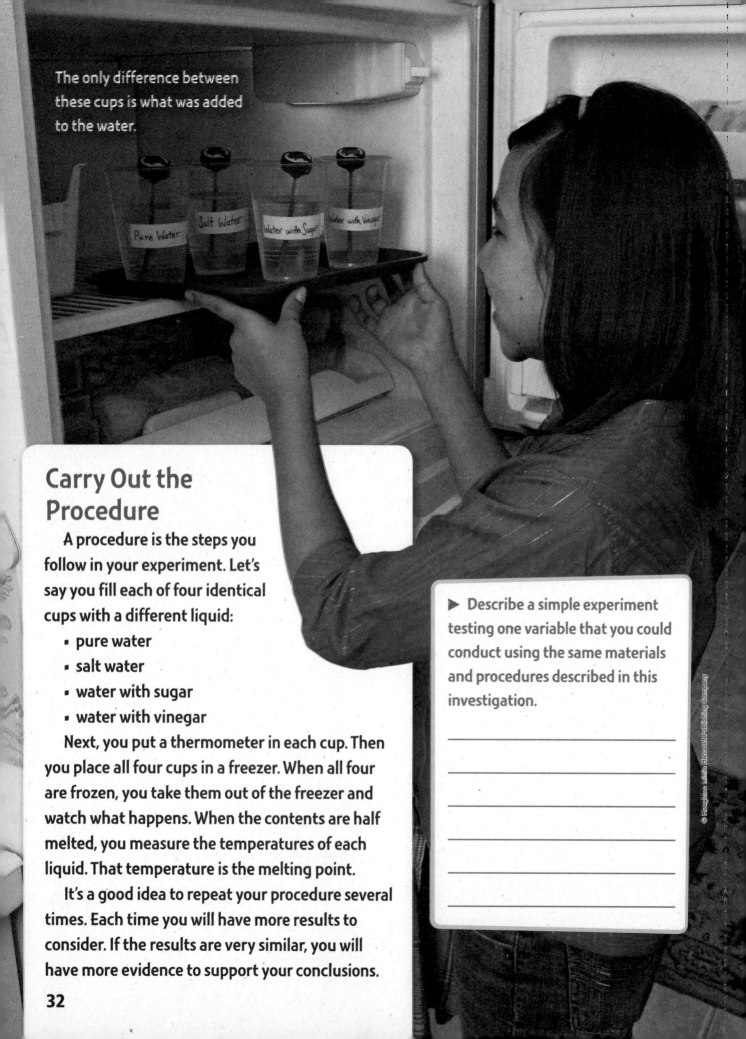

The only difference between these cups is what was added to the water.

Carry Out the Procedure

A procedure is the steps you follow in your experiment. Let's say you fill each of four identical cups with a different liquid:

- pure water
- salt water
- water with sugar
- water with vinegar

Next, you put a thermometer in each cup. Then you place all four cups in a freezer. When all four are frozen, you take them out of the freezer and watch what happens. When the contents are half melted, you measure the temperatures of each liquid. That temperature is the melting point.

It's a good idea to repeat your procedure several times. Each time you will have more results to consider. If the results are very similar, you will have more evidence to support your conclusions.

▶ Describe a simple experiment testing one variable that you could conduct using the same materials and procedures described in this investigation.

_____

_____

_____

_____

_____

_____

Record and Analyze Data

You could write down your observations as sentences. Or you could make a table to fill in. No matter how you do it, make sure you record correctly. Check twice or have a team member check.

Once the experiment is completed and the data recorded, you can analyze your results. If your data is in the form of numbers, math skills will come in handy. For example, in the data table below, you'll need to know how to write, read, and compare decimals.

Melting Point Experiment	
Substance	Melting Point (°C)
Pure water	0.0
Salt water	−3.7
Sugar water	−1.8
Vinegar water	−1.1

Draw Conclusions and Evaluate the Hypothesis

You draw conclusions based on your results. Remember that all conclusions must be supported with evidence. The more evidence you have, the stronger your conclusion. What conclusion can you draw based on this experiment?

Once you've reached a conclusion, look at your hypothesis. Decide if the hypothesis is supported or not. If not, try rethinking your hypothesis. Then design a new experiment to test it. That's what scientists do—build on what they learn.

Experiment!

Ask a well-defined question you could answer using experimental testing.

_____

_____

_____

Plan, describe, and implement an experiment that tests the effect of only one variable.

Special Delivery:
Data Displays

Once you've completed a science investigation, you'll want to share it. What's the best way to communicate the data you collected?

As part of their investigations, scientists collect, record, and interpret data. They use technology, including computers, to construct graphs, tables, maps, and charts. These kinds of displays help scientists organize, examine, and evaluate lots of information. Some kinds of displays are more suited to certain kinds of data than others.

Food Eaten by Orangutans

- Other 5%
- Flowers 5%
- Insects 10%
- Leaves 15%
- Fruits 65%

Estimated Number of Orangutans in Sumatra

(Line graph: Number of Individuals vs. Year, 1990–2010, values from 14,000 down to about 7,000)

Line graphs are suited to show change over time, especially small changes, such as the amount you grow each year.

Circle graphs are suited to comparing parts to the whole. If you want to show fractions or percents, use a circle graph.

Orangutan Using Tool to Feed

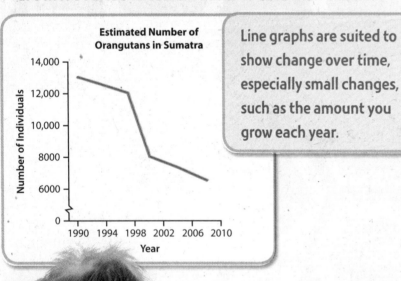

Diagrams are suited to show data that do not include numbers. This diagram shows how an orangutan uses a tool to eat seeds in fruit.

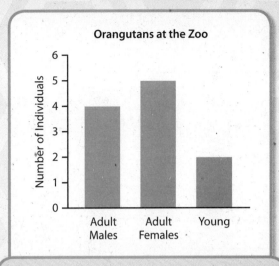

Orangutans at the Zoo

Number of Individuals

Adult Males — 4
Adult Females — 5
Young — 2

Bar graphs are suited to compare things or groups of things. When your data are in categories, use a bar graph.

Do the Math!
Construct a Bar Graph

Use technology to construct a bar graph using the data in the table. Decide whether you want the bars to be vertical or horizontal. Carefully label the intervals on each axis. Draw the bars. Then title and label all the parts of your graph. Attach your graph in the space below.

Number of Orangutans Counted	
Day	Number
Monday	7
Tuesday	13
Wednesday	10
Thursday	2
Friday	6

Sum It Up!

When you're done, use the answer key to check and revise your work.

**The outline below is a summary of the lesson. Complete the outline.
When you are done, check and revise your work.**

Summarize

I. Scientific Methods

  A. All start with a question

  B. Investigations differ

    1. experiments

    2. **①** _____

    3. **②** _____

  C. All have results from which to

    ③ _____

II. Observational Testing

  A. Some things are just too big, too far away, or too uncontrollable for experiments

  B. Examples

    1. volcanoes

    2. **④** _____

III. Using Models

  A. Needed to understand systems that have many hidden parts

  B. Types of models

    1. diagrams and flow charts

    2. **⑤** _____

    3. **⑥** _____

IV. Experiments

  A. Ask well-defined questions

  B. Hypothesize

  C. **⑦** _____

  D. Carry out the procedure

  E. **⑧** _____

  F. Draw conclusions

V. Organizing and Displaying Data

  A. Data displays help communicate

  B. Kinds of data displays

    1. circle graphs

    2. **⑨** _____

    3. **⑩** _____

    4. **⑪** _____

 **Brain Check**

Name _____

Word Play

1 Read each clue. Then find and circle the term in the word search puzzle.

Clues

1. All the ways scientists do investigations:
   _ _ _ _ _ _ _ _ _ _
   _ _ _ _ _ _ _

2. These show how something works that can't be seen: _ _ _ _ _ _

3. The part of an experiment used to compare all the other groups:
   _ _ _ _ _ _ _

4. What scientists do that is the basis for their investigations:
   _ _ _ _ _ _ _ _ _ _ _ _

5. Any condition in an experiment that can be changed: _ _ _ _ _ _ _ _

6. A type of graph suited to show change over time: _ _ _ _ _   _ _ _ _ _ _

7. A statement that can be tested and that explains what you think will happen in an experiment:
   _ _ _ _ _ _ _ _ _ _

8. The steps you follow in your experiment:
   _ _ _ _ _ _ _ _ _

9. To use patterns in observations to say what may happen next:
   _ _ _ _ _ _ _

10. An investigation that is controlled:
    _ _ _ _ _ _ _ _ _ _

```
R T A S N O I T S E U Q K S A R S
C O L L E C T D A T A R S A T S I
S C I E N T I F I C M E T H O D S
B B N Z X E J E O E S T S A U Y E
A Z E Y N P I D D V U L O T Q S H
R F G L A C E A A U F Q E A T V T
G W R A M D N R E P L P T D V L O
R C A N C I I R I W N C I D O D P
A E P A C A D G R M I U N R A M Y
P I H A B G K N I D E P T O B Z H
H N K L Y R H L E A H N Y C C U A
R Y E W D A X R V M O A T E N R A
A N G L B M P R O C E D U R E Y D
```

CHALLENGE: How many other important words from this lesson can you find in the word search? Write them below.

_____

_____

_____

_____

_____

Apply Concepts

2 For each question, state which kind of investigation works best: observational testing, using models, or experimental testing. Then explain how you would do the investigation.

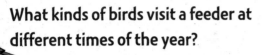

What kinds of birds visit a feeder at different times of the year?

_____

_____

Does hot water or cold water boil faster?

_____

_____

What are the parts of an elevator and how does it work?

_____

_____

_____

How does the length of a kite's tail affect the way it flies?

_____

_____

_____

3 Ryan hypothesizes that darker colors heat up faster. He places a thermometer inside a red wool sock, a green cotton glove, and a black nylon hat. What's wrong with his procedure?

_____

_____

_____

Take It Home!

Use scientific methods to help your family enjoy a healthy snack. Design an experiment to find out whether coating apple slices in lemon juice can stop them from turning brown. Perform your experiment.

Inquiry Flipchart page 6

OHIO **5.SIA.1** Identify questions that can be answered through scientific investigations. **5.SIA.2** Design and conduct a scientific investigation. **5.SIA.3** Use appropriate mathematics, tools and techniques to gather data and information. **5.SIA.4** Analyze and interpret data. **5.SIA.5** Develop descriptions, models, explanations and predictions. **5.SIA.6** Think critically and logically to connect evidence and explanations. **5.SIA.7** Recognize and analyze alternative explanations and predictions. **5.SIA.8** Communicate scientific procedures and explanations.

Name _____

Essential Question

How Do You Perform a Controlled Experiment?

Set a Purpose

What will you learn from this experiment?

_____

_____

_____

_____

_____

Think About the Procedure

What is the tested variable in this experiment?

_____

Each time you try the same test, it is called a trial. Why is it important to do repeated trials of this experiment?

_____

_____

_____

Record Your Data

In the table below, record your results.

Surface Material	Height Ball Bounced					
	Trial 1	Trial 2	Trial 3	Trial 4	Trial 5	Average

Draw Conclusions

Based on the empirical evidence from your experiment, what can you conclude?

_____

_____

_____

_____

Analyze and Extend

1. Analyze and interpret information using direct (observable) evidence. Think about the materials the ball bounced on. What was it about them that affected the height of the bounce?

_____

_____

2. Analyze and interpret information using indirect (inferred) evidence. Tennis is played on three types of surfaces: grass, packed clay, and hard courts. Hard courts are often made from asphalt, the black road surface material. How do these surfaces compare to the surfaces that you tested? How would they affect the bounce of your ball?

_____

_____

_____

3. **REVIEW** Suppose your data are different from other groups. How could you demonstrate that the data you obtained are reliable?

_____

_____

_____

_____

4. **REVIEW** Ask a well-defined question about how a ball bounces. Remember, a well-defined question is specific and testable.

_____

_____

_____

_____

_____

_____

_____

OHIO **5.SIA.1** Identify questions that can be answered through scientific investigations.
5.SIA.3 Use appropriate mathematics, tools and techniques to gather data and information.

Lesson **5**

Essential Question

What Are Some Science Tools?

Engage Your Brain!

Find the answer to the following question in this lesson and write it here.

This scientific equipment is filled with liquids. What tools can scientists use to measure the volume of a liquid?

_____

_____

_____

Active Reading

Lesson Vocabulary

List the terms. As you learn about each one, make notes in the Interactive Glossary.

_____

_____

_____

_____

Compare and Contrast

Many ideas in this lesson are connected because they explain comparisons and contrasts—how things are alike and different. Active readers stay focused on comparisons and contrasts when they ask themselves, How are these things alike? How are they different?

Inquiry Flipchart   p. 7 — Making Measurements/Get Detailed
pp. 8–11 — Science Tools Activities

41

Field Trips

If you like school field trips, you might want to become a field scientist. Field scientists travel around the world studying science in the wild. They pack their tools and take them along.

Active Reading As you read these two pages, box the names of all the science tools.

Field scientists go "on location" to investigate the natural world. Their investigations are often in the form of repeated observations. They use observational testing to evaluate scientific explantions. Choosing appropriate tools and technology to extend their senses is often their first step.

Collecting Net

What kinds of animals swim near the shore of a pond? A scientist might use a collecting net and an observation pan to answer this question. By carefully pulling the net through the water, they can catch small animals without harming them.

Hand Lens

How does an ant move? How does it use its mouthparts? A hand lens might help answer these questions. Hold the hand lens near your eye. Then move your other hand to bring the object into view. Move the object back and forth until it is in sharp focus.

Cameras

What do lionfish eat? How do they catch their food? To investigate, a scientist might use an underwater video camera. Cameras help scientists record events.

Do the Math!
Estimate by Sampling

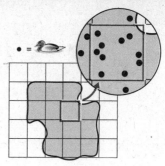

Scientists photograph ducks from a plane and then draw a grid over the photo. How many ducks do you estimate are on the whole lake?

_____

Why might your estimate differ from the actual number of ducks?

_____

_____

_____

Into the Lab

What's living in a drop of pond water? Lots of tiny critters! Some behave like animals. Others are like plants. All are too small to be seen with only a hand lens.

Active Reading As you read these two pages, draw lines connecting the pairs of tools being compared to each other.

Science tools can be heavy and expensive. If you want to observe the tiniest pond life, you'll need science tools that are too big or too delicate to be carried into the field. For example, scientists use computers to record and analyze data, construct models, and communicate with other scientists.

Use Numbers

Some tools help scientists count things. Some scientists estimate, while others perform complex mathematical calculations. All scientists must be comfortable **using numbers**.

▶ To find the magnification of a light microscope, multiply the power of the eyepiece lens by the power of the objective lens. The letter X stands for how many times bigger objects appear.

Eyepiece Magnification	Objective Magnification	Total Magnification
10X	40X	
15X	60X	
8X	100X	

Light Microscope

The tiny living things in pond water are **microscopic**, or too small to see with just your eyes. A light microscope magnifies things, or makes them look bigger. The object to be viewed is placed on a clear slide. Light passes through the object and two lenses. You look through the eyepiece and turn knobs to focus an image.

Dropper

A dropper is a tube with a rubber bulb on one end. Squeeze the bulb and then dip the tip into a liquid. Release the bulb, and the liquid will be sucked up the tube. When you slowly squeeze the bulb, the liquid drops out.

Electron Microscope

Light microscopes have been around for 500 years. But technology, or people's use of tools, has improved. Today a scanning electron microscope (SEM) can magnify an object up to one million times. The SEM shoots a beam of electrons at the object. An image of the surface of the object appears on a computer screen.

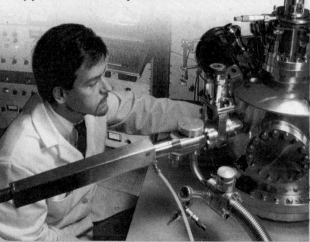

Pipette

A pipette is a tool like a dropper, but it's more exact. It is used to add or remove very small amounts of liquids. Pipettes often have marks on the side to measure volume. One kind of pipette makes drops so tiny that they can only be seen with a scanning electron microscope!

Measuring Up

What do a digit, a palm, a hand, a dram, a peck, a rod, and a stone have in common? They all are, or were at one time, units of measurement!

Active Reading As you read the next four pages, circle all the units of measurement.

When you **measure**, you make observations involving numbers and units. Today most countries use the International System (SI) units in daily life. If you were to visit these countries, you'd purchase fruit or cheese by the *kilogram*. In the United States, most everyday measurements use units from the time when English colonists lived in America.

However, scientists around the world—including those in the United States—use the SI, or metric system.

The metric system is based on multiples of 10. In the metric system, base units are divided into smaller units using prefixes such as *milli-, centi-,* and *deci-*. Base units are changed to bigger units using prefixes such as *deca-* and *kilo-*.

Measuring Length

Length is the distance between two points. The base metric unit of length is the *meter*. Rulers, metersticks, and tape measures are tools used to measure length.

A caliper can be used to measure the distance between the two sides of an object.

Measuring Time

Time describes how long events take. The base unit of time is the second. Larger units are the minute, the hour, and the day. Smaller units include the millisecond and microsecond. Clocks, stopwatches, timers, and calendars are some of the tools used to measure time.

Measure Your Science Book

Use a metric ruler and units to measure the length, width, and thickness of your science book.

Length: _____

Width: _____

Thickness: _____

Measuring Temperature

Temperature describes how hot something is. Thermometers are used to measure temperature. Scientists measure temperature in degrees Celsius. So do most other people around the world. In the United States, degrees Fahrenheit are often used to report the weather, to measure body temperatures, and in cooking.

Pan Balance

A **balance** is a tool used to measure mass. *Mass* is the amount of matter in an object. The base unit of mass is the kilogram. One kilogram equals 1,000 grams.

With this balance, you can directly compare the masses of two objects. Put one object in each pan. The pan that sinks lower contains the greater mass.

To measure in grams, place an object in one pan.

Always carry a balance by holding its base.

This pan balance has drawers where the masses are stored.

Add gram masses to the other pan until the two pans are balanced. Then add the values of the gram masses to find the total mass.

Three Beams

A triple-beam balance measures mass more exactly than the pan balance. It has one pan and three beams. To find the number of grams, move the sliders until the beam balances.

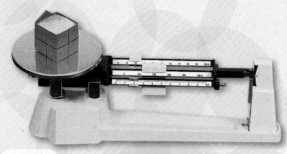

Digital Mass

An electronic balance calculates the mass of an object for you. It displays an object's mass on a screen.

How Strong?

A **spring scale** is a tool used to measure force. Force is a push or a pull. When an object hangs down from the scale, the force of gravity, or weight, is measured. When the spring scale is used to pull an object, it measures the force needed to move the object. Either way, the base unit is called a newton.

▶ Draw lines to match the tools to what they measure and the units.

Tool	What It Measures	Units
	• force •	• seconds, minutes, hours, days, years, etc.
	• temperature •	• grams, milligrams, kilograms, etc.
	• length •	• newtons
	• mass •	• degrees Celsius, degrees Fahrenheit
	• time •	• meters, kilometers, millimeters, etc.

More Measuring

It's a hot day and you're thirsty. Would you prefer 1,000 milliliters or 1,000 cubic centimeters of lemonade? Not sure? Read on!

Units of Volume

Volume is the amount of space a solid, liquid, or gas takes up. There are two base metric units for measuring volume. A *cubic meter* is one meter long, one meter high, and one meter wide. The *liter* is the base unit often used for measuring the volume of liquids. You're probably familiar with liters because many drinks are sold in 1-liter or 2-liter bottles. These two metric units of volume are closely related. There are 1,000 liters (L) in one cubic meter (m^3).

> ▶ One cubic centimeter (cm^3) is equal to 1 milliliter (mL). Both are equal to about 20 drops from a dropper.
> Which is greater—1,000 mL or 1,000 cm^3?
>
> _____

1 cm
1 cm
1 cm

Finding Volume

You can find the volume of a rectangular prism by multiplying length times width times height. To find the volume of a liquid, use a measuring cup, beaker, or graduated cylinder. Use water to find the volume of an irregular solid. Put water in a graduated cylinder. Note the volume. Then drop the object in and note the new volume. Subtract the two numbers to find the volume of the object.

> The surface of a liquid in a graduated cylinder is curved. This curve is called a *meniscus*. Always measure volume at the bottom of the meniscus.

Accurate Measurements

When a measurement is close to the true size, it is **accurate**. Try to measure as accurately as you can with the tools you have. Make sure a tool is not broken and that you know how to use it properly. Also pay attention to the units on the tools you use. Accurate measurements are important when doing science investigations, when baking, and when taking medicines.

Follow these tips to improve your accuracy:

- ☑ Handle each tool properly.
- ☑ Use each tool the same way every time. For example, read the measurement at eye level.
- ☑ Measure to the smallest place value the tool allows.
- ☑ Measure twice.
- ☑ Record your measurements carefully, including the units.

▶ Write the math sentence for finding the volume of the toy.

_____

51

Computing
Information

Out in the field or in the lab, you may measure properties of objects or count how often something happens. What modern tools can help organize and make sense of all these data? Let's find out.

Active Reading As you read these two pages, circle the main idea in each section.

Calculators and computers are tools that can help you make sense of data. You can use these computing tools to make precise calculations. You can also use them to record, organize, and communicate information. Computers can be used to make bar, line, or circle graphs to display numerical data. This makes patterns and trends in the data easier to recognize.

Computers

Computers are used to record and organize information during indoor and outdoor investigations. Scientists and engineers can use computers to:

- analyze their data;
- write up their results; and
- share the results of their investigations with others.

Probes

A *digital probe* is an electronic tool used to make observations, or measurements. Some digital probes can do more than one thing. The probe shown here measures temperature. The data it collects can be downloaded into a computer to make a graph. Other kinds of probes can measure the amount of oxygen dissolved in a stream or the current in an electric circuit.

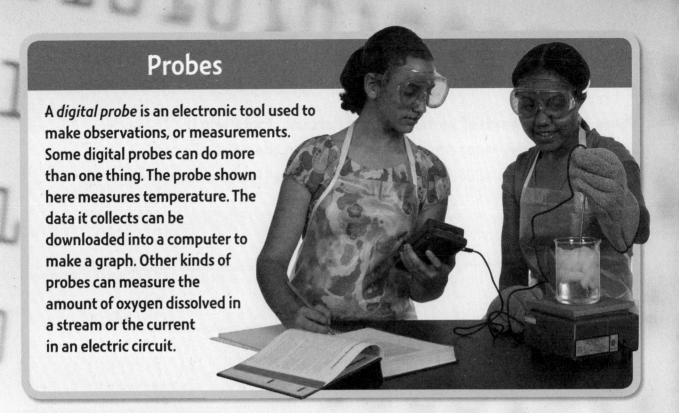

Data from outdoor investigations can be quickly shared with others using portable computers.

Analyze Data

The table shows data collected by a temperature probe placed in an oven. Use a computer to plot the data on a graph. Then write a conclusion about what is happening in the oven.

Time (min)	0	5	10	15	20
Temp. °C	25	65	175	175	175

_____

_____

_____

_____

Sum It Up!

When you're done, use the answer key to check and revise your work.

There are many kinds of tools that scientists use. Tools help scientists observe, measure, and study things in the natural world. Fill in the blank boxes with examples of tools that scientists use.

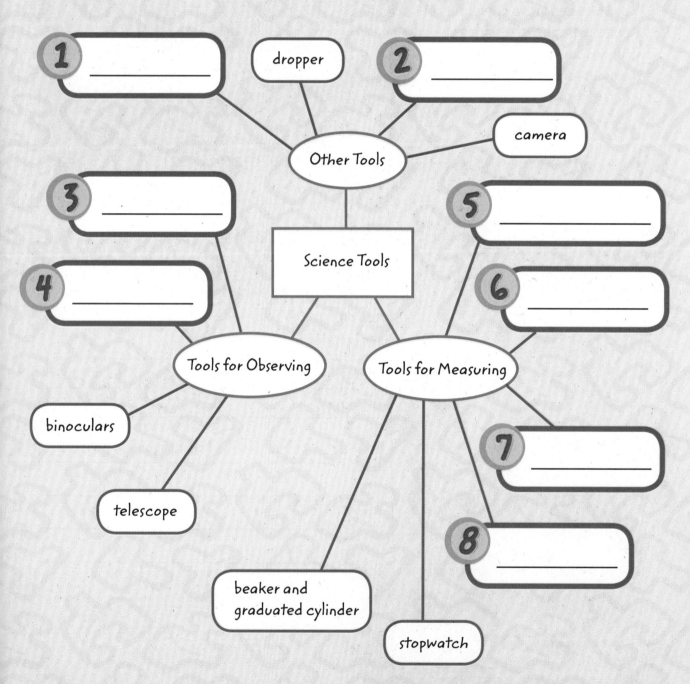

1. _____

dropper

2. _____

camera

Other Tools

3. _____

4. _____

Science Tools

5. _____

6. _____

Tools for Observing

binoculars

telescope

Tools for Measuring

7. _____

8. _____

beaker and graduated cylinder

stopwatch

Answer Key: 1 and 2—computer or collecting net; 3 and 4—microscope or hand lens; 5, 6, 7, and 8—thermometer, balance, spring scale, and ruler or meterstick.

Name _____

Word Play

1 Put the scrambled letters in order to spell a science term.

1. treem

   ◯ _ _ ◯ _   A metric unit of length

2. amrg

   _ _ ◯ _   A metric unit of mass

3. rdsgeee seCisul

   _ _ _ _ _ _ ◯   A metric unit for temperature
   _ _ ◯ _ _ _ _

4. taceurca

   _ _ _ ◯ _ _ ◯   A measurement close to the true size

5. townne

   _ _ ◯ _ _ _   A unit used to measure force

6. trile

   _ _ _ _ ◯   A metric unit of volume

7. inpsrg casel

   _ _ _ _ _ ◯   A tool used to measure force

8. nap cablane

   _ ◯ _ _ _   A tool used to measure mass
   _ _ _ _ _ _

9. dceson

   ◯ _ _ _ _ _   A metric unit of time

10. veumol

    _ _ _ ◯ _ _   The amount of space a solid, liquid, or gas takes up

11. tagurdade lycnidre

    ◯ _ _ _ _ _ _   A tool used to measure volume
    _ _ _ _ ◯ _ _

Riddle: Place the circled letters in order to solve the riddle below.

Why did the captain ask for a balance?

He wanted to _ _ _ _ _ _ _ _ _ _

the mass of the _ _ _ _ _ _ _ _ _ _ _ _ .

Apply Concepts

2 Tell how you use one or more of these tools to investigate each question.

How are two fossil teeth similar and different?

_____

_____

_____

Which kinds of butterflies are found in a field?

_____

_____

_____

What do scientists already know about the bottom of the ocean?

_____

_____

_____

Does the mass of a ball affect how far it rolls?

_____

_____

_____

3 Identify what each tool measures and the metric units it uses.

_____   _____   _____

_____   _____   _____

Take It Home!

At your school or public library, find a book about how scientists work or the tools they use. Read and discuss the book with your family. Prepare a brief summary to present to your classmates.

OHIO **5.SIA.2** Design and conduct a scientific investigation. **5.SIA.3** Use appropriate mathematics, tools and techniques to gather data and information. **5.SIA.4** Analyze and interpret data. **5.SIA.5** Develop descriptions, models, explanations and predictions. **5.SIA.6** Think critically and logically to connect evidence and explanations. **5.SIA.8** Communicate scientific procedures and explanations.

Name _____

Essential Question

How Can Scientists Learn from Observations?

Set a Purpose
What will you learn from this investigation?

_____

_____

_____

_____

Think About the Procedure
What planning must I do before this investigation?

_____

_____

_____

What is a safety tool used in this investigation? What is a safety practice?

_____

_____

_____

What properties of objects are measured in this investigation? What tools are used to measure them?

_____

_____

_____

_____

_____

Record Your Data
In the space below, record your results.

Soil Sample: _____

My Observations:

Amount of water held by
100 mL of soil: _____

Mass Before Drying: _____

Mass After Drying: _____

Draw Conclusions

Compare your data with the data from other groups. What can you conclude?

_____

_____

_____

_____

Analyze and Extend

1. Few plants can survive in sandy soil. Use empirical evidence and logical reasoning to identify a characteristic of sandy soil.

_____

_____

_____

_____

2. Why would a farmer want to know about the soil on his or her farm?

_____

_____

_____

_____

3. How was this investigation different from a controlled experiment?

_____

_____

_____

_____

4. Why was it important to know the mass of the soil before it was dried for one week?

_____

_____

_____

_____

5. What else would you like to find out about different types of soils?

_____

_____

_____

_____

_____

Unit 1 Review

Vocabulary Review

Use the terms in the box to complete the sentences.

> balance
> control
> evidence
> experiment
> spring scale
> variable

1. An investigation in which all conditions are controlled

   is a(n) _____.

2. Jane wants to measure the mass of a rock. The tool she

   should use is a(n) _____.

3. Any condition in an experiment that can be changed

   is a(n) _____.

4. The information that scientists gather during an

   investigation is called _____.

5. The setup or condition to which you compare all the others

   in an experiment is the _____.

6. Jaime wants to find out how much force it takes to
   pull a toy car up a ramp. The tool he should use is

   a(n) _____.

Science Concepts

Fill in the letter of the choice that best answers the question.

7. Which of the following is the best testable hypothesis related to friction?

   (A) You can use a spring scale to measure friction.

   (B) Many different objects can produce friction.

   (C) Friction increases as the roughness of the surface increases.

   (D) Friction is caused by the attraction between particles.

8. Students look out the window for 5 minutes. In their notebooks, they record the number, type, and color of the vehicles that pass. What are students doing?

   (A) concluding

   (B) observing

   (C) hypothesizing

   (D) experimenting

Analyze and evaluate the information below to answer questions 9 and 10.

Abe built this setup to investigate how far a toy car would travel after it left the ramp. He used a meterstick to measure distance.

Number of Books	Distance Traveled (m)
2	1.50
4	2.50
6	3.75

9. Which is a conclusion that Abe can draw?

(A) The toy car would have traveled farther if Abe had used a different ramp.

(B) Adding two books to the height doubled the distance the car traveled.

(C) A toy car will travel 6 meters if there are 8 books under the end of the ramp.

(D) The greater the number of books under the ramp, the farther the car traveled.

10. How could Abe increase the reliability of his results?

(A) Do the same experiment with different cars.

(B) Do the experiment more times at each height.

(C) Do the same experiment with different ramps.

(D) Do the experiment on a different surface.

Use the following information to answer questions 11 and 12.

Jen wants to find out how the temperature of water affects the amount of sugar it can dissolve. She places 100 mL of water at 25 °C, 50 °C, and 75 °C into three containers. Jen adds measured masses of sugar to each container until no more will dissolve. She records all her data in a notebook.

11. Which of the following tools will Jen use in her experiment?

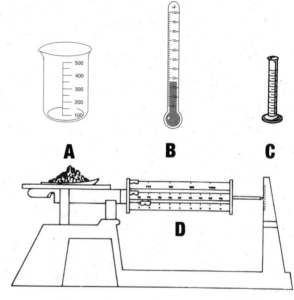

(A) Only A and C

(B) Only B and D

(C) A, B, and C

(D) A, B, C, and D

12. Which would be the best way for Jen to record her observations and data?

(A) in a table

(B) as a line graph

(C) as a circle graph

(D) in a Venn diagram

Name _____

UNIT 1

13. Lena adds 5 g of fertilizer and 1 cup of water to Plant A and places it in the shade. She adds no fertilizer and 1 cup of water to Plant B and places it in the sun. She measures and records the growth of the two plants every other day for 10 days. Which of the following best describes Lena's experimental design?

Ⓐ It is a well designed experiment to test the effect of fertilizer on plant growth.

Ⓑ It is a well designed experiment to test the effect of sunshine on plant growth.

Ⓒ It is a poorly designed experiment because she only measured the growth for 10 days.

Ⓓ It is a poorly designed experiment because it has no control and too many tested variables.

14. Which is the best explanation for the observation that clothes hung in the sun dry faster than those hung in the shade?

Ⓐ Sunshine causes air to flow around the clothes, carrying the water away.

Ⓑ Air in the shade is more humid than air in the sun, so water can't change to a gas as quickly.

Ⓒ More energy strikes the clothes in the sun, so water changes to a gas more quickly.

Ⓓ The light from the sun works with the heat to make the clothes dry faster.

15. The table below shows the results of an experiment designed to study how exercise affects heart rate.

Time	Person A Heart Rate (beats/min)	Person B Heart Rate (beats/min)	Person C Heart Rate (beats/min)
Before exercise	75	62	70
After exercise	120	110	130

Which of the following statements is the best conclusion for this experiment?

Ⓐ Heart rate is not affected by exercise.

Ⓑ Heart rate is increased by exercise.

Ⓒ Exercise triples a person's heart rate.

Ⓓ Exercise decreases a person's heart rate.

16. Fahim wants to know more about how birds protect their nests. Which equipment should Fahim choose for his experiment?

Ⓐ a recorder and a collecting net

Ⓑ a camera and a notebook

Ⓒ a hand lens and a stopwatch

Ⓓ a calculator and a clock

© Houghton Mifflin Harcourt Publishing Company ©NDisc/Age Fotostock

Unit 1 **61**

Apply Inquiry and Review the Big Idea

Write the answers to these questions.

17. Maria counts the number of people who attend several basketball games. She uses a computer to create the bar graph.

How many more people did Maria observe at Game 2 than at Game 1?

_____

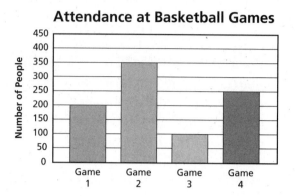

Attendance at Basketball Games

18. Keisha observes that sliced apples turn brown when exposed to air. She thinks that pouring a liquid, such as water, ginger ale, or lemon juice, over the apple slices will keep them from turning brown. What is Keisha's hypothesis? How could she set up a controlled experiment to test it? What variables will she control? How would she know if her hypothesis is correct?

_____

_____

_____

_____

19. Draw a diagram to show why a pot of boiling water left for too long over a stove dries up. Use your diagram to explain the process.

_____

_____

20. Tia is observing a worm she found on a branch. What tools might Tia use to make observations about the worm?

_____

_____

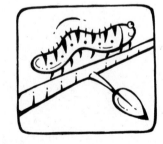

The Engineering Process

Big Idea

Technology is all around us. Engineers apply their knowledge of science to design solutions to practical problems.

OHIO 5.SIA.2, 5.SIA.3, 5.SIA.4, 5.SIA.5, 5.SIA.6, 5.SIA.8

I Wonder Why

Mixers, rollers, cutters, tumblers, and hoppers, all run by electricity! I wonder why it takes so many machines to make a gumball?

Here's Why Food processing relies on technology. Machines produce treats that always have the same taste, color, smell, and size. When a gumball pops out of the dispenser, you know exactly what you're getting!

In this unit, you will explore the Big Idea, the Essential Questions, and the Investigations on the Inquiry Flipchart.

Levels of Inquiry Key ■ DIRECTED ■ GUIDED ■ INDEPENDENT

Big Idea Technology is all around us. Engineers apply their knowledge of science to design solutions to practical problems.

Essential Questions

Now I Get the Big Idea!

Science Notebook

Before you begin each lesson, be sure to write your thoughts about the Essential Question.

OHIO **5.SIA.3** Use appropriate mathematics, tools and techniques to gather data and information. **5.SIA.4** Analyze and interpret data. **5.SIA.5** Develop descriptions, models, explanations and predictions. **5.SIA.6** Think critically and logically to connect evidence and explanations. **5.SIA.8** Communicate scientific procedures and explanations.

Essential Question

What Is the Design Process?

Engage Your Brain!

Find the answer to the following question in this lesson and record it here.

What are the steps for designing technology such as the robot arm you see here?

_____

_____

_____

_____

_____

_____

Active Reading

Lesson Vocabulary
List the terms. As you learn about each one, make notes in the Interactive Glossary.

_____   _____

_____   _____

Problem-Solution
Ideas in this lesson may be connected by a problem-solution relationship. Active readers mark a problem with a *P* to help them stay focused on the way information is organized. When multiple solutions are described, they mark each solution with an *S*.

Works of Ingenuity

Did you brush your teeth this morning? Did you run water from a faucet? Did you ride to school in a car or bus? If you did any of those things, you used a product of engineering.

Active Reading As you read these pages, underline the names of engineered devices.

Engineered devices, such as computers, help us solve many problems. Engineers use computers and hand-drawn diagrams to plan their designs.

Engineers are problem solvers. They invent or improve products that help us meet our needs. Engineers use their knowledge of science and mathematics to find solutions to everyday problems. This process is called **engineering**.

From the start of each day, we use the products of engineering. Engineered devices are found all around us. They include simple tools and complex machines.

Engineers work in many fields. Some design and test new kinds of materials. Some work in factories or on farms. Others work in medical laboratories. Engineers also design the engines that may one day fly people to Mars!

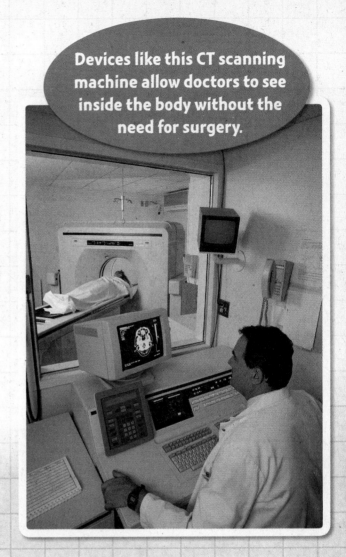

Devices like this CT scanning machine allow doctors to see inside the body without the need for surgery.

Sometimes engineers design devices with one purpose in mind—fun!

Engineering Diary

In the space below, draw or attach a chart constructed on a computer that lists some of the engineered devices you use every day. Explain the need that each device meets.

The Right Tool for the Right Job

When you see or hear the word *technology*, you may think of things such as flat screen TVs, computers, and cell phones. But technology includes more than just modern inventions.

Active Reading As you read these two pages, underline sentences that describe how technology affects our lives.

Stone tools, the wheel, and candles were invented a long time ago. They are examples of technology. **Technology** is any device that people use to meet their needs and solve practical problems.

Technology plays an important role in improving our lives. Tools and machines make our work easier or faster. Medicines help us restore our health and live longer. Satellites help us predict weather and communicate.

Technology changes as people's knowledge increases and they find better ways to meet their needs. For example, as people's knowledge of materials increased, stone tools gave way to metal tools. As people learned more about electricity, washboards and hand-cranked washing machines gave way to electric washers.

Centuries ago, many people washed their clothes on rocks in a river. The invention of the washboard allowed people to wash their clothes at home.

Over the past 150 years, engineers have improved washing machines. Even today, new washers are being designed to work faster and more efficiently.

The washboard helped make washing clothes easier, but it was still hard work. In the 1800s, engineers designed machines that could be filled with water and had a hand-cranked wringer. The wringer made getting the water out of clothes easier.

Use Inferred Evidence

Look at the washboard. They were made of a wooden frame and a corrugated, or wavy, metal body. What technologies must have been developed before washboards were invented?

_____

_____

_____

_____

The Design Process (Part 1)

Technology is all over—video games, 3D TVs, microwaves. But technology doesn't just happen. It comes about through a step-by-step process.

Active Reading As you read these pages, bracket sentences that describe a problem. Write *P* in the margin. Underline sentences that describe a solution. Write *S* by them.

When engineers design new technologies, they follow a *design process.* The process includes several steps. Here's how the process starts.

1. Find a Problem Engineers must first identify a need, or a problem to be solved. They brainstorm possible solutions. There may be more than one good solution.

2. Plan and Build Engineers choose the solution they think is most practical. They build a working model, or **prototype**, to test.

Throughout the design process, engineers keep careful records. Good records include detailed notes and drawings. Records help them remember what they have done and provide information to others working on similar problems. If the prototype doesn't work, the records can provide clues to a solution that *might* work next time.

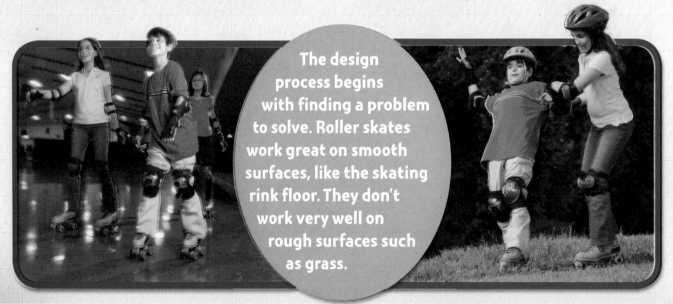

The design process begins with finding a problem to solve. Roller skates work great on smooth surfaces, like the skating rink floor. They don't work very well on rough surfaces such as grass.

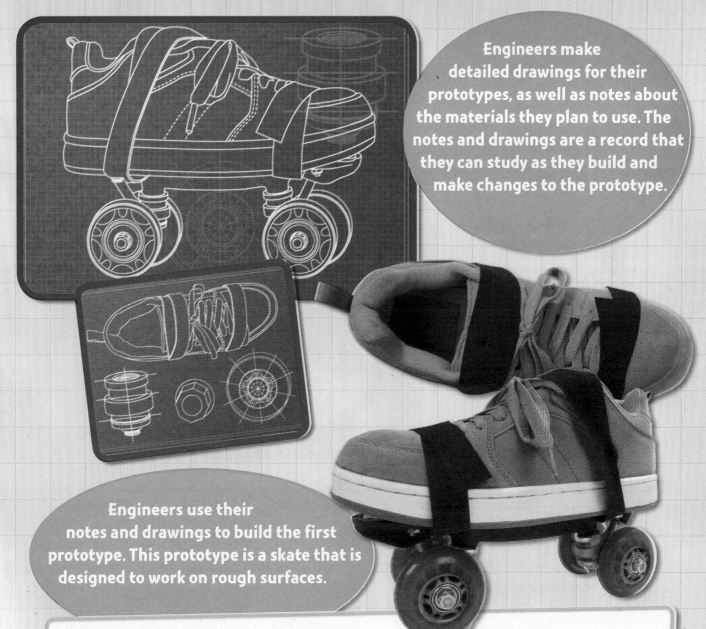

Engineers make detailed drawings for their prototypes, as well as notes about the materials they plan to use. The notes and drawings are a record that they can study as they build and make changes to the prototype.

Engineers use their notes and drawings to build the first prototype. This prototype is a skate that is designed to work on rough surfaces.

Problem Solved!

The first step in the design process is identifying a problem and thinking up solutions. Complete the chart with a problem or a solution.

Problem	Solution
Cord for the computer mouse keeps getting tangled	
	Watch face that lights up
	Hand-held electronic reader
Injuries in car crashes	

The Design Process (Part 2)

Do you get nervous when you hear the word *test*? A test is a useful way to decide both if you understand science and if a prototype works.

The skate designers are steadily working through the steps of the design process. They have found a problem and built a prototype. What's next?

3. Test and Improve After engineers build a prototype, they test it. **Criteria** are standards that help engineers measure how well their design is doing its job. The tests gather data based on the criteria. The data often reveal areas that need improvement.

4. Redesign After testing, engineers may decide that they need to adjust the design. A new design will require a new prototype and more testing.

A prototype is usually tested and redesigned many times before a product is made on a large scale and sold to consumers.

5. Communicate Finally, engineers communicate their results orally and in written reports.

Engineers use criteria to test a prototype. They may gather data on how fast someone can skate on a rough surface or the number of times the person falls. Speed and safety are two criteria in the test you see here.

The design is modified if it doesn't meet all criteria. An unsafe design will be reworked even if the design meets all other criteria. The engineers focus on improvements. They revise their drawings and keep notes on design changes.

This is the redesigned skate. It has larger wheels that work better on rough surfaces. The skater can skate faster for longer distances without falling.

Do the Math!
Solve a Problem

Engineers tested a wheel that was 100 mm in diameter. Then they tested a wheel that was 0.15 larger.

Convert 0.15 to a fraction.

_____

What is the size of the larger wheel?

_____

If At First You Don't Succeed...

Suppose Thomas Edison asked himself, "How many times must I make a new prototype?" What do you think his answer was?

Many things affect how long it takes to reach the final product for new technology. The kinds of materials needed, the cost, the time it takes to produce each prototype, and safety are just some of the criteria engineers consider.

Thomas Edison tried 1,000 times to develop a light bulb that didn't burn out quickly. It took him nearly two years to develop a bulb that met the criterion of being long-lasting.

Some of Edison's early bulb prototypes

Cars must pass crash tests before they can be sold to the public.

Cars of the future may look different or run on fuels different from those of today. Years of testing and redesign occur before a new car is brought to market.

Finding materials that work well affects the design process. Edison found that the materials used to make light bulbs must stand up to heat.

Some technologies cost a lot of money to develop. For example, prototypes for many electronic devices are expensive to build. The cost of building the prototype, in turn, affects the cost of the final product.

It may take many years to develop new cars, because they must undergo safety and environmental testing. Environmental laws limit the pollutants that a car may release and determine the gas mileage it must get.

Criteria Match Up

Draw a line from the technology to criteria that must be considered during the design process.

Technology	Must Be Considered
Hydrogen car	Lightweight, sturdy
Laptop computer	Finding fuel
Bicycle	Portable, long battery life

Sum It Up!

When you're done, use the answer key to check and revise your work.

In the blanks, write the word that makes the sentence correct.

engineering	technology

1. The things that engineers design to meet human needs are _____

2. _____ is the process of designing and testing new technologies.

3. Toothbrushes, washing machines, and computers are examples of _____

4. _____ uses math and science to test devices and designs.

Summarize

Fill in the missing words to explain how engineers conduct the design process. Use the words in the box if you need help.

communicating	engineering	keep good records
needs	problem	prototype

5. _____ is the use of science and math to solve everyday problems. Engineers invent and improve things that meet human 6. _____ . The design process that engineers follow includes finding a 7. _____ , building and testing a 8. _____ , and 9. _____ results. During each step of the design process, engineers 10. _____ .

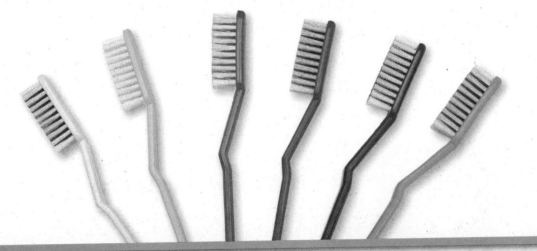

Answer Key: 1. technology 2. Engineering 3. technology 4. Engineering 5. Engineering 6. needs 7. problem 8. prototype 9. communicating 10. keep good records

Name _____

Word Play

1 Beside each sentence, write *T* if the sentence is mostly about using technology. Write *E* if the sentence is mostly about the engineering design process.

_____ 1. Sarah sent a text message to Sam on her cell phone.

_____ 2. The nurse used a digital thermometer to measure the patient's temperature.

_____ 3. Henry tested three brands of blender. He wanted to see which one made the creamiest smoothies.

_____ 4. Workers at the factory use machines to bottle spring water.

_____ 5. Jessica invented a better mousetrap. She patented her invention.

_____ 6. Eli used math to figure out how much weight a bridge could hold.

_____ 7. The nurse is using a new x-ray machine.

_____ 8. Mayling is designing a refrigerator that uses less electricity.

_____ 9. Guillermo's new snowblower makes snow removal faster and easier.

_____ 10. Laptop computers are designed to be smaller, lighter, and easier to carry.

Apply Concepts

2 Match the picture of the technology to the need it fulfills. Draw a line from the picture to the matching need.

go to school

get up on time

see clearly

make a cake

fix a broken bone

keep papers together

3 Write the missing words in the sentences below. Use the word box if you need help.

| brainstormed | good records | problem | prototype |

Jeremy had a _____ that he wanted to solve—his go-cart was too slow. Jeremy and his friend Todd _____ ideas to make it faster. Together, they designed a _____ and tested it. They kept _____ that showed that the go-cart really was faster.

4 Circle the words or phrases that are criteria for designing skates that will be safe. Cross out those that are *not* criteria for safety.

roll smoothly   brake easily   come in different styles

fit snugly   come in different colors   sturdy

5 Look at the flow chart showing the steps of the design process. Then read the list of steps for designing a thermos. These steps are not in order. Write the letter of each step in the appropriate box of the flow chart.

The Design Process

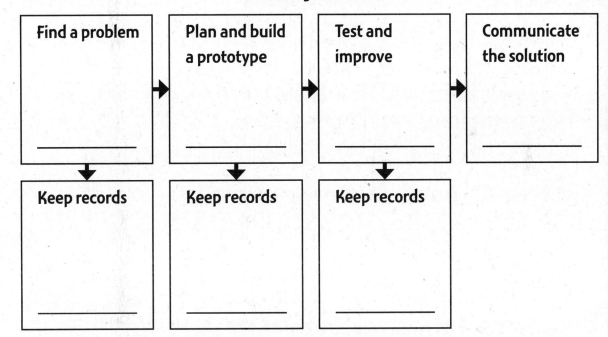

| Find a problem | Plan and build a prototype | Test and improve | Communicate the solution |

| Keep records | Keep records | Keep records |

Steps for Designing a Thermos

A Keep data tables.

B Write a report

C Write down ideas.

D Make drawings.

E Measure the temperature inside the container.

F Keep hot things hot and cold things cold.

G Use insulating materials to make a container.

6 Sylvia is an engineer. Her friend Martin is an artist who paints with oil paints. Martin tells Sylvia that cleaning oil paint out of brushes takes a lot of time. It's messy, too. Write three or more sentences explaining what Sylvia would do to engineer a solution to Martin's problem.

_____

_____

_____

_____

_____

_____

7 Michaela's grandparents used to have a record player. When they were her age, they listened to songs recorded on vinyl records. Michaela's parents listened to cassette tapes when they were young. Later, they got a CD player. Now, Michaela's family members upload music onto MP3 players.

Explain how these changes are examples of engineering and technology.

_____

_____

_____

_____

Take It Home! Ask an older person about a technology that has changed since he or she was young. Discuss how engineering has changed that technology over the years.

OHIO **5.SIA.2** Design and
conduct a scientific investigation.
5.SIA.4 Analyze and interpret data.
5.SIA.5 Develop descriptions... and
predictions. **5.SIA.6** Think critically
and logically to connect evidence and
explanations. **5.SIA.8** Communicate
scientific procedures and explanations.

Name _____

Essential Question

How Can You Design a Solution to a Problem?

Set a Purpose
What is the purpose of this investigation?

_____

_____

State Your Hypothesis
Sketch a raft with pennies on it to show
what you think will be the best design.
Write a brief description of your raft's
key features.

_____

_____

Think About the Procedure
What variables can affect the results of
this investigation?

_____

_____

_____

_____

Record Your Data
In the space below, construct a chart to
organize, evaluate, and examine
information. Include information about
each raft design and its performance.

Draw Conclusions

Why did some of your model rafts work better than others?

_____

_____

_____

_____

Analyze and Extend

1. Based on evidence from your investigation, sketch a raft design you think would NOT float. Explain why.

_____

_____

_____

_____

2. Mary and Sarah built identical raft models. Mary's raft sank after adding only 6 pennies. Sarah's raft held 12 pennies before it sank. Infer a possible reason for the difference.

_____

_____

_____

_____

3. Scientists often build and test models to solve problems. Based on this investigation, explain what are the advantages of solving problems in that way.

_____

_____

_____

_____

_____

4. **REVIEW** Formulate another testable hypothesis related to how you can build a raft to carry a heavy load.

_____

_____

_____

_____

_____

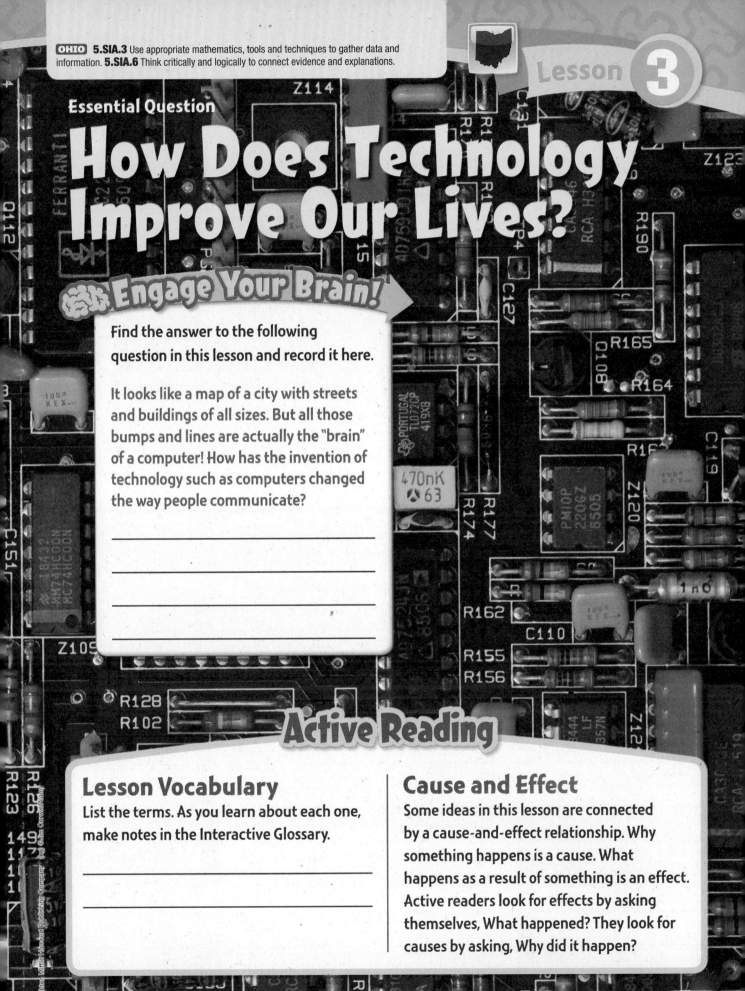

OHIO **5.SIA.3** Use appropriate mathematics, tools and techniques to gather data and information. **5.SIA.6** Think critically and logically to connect evidence and explanations.

Lesson **3**

Essential Question

How Does Technology Improve Our Lives?

Engage Your Brain!

Find the answer to the following question in this lesson and record it here.

It looks like a map of a city with streets and buildings of all sizes. But all those bumps and lines are actually the "brain" of a computer! How has the invention of technology such as computers changed the way people communicate?

_____

_____

_____

Active Reading

Lesson Vocabulary
List the terms. As you learn about each one, make notes in the Interactive Glossary.

_____

_____

Cause and Effect
Some ideas in this lesson are connected by a cause-and-effect relationship. Why something happens is a cause. What happens as a result of something is an effect. Active readers look for effects by asking themselves, What happened? They look for causes by asking, Why did it happen?

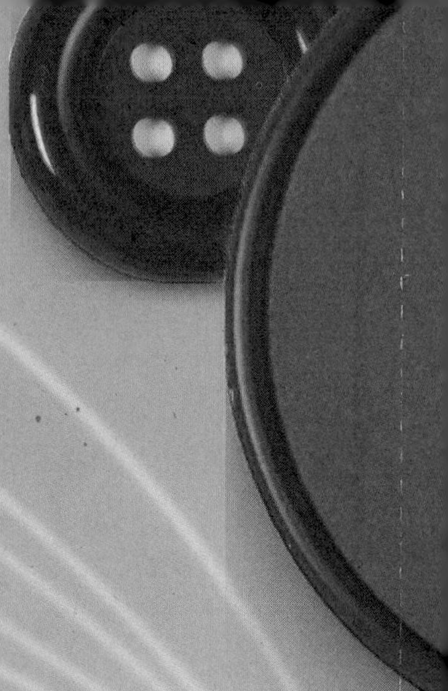

The Technology Zone

Pick up your pencil and look at it carefully. You are holding technology in your hand.

Active Reading As you read these two pages, draw boxes around the names of two things that are being compared.

Most of the things you use every day are *technology*. Pencils, bikes, light bulbs, even the clothes you wear are technology. Cooking food uses technology. What makes something a technology is not how modern it is. Technology doesn't need to be complex or require electricity to operate.

What technology must do is meet a human need. A pencil lets you write your thoughts or work math problems. Think about what needs are being met as you read about the technologies on these two pages. How would you meet those needs without these items?

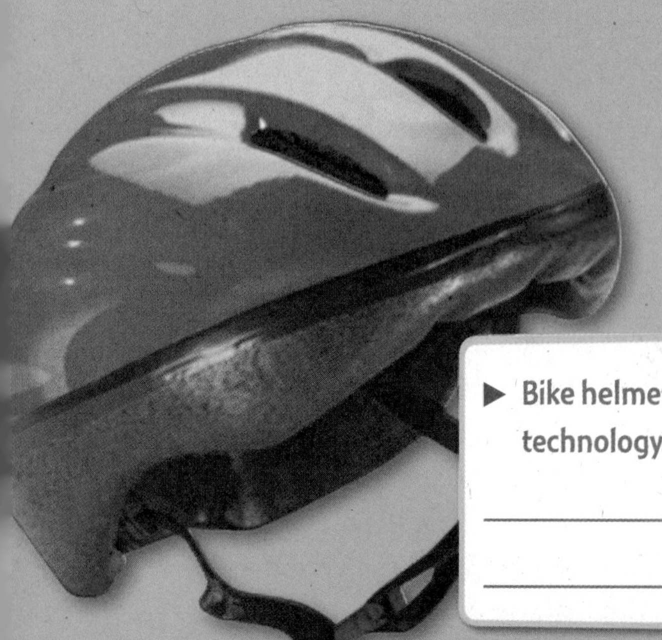

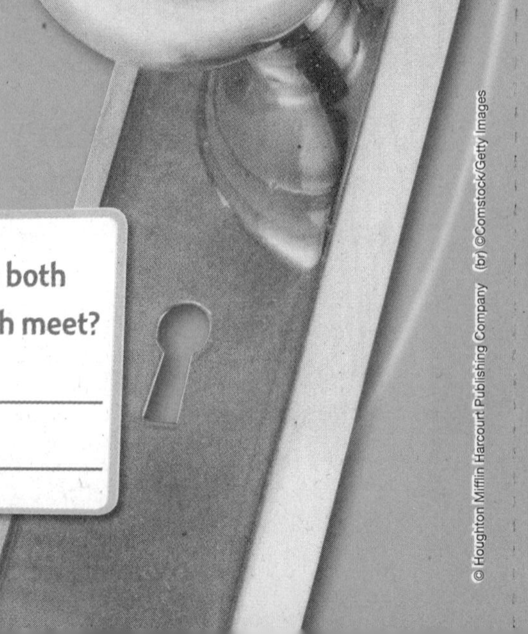

▶ Bike helmets and doorknobs are both technology. What need does each meet?

____

____

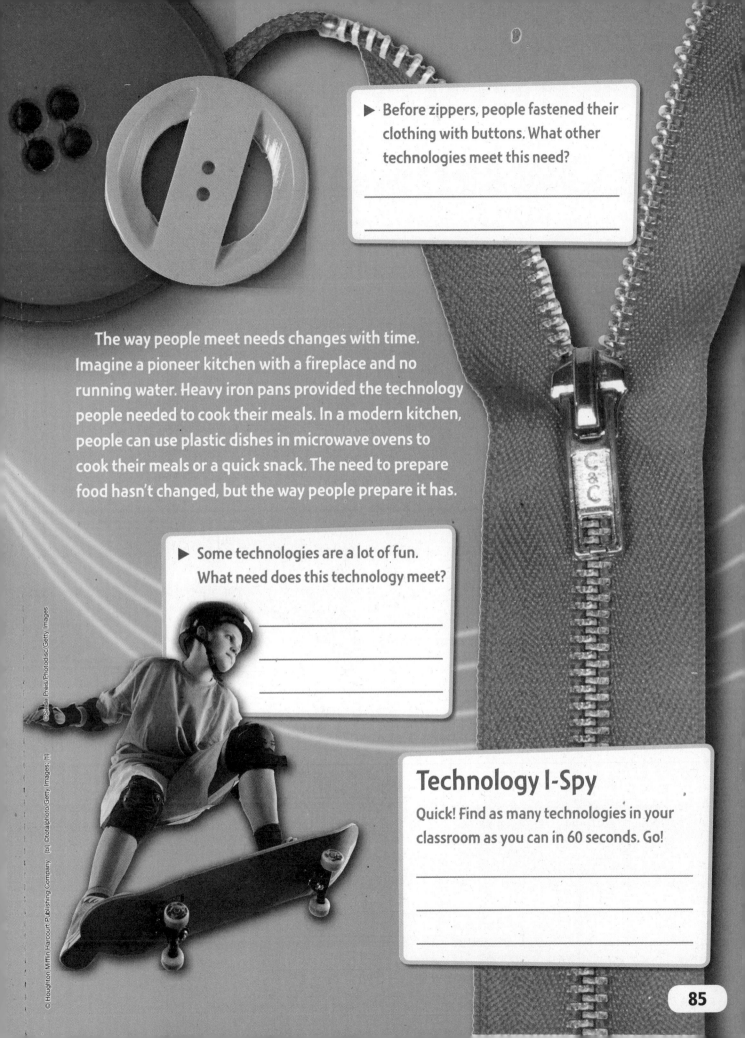

▶ Before zippers, people fastened their clothing with buttons. What other technologies meet this need?

_____

_____

The way people meet needs changes with time. Imagine a pioneer kitchen with a fireplace and no running water. Heavy iron pans provided the technology people needed to cook their meals. In a modern kitchen, people can use plastic dishes in microwave ovens to cook their meals or a quick snack. The need to prepare food hasn't changed, but the way people prepare it has.

▶ Some technologies are a lot of fun. What need does this technology meet?

_____

_____

_____

Technology I-Spy

Quick! Find as many technologies in your classroom as you can in 60 seconds. Go!

_____

_____

_____

Meeting People's Needs

It's 1860. You want to contact a distant friend. Today, you might send a text message. What about then?

Active Reading As you read these two pages, draw one line under a cause. Draw two lines under its effect.

1858

In the early 1800s, long-distance mail was carried by horseback riders, steamboats, and stagecoaches. A stagecoach took 25 days to carry a letter 3,000 km (1,700 mi) from St. Louis to San Francisco.

1869

When the transcontinental railroad opened, the time it took to move a letter across the country was cut down to a week or less.

1881

The time it took to send a message across the country was reduced to minutes with the invention of the telegraph.

In the early 1800s, communicating with someone far away might take weeks or months. Sometimes such communications were not possible at all. As people began to move westward across the growing United States, the need for reliable communication increased. The timeline on these pages shows ways technology changed in response to this need.

The time it took to communicate with someone across the country decreased as new technologies developed. What once took weeks, then days, then minutes now happens almost instantly! Today, people text back and forth almost as fast as they can talk in person. E-mails can be sent to many people at one time. New technologies for communicating seem to develop faster and faster. What could be next?

1915

Cross-country telephone service began in the United States.

1993

The first smartphone was developed.

07:00 AM

CONNECTED

Do the Math!
Solve a Problem

Suppose you send two text messages per minute. How many text messages could you send in the time it took to carry a letter by stagecoach from St. Louis to San Francisco in 1858?

_____

_____

_____

Technology Risks and Benefits

A cell phone lets you communicate from almost anywhere. What happens when the phone dies or a newer, better model comes out?

Active Reading As you read these two pages, **underline** the things that are being contrasted .

Technology can have both positive and negative effects. Positive effects are called *benefits*. Benefits are the ways that a technology fills a need. For example, a cell phone lets friends and family communicate with you wherever you are. It might let you surf the Internet or download useful applications, too.

Negative effects are called *risks*. Cell phone technology changes fast, and some people switch to new models after just a few months. More resources are used up, and the old phones sometimes end up in a landfill. This risk is environmental.

No matter what the technology, there are both risks and benefits. Think about how each technology described here impacts your life. Are the benefits worth the risks?

Computers

BENEFITS	RISKS
Computers let you communicate with friends and family. They let you surf the Internet for information that can help with homework, and they let you play games.	Computer technology changes quickly, and many computers end up in landfills. Computers are expensive, and using the Internet can expose you to sites that are unsafe.

Automobiles

BENEFITS	RISKS
Cars allow personal freedom by letting you go almost anywhere. They carry heavy items that you could not move on your own.	Cars use gasoline that is made from a limited resource—oil. They cause air pollution, and they can be dangerous if not driven properly.

MP3 Players

BENEFITS	RISKS
MP3 players let you download and listen to your favorite music without disturbing others.	Turning up the volume can damage your hearing. You may not be able to download some songs.

Risks Versus Benefits

New technologies are being invented every day. One relatively new kind is digital print materials. List some benefits and risks associated with this new technology.

BENEFITS	RISKS
_____	_____
_____	_____
_____	_____

Smart Choices

There are many new products and services today. How do you decide which ones to choose?

Active Reading As you read these two pages, underline types of information you can use to make smart choices.

Many more products and services come to market as new technologies develop. Companies with similar products or services compete against one another. Each claims that its product or service is best. Companies use *promotional materials*, such as the ones shown below, to catch your interest. But are the claims true? Before buying, smart shoppers clearly identify their own needs and wants. Then they evaluate the accuracy of the claims. Smart shoppers compare prices and features between similar products or services. They weigh the pros and cons of a product before buying.

These promotional materials make claims about the benefits of renting or buying computer games. How do you decide which one is best for you?

GAMES R US

Don't Pay More for New Games
When You Could Rent for Less!

When you subscribe to our service, you could rent up to SIX Brand-New games for just $20 each!

So, why wait? Act Now!

Just pay an annual membership and renewal fee of $120 and start renting!

GAMEGARAGE
Buy It Now! Keep It Forever!

New bestsellers starting at $40!
Used classics as low as $15!
Build your collection!
Play over and over with your friends!

Preorder the hottest upcoming titles!

Promotional labels on products in the grocery store also try to catch your eye. These products may make claims about being healthful, having great taste, or being low in fat. Evaluating product claims may be a challenge. Luckily, there is a *nutritional label* on each. It tells you about a product's essential ingredients. Nutritional labels are designed to help you compare foods so that you can make healthful food choices.

Fresh fruits and vegetables are healthful. Yet processed, prepackaged, ready-to-eat foods may seem more convenient if you're on the go. Look at nutritional labels to decide which is best for you.

Nutrition Facts

Serving Size 1 strip (14g)
Servings per Container — 10

Amount per Serving

Calories	60
Calories from Fat	9

% Daily Value*

Total Fat 1g	**1%**
Saturated Fat 0g	**0%**
Trans Fat 0g	
Cholesterol 0mg	**0%**
Sodium 55mg	**2%**
Total Carbohydrate 12g	**4%**
Sugars 8g	
Protein 0g	
Vitamin C	10%

Not a significant source of dietary fiber, vitamin A, calcium, and iron.

*Percent Daily Values are based on a 2,000 calorie diet.

Ingredients: Apples from Concentrate, Corn Syrup, Dried Corn Syrup, Sugar, Partially Hydrogenated Cottonseed Oil. Contains 2% or less of: Citric Acid, Sodium Citrate, Acetylated Monoglycerides, Fruit Pectin, Dextrose, Malic Acid, Vitamin C (ascorbic Acid), Natural Flavor, Color (red 40, yellows 5 & 6, blue 1).

Make a Choice!

Look at the three apple products on this page. Read the claims. Weigh the pros and cons. Which one will you choose? Explain why you made your decision.

_____

_____

_____

Living Technology

The many branches of science are often connected. Engineered devices are sometimes used on living things. This connects engineering and biology.

This plant cleans wastewater to make it safe to return to the environment.

Engineers who work with living things are called bioengineers. When bioengineers apply the engineering design process to living things, they are practicing **bioengineering**.

A bioengineer may design a fish farm to raise large numbers of fish for food or other uses.

92

An important part of bioengineering has to do with the environment. Bioengineers design tools to prevent or clean up pollution, for example. Any product used to benefit organisms or their environment is an example of **biotechnology**.

Bioengineering also deals with health and nutrition. For instance, plants can be engineered to grow faster or larger to feed more people. Food for livestock may be engineered to make the animals healthier.

Bioengineers also design biotechnology that helps detect or treat diseases. For example, scanners in hospitals can look inside the body. They let doctors see a diseased or damaged organ. Other devices help surgeons perform operations.

Some bioengineers design devices that replace human body parts. Artificial legs help people who have lost their own. Artificial skin helps people with burns. Bioengineers have even developed artificial hearts.

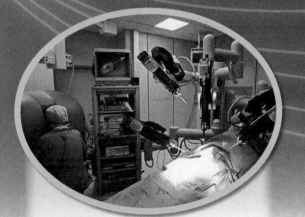

Surgeons today can use computer-assisted machines in delicate operations.

This artificial heart may not look like a real human heart, but it works nearly the same.

Bioengineering and Human Needs

Identify the human need met by each of these biotechnologies.

Biotechnology	Need
Water treatment plant	
Fish farm	
Robotic surgery	
Artificial heart	

Sum It Up!

When you're done, use the answer key to check and revise your work.

Summarize

Fill in the missing words to explain how technology improves our lives. Use the words in the box if you need help.

benefits	bioengineering	risks
promotional materials	need	technology

Technology may be simple or complex, but all technology meets a 1. _____ .

2. _____ changes as the needs of people change. Technology may have both a positive and a negative effect on people. Positive effects are called 3. _____ .

Negative effects are called 4. _____ . 5. _____ make claims about products, but smart shoppers should always evaluate the accuracy of the claims. The application of the engineering design process to living things is 6. _____ .

Draw a line from the picture to the statement that best summarizes what the picture shows.

7. Bioengineering may develop technologies that protect the environment, improve nutrition, or replace body parts.

8. A benefit of packaged food is convenience. A risk is an increase in the amount of trash.

9. Even a simple fastener is technology because it meets a human need.

10. Communication technology has changed greatly over time.

Answer Key: 1. need 2. Technology 3. benefits 4. risks 5. promotional materials 6. bioengineering 7. line to artificial heart 8. line to dried apples 9. line to zipper 10. line to smartphone

Name _____

Word Play

1 Use the words in the box below to help you unscramble the highlighted words in each statement. Then, write the unscrambled word on the line.

One **irsk** of using a computer is being exposed to unsafe Internet sites.

_____

A fish farm is an example of **hetooblyincgo**.

_____

otyleonchg is anything that meets a need or solves a problem.

_____

Engineers work with living organisms in the process of **nnneeeiiiggbor**.

_____

mintroooalpaalsiremt make claims about products.

_____

benefit	bioengineering*	biotechnology*
risk	promotional materials	technology

* Key Lesson Vocabulary

Apply Concepts

2 Describe how changes in transportation have affected communication over long distances. Give an example.

_____

_____

3 Name two benefits and two risks for each of these technologies.

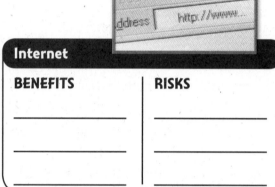

Plastic Grocery Bags	
BENEFITS	**RISKS**
_____	_____
_____	_____
_____	_____

Internet	
BENEFITS	**RISKS**
_____	_____
_____	_____
_____	_____

4 Evaluate the accuracy of the label on this product. Explain if the label is accurate, or if it isn't.

_____

_____

_____

Take It Home!

With a family member, identify five examples of technology in your home. Explain to the family member what needs are met by each of the technologies. Try to identify the risks and benefits of each one.

1 Prosthetic designers help people who are missing a body part, such as a hand, arm, or leg.

2 The people they help may have lost a body part from an injury or a disease. Or it may have been missing from birth.

3 Prosthetic designers create the prosthesis that replaces the missing body part.

4 To design a prosthesis, prosthetic designers need to study how the human body moves.

5 A prosthetic designer looks for new ways to improve how a prosthesis is made.

6 They use both computers and traditional tools including drills.

7 A prosthesis is made to meet the needs of each user.

8 A person may need a special prosthesis to swim, run, bike, or golf.

9 A prosthesis is designed to move easily, naturally, and under the wearer's control.

10 Prosthetic designers can change people's lives!

10 THINGS
YOU SHOULD KNOW ABOUT
Prosthetic Designers

Designing Sports Prostheses

For each image, write the number of the design criteria that meet each person's needs.

1 It should allow the leg to bend forward and the knee to lock.

2 It should fit comfortably at the knee and allow the ankle to rotate.

3 It should be lightweight, flexible, and resist high-force impacts.

4 It should be lightweight and able to rotate 180°.

5 It should be waterproof and allow the ankle to lock.

6 It should have attachments for gripping different objects.

7 It should be able to rotate 90° and have good traction.

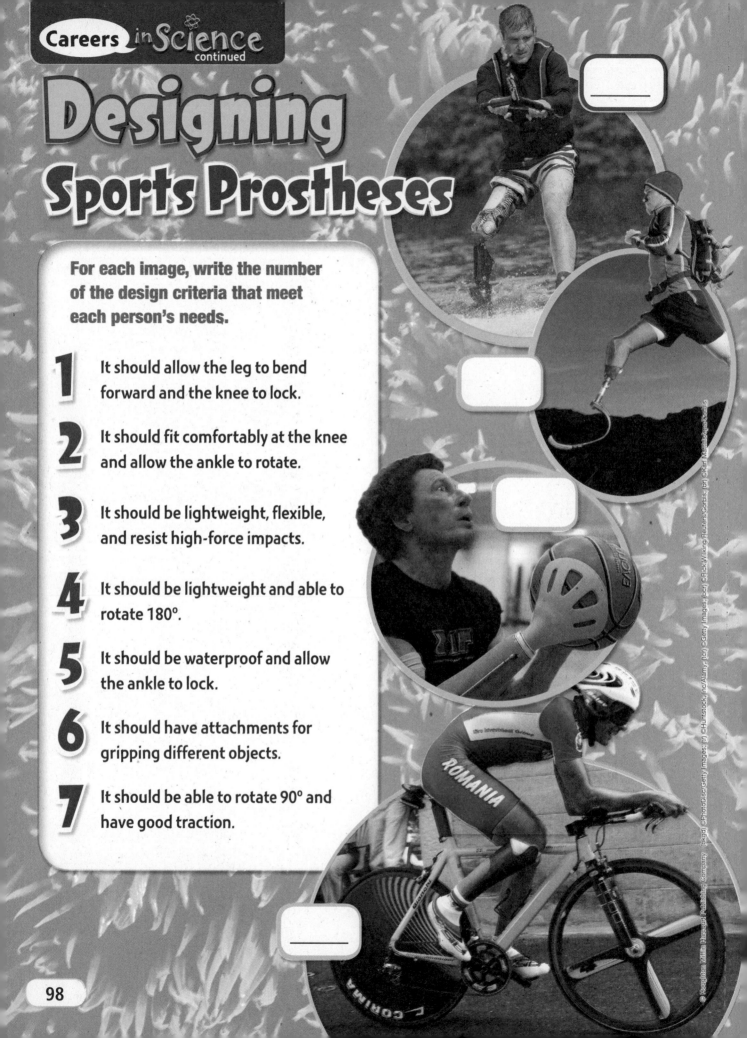

Inquiry Flipchart page 16

Lesson 4

INQUIRY

OHIO **5.SIA.4** Analyze and interpret data, **5.SIA.8** Communicate scientific procedures and explanations.

Name _____

Essential Question

How Can You Use Engineering to Solve a Problem?

Set a Purpose

What problem are you trying to solve?

_____

_____

How would a jar opener be useful?

_____

_____

_____

Think About the Procedure

What is a prototype?

_____

Describe two ideas for your prototype.

_____

_____

_____

_____

Record Your Data

Draw a detailed plan for your jar opener. Label the materials. Describe how it will work. Then build and test your prototype.

_____

_____

_____

Draw Conclusions

What criteria did you use to test your
prototype?

_____

_____

_____

_____

Based on the tested criteria, write a valid
conclusion about the results of your
investigation. Then, communicate your
conclusion in verbal form to your class.

_____

_____

_____

Describe how you tested your prototype.
Record any data you collected.

_____

_____

_____

_____

Analyze and Extend

1. Did your prototype need
   improvements? Describe them.

_____

_____

_____

_____

_____

2. Summarize how you designed and
   tested your jar opener.

_____

_____

_____

_____

_____

_____

3. Describe another jar opener
   design that is possible using the
   materials provided.

_____

_____

_____

_____

_____

4. Think of other designs you might
   make if you had different materials.
   How would that design work?

_____

_____

_____

_____

_____

Name _____

Vocabulary Review

Use the terms in the box to complete the sentences.

> bioengineering
> biotechnology
> criteria
> engineer
> prototype
> technology

1. People who use scientific knowledge to solve practical problems are producing _____.

2. A person who uses science and math for practical purposes, such as designing structures, machines, and systems, is a(n) _____.

3. The standards a designer uses to measure the success of a design are _____.

4. The process of applying the engineering design process to living things is _____.

5. The original or test model a designer builds for a new product is a(n) _____.

6. An engineer who designs artificial legs is engaged in the field of _____.

Science Concepts

Fill in the letter of the choice that best answers the question.

7. Suppose you are a bioengineer designing an artificial hand that can perform everyday tasks, such as picking up a spoon. What would you do first?

   (A) Build a prototype and have someone use it.

   (B) Make the hand lighter and more flexible.

   (C) Build a computer model to observe how the human hand works.

   (D) Take a survey to see how many people are interested.

8. What is the first step in the design process?

   (A) Brainstorm ideas for a product.

   (B) Ask questions to establish a need.

   (C) Identify criteria for the product.

   (D) Build a prototype and test it.

9. Engineers study materials for possible use in an artificial knee joint. They need a strong material with a mass/volume ratio in the range of 2.3–2.6. The graph shows data they collected on three materials.

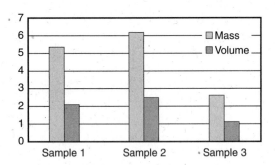

What can the engineers conclude using the data from the graph?

(A) All of the samples meet the material design criterion that the engineers identified.

(B) Sample 3 has the least volume and should not be considered for the knee.

(C) Sample 2 has the greatest mass per volume ratio and is the densest material.

(D) All samples are outside the acceptable range and show a mass of 5–6.

10. Use logical reasoning. Suppose you are designing a prosthetic shoulder joint. Which is the most important design criterion that you should include?

(A) It should be realistic in color and appearance.

(B) It should be capable of full movement within a shoulder socket.

(C) It should keep the user from injuring himself again.

(D) It should be stronger and more flexible than a natural shoulder joint.

11. A sports company wants to produce a profitable product that will benefit the wearer. The data below show the results of a survey about students' favorite sports activities.

Sports Participation in High School

Sport	Fraction of Students
basketball	$\frac{4}{5}$
bicycling	$\frac{3}{5}$
soccer	$\frac{1}{2}$
swimming	$\frac{3}{10}$

Which can you infer would be the most needed product among those students surveyed?

(A) a helmet to protect against accidental head injuries

(B) water-repelling racing swim trunks

(C) shorts with padded backs

(D) high-impact, ankle-supporting shoes

12. Which of the following is a testable hypothesis related to a new fabric prototype?

(A) The fabric can be used for many products.

(B) The fabric will be popular for use in clothing.

(C) The fabric is stronger than other fabrics.

(D) The fabric is easy to make and inexpensive.

13. Engineers want to develop a more efficient dishwasher by decreasing cycle time and the amount of water used per cycle. They design and test four different prototypes. The bar graph shows their results.

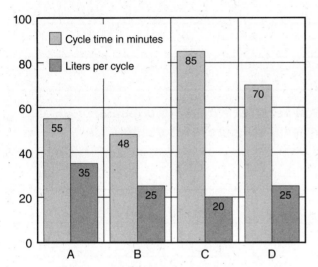

Based on this data, which model best meets the engineers' design criteria?

Ⓐ Model A   Ⓒ Model C

Ⓑ Model B   Ⓓ Model D

14. With further testing, engineers discover that the dishwasher model that best met the criteria didn't clean the dishes thoroughly. Which is the best next step for the engineers?

Ⓐ Start all over with a new dishwasher design.

Ⓑ Build another prototype and test it again.

Ⓒ Choose one of the other models to manufacture.

Ⓓ Figure out what is wrong with the model and redesign it.

15. A company claims that their MP3 players produce better sound than that of a competitor.

Which of the following best describes this claim?

Ⓐ If the company is reputable, it is probably true.

Ⓑ It can't be proven because "better" is an opinion.

Ⓒ It can be evaluated by experimental testing.

Ⓓ You could decide if it's true by testing the players.

16. A satellite TV company claims that they have more satisfied users than their competitor. How would you evaluate the accuracy of this claim?

Ⓐ Ask all of your friends and neighbors if they are satisfied with their company.

Ⓑ Read the claims of both companies and compare them.

Ⓒ Try both companies and decide which you like better.

Ⓓ Analyze a survey of satisfied satellite TV users.

Apply Inquiry and Review the Big Idea

17. Javier wants to design a better pack to carry his books and sporting equipment back and forth to school.

a. What criteria will Javier use when choosing material for his bag? How will he test the criteria? What tools will he use?

_____

_____

_____

_____

b. Describe Javier's procedure in testing his prototype. What types of information will he collect? How will he decide whether he needs to improve his design? How will he select the final design?

_____

_____

_____

_____

Use the table to answer questions 18 and 19. It shows the result of an investigation to determine the range of the signal of four models of garage door remote openers and the time it takes for the doors to lift.

Remote Range and Door Lift Time		
Model	Range (m)	Time (sec)
A	18	10
B	10	8
C	15	12
D	6	15

18. Analyze and interpret data. Which opener best meets the criteria for longest range and shortest lift time? Explain your answer.

_____

_____

19. How many times farther than the shortest-range remote was the longest-range remote able to activate the garage door?

_____

The Solar System and the Universe

Big Idea

Earth is part of a solar system, which is made up of many different objects orbiting a sun.

OHIO 5.ESS.1, 5.ESS.2, 5.ESS.3, 5.SIA.1, 5.SIA.2, 5.SIA.3, 5.SIA.4, 5.SIA.6, 5.SIA.8

I Wonder Why

Why are most observatories built far from large cities? *Turn the page to find out.*

Here's why Most observatories are built far from cities to avoid the brightening of the night sky caused by artificial outdoor lighting, which can make it impossible to see dim lights from stars.

In this unit, you will explore the Big Idea, the Essential Questions, and the Investigations on the Inquiry Flipchart.

Levels of Inquiry Key ■ DIRECTED ■ GUIDED ■ INDEPENDENT

Track Your Progress

Big Idea Earth is part of a solar system, which is made up of many different objects orbiting a sun.

Essential Questions

Now I Get the Big Idea!

Science Notebook

Before you begin each lesson, be sure to write your thoughts about the Essential Question.

Lesson 1

Essential Question

How Do the Sun, Earth, and Moon Differ?

Engage Your Brain!

Find the answer to the following question in this lesson and record it here.

The picture shows a solar flare on the sun. How can solar flares affect you on Earth?

_____

_____

_____

_____

Active Reading

Lesson Vocabulary
List each term. As you learn about each one, make notes in the Interactive Glossary.

_____

_____

_____

Signal Words: Cause and Effect
Signal words show connections between ideas. Words signaling a cause include *because* and *if*. Words signaling an effect include *so* and *thus*. Active readers recall what they read because they are alert to signal words that identify causes and effects.

Very Different Orbs

You can't help but notice that the sun and moon are very different from Earth and from each other. What makes them so different? Read on to find out!

Active Reading As you read this page, draw boxes around words or phrases that signal comparison, such as *like*, *unlike*, *larger*, and *smaller*.

There are millions of kilometers between the sun, moon, and Earth. Yet we feel heat from the sun and see the whitish color of the moon. These are direct evidence that these bodies are different from our planet.

Earth is often called the "blue planet" because most of its surface is covered by water. On the moon's surface, water wouldn't last long. Without a thick atmosphere like Earth's, water on the moon would freeze or be lost to space.

The sun is a star, which is a huge, hot ball of gases that produces its own light. It's about 109 times larger than Earth. Unlike Earth and the moon, the sun does not have a solid surface. Its atmosphere extends out millions of kilometers. From the sun's surface, solar flares explode into space.

The moon is tiny when compared in size to the sun. Unlike Earth, its temperatures are scorching hot during the day and freezing cold at night. Like Earth, it has features such as mountains and flat plains.

EARTH

Earth is a *planet*, an object that moves around a star, has a nearly round shape, and has cleared its path of most debris. Its characteristics include:

- Diameter: 12,742 km
- Structure: mainly rocky layers, partly liquid core
- Composition: mainly iron, oxygen, silicon, and magnesium
- Atmosphere: mainly nitrogen and oxygen
- Notable features: Lots of liquid water and diverse life forms
- Minimum surface temperature: -88 °C
- Maximum surface temperature: 58 °C

The green hue shows plant life that Earth's waters help support.

SUN

The sun produces energy deep in its core. This energy makes the sun glow and provides Earth with heat and light.

- Diameter: 1,391,016 km
- Structure: gaseous layers
- Composition: hydrogen and helium
- Atmosphere: hydrogen and helium
- Notable surface features: sunspots, solar flares
- Average surface temperature: 5,500 °C

Solar flares can disrupt energy distribution systems on Earth.

How Do They Compare?

This circle is a model of Earth. It is 4 cm in diameter. Use a calculator and data on this page to find the diameter for a moon model. Would the moon model fit inside Earth's model? If so, draw it in.

4 cm

_____

Without water or wind, moon landforms do not change.

MOON

The moon is visible from Earth because it reflects light from the sun.

- Diameter: 3,475 km
- Structure: rocky layers
- Composition: mainly oxygen, silicon, magnesium, and iron
- Atmosphere: none
- Notable surface features: craters, mountains, plains
- Minimum surface temperature: –233 °C
- Maximum surface temperature: 123 °C

Beyond the Book

Use the information on these pages to construct a 3-ring Venn diagram to compare the physical characteristics of the sun, Earth, and moon. What makes each object unique?

Images are not to scale.

The Sun-Earth-Moon System

The moon moves around Earth as Earth moves around the sun. What keeps these objects from flying off in space?

Active Reading As you read these two pages, draw boxes around clue words that signal a cause.

What defines the unit of time we call a year? A year is the time it takes for Earth to **revolve**, or go around, the sun. Any object that revolves around another object in space is called a *satellite*. Earth is a satellite of the sun. Because the moon revolves around Earth, it is a satellite of Earth.

The path one space object takes around another is called an **orbit**. It takes Earth about 365 days to complete its orbit around the sun. The moon's orbit is shorter than Earth's. As a result, it takes the moon just 27 days to revolve once around Earth.

The Earth and moon motion around the sun is in part because of gravity. *Gravity* is the force of attraction that exists between all objects. Gravitational attraction between objects depends on two things: the distance between the objects and the masses of the objects.

Sun

Gravitational Pull The sun is about 330,000 times more massive than Earth. Its strong gravitational pull keeps all objects near it from flying off into space. Gravity also keeps the moon in its orbit around Earth. Gravitational pull decreases with distance.

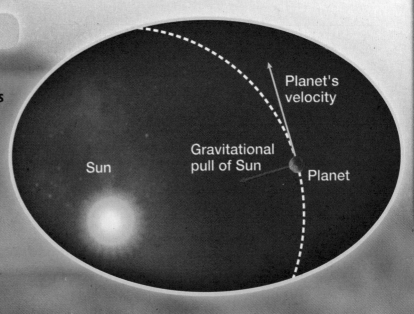

Planet's velocity

Gravitational pull of Sun

Sun

Planet

Moon

Earth

▶ Scientists have observed that every year the moon gets farther away from Earth. Predict what could happen if the moon gets too far away.

_____

_____

_____

_____

Orbits Earth revolves around the sun in a counterclockwise orbit. The moon also revolves in a counterclockwise orbit around Earth. Earth's orbit around the sun is nearly circular in shape, with the sun nearly in the center of the circle.

▶ Draw arrows to show how Earth revolves around the sun and the moon around Earth.

Sun

Moon

Earth

© Houghton Mifflin Harcourt Publishing Company (bg) ©Pearson Co Ltd/Getty Images; (t) ©Grand X Pictures/Getty Images; (c) ©Photodisc/Getty Images

Images are not to scale.

Clear As Day and Night

You've learned that Earth revolves around the sun. What other movement does Earth have?

Active Reading As you read these two pages, find and underline the definitions of *rotates* and *axis*.

Each morning, you see the sun appear to rise in the east. At first, the sun is low in the sky. As the day goes on, it seems to move higher, cross the sky, and set in the west.

The sun is not actually moving. Instead, Earth **rotates**, or spins around its axis, once every 24 hours. The **axis** is the imaginary line that goes through Earth from pole to pole. The rotation of Earth around its axis also causes the moon and the stars to appear to move across the sky.

Evidence of Rotation You can see evidence of Earth's rotation if you look at the stars at night. The North Star is nearly directly above the North Pole. It does not appear to move as Earth rotates. It's like the hub of a wheel—the stars around it seem to circle around the North Star.

North Star

The North Star does not seem to rise, set, or move across the sky.

As Earth rotates, one half of Earth experiences daylight while the other half is in darkness.

Day/Night Cycle

The rotation of Earth around its axis causes day and night. Look at the diagrams on the right. At 12 a.m., Houston, Texas, faces away from the sun. The people who live there are most likely sleeping. However, Earth is constantly rotating. In the bottom diagram, it is 12 p.m. and Texas is facing the sun. People there may now be outside in the sunshine. While it is day in Texas, it is nighttime on the opposite side of the world.

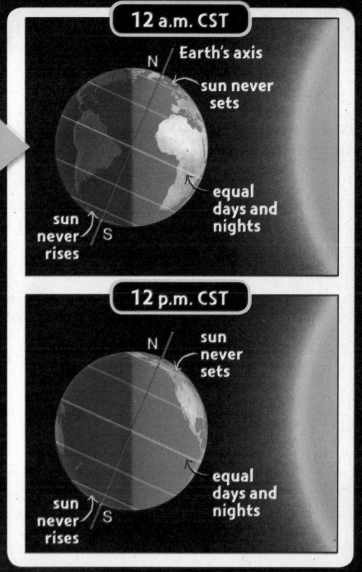

12 a.m. CST

Earth's axis

sun never sets

N

equal days and nights

sun never rises

S

12 p.m. CST

sun never sets

N

equal days and nights

sun never rises

S

North Star

This time-lapse photo shows the circular path stars appear to take around the North Star throughout the night.

Do the Math!
Calculate Circumference

Earth takes 24 hours to complete one rotation. It rotates at an average speed of 1,670 km/hour. Calculate Earth's circumference at the equator based on its rotational speed. Show your work below.

1,670 × 24 =

24 × 1000 = 2400

24 × 600 =

24 × 70 =

Images are not to scale.

More Earth-Sun Interaction

Earth's rotation around its axis causes night and day. What changes happen on Earth as it also revolves around the sun?

Summer Solstice

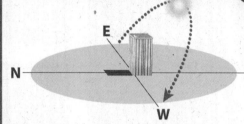

During summer, Earth's axis points toward the sun. The Northern Hemisphere's summer solstice occurs June 20 or 21. It is the longest day of the year and marks the start of the summer season. Summer days are the longest and warmest. The noon sun is high in the sky, causing shadows to be short.

Fall Equinox

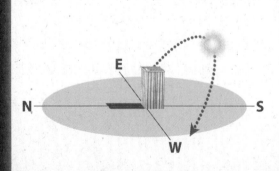

During fall and spring, Earth's axis points neither away nor toward the sun. The fall equinox occurs September 22 or 23 in the Northern Hemisphere. This day marks the start of fall and has equal hours of day and night. In fall, daylight hours grow shorter and the noon sun's height is lower than in summer.

Images are not to scale.

Earth's Orbit

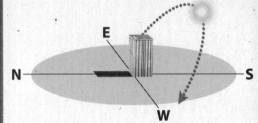

Look at the diagrams of Earth on these pages. Notice that Earth's axis is not straight up and down. Instead, it is tilted at a 23.5 degree angle. The tilt of Earth's axis as it revolves around the sun causes seasons. *Seasons* are short-term changes in climate. Most places on Earth have four seasons: summer, fall, winter, and spring. Seasons happen because different parts of Earth get different amounts of sunlight throughout the year. This causes changes in temperature and length of day.

Spring Equinox

In the Northern Hemisphere, the spring equinox occurs March 20 or 21. In spring, the sun appears higher in the sky than it did in winter, daylight hours grow longer, and temperatures get warmer.

▶ To complete the model, draw the path of the sun as it appears to rise, cross the sky, and set during winter. Then draw the shadow cast by the building.

Winter Solstice

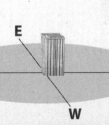

During winter, Earth's axis points away from the sun. The Northern Hemisphere's winter solstice occurs December 21 or 22. It is the shortest day of the year and marks the start of the winter season. Winter days are the shortest and coldest of the year. The sun is never high in the sky.

What if Earth Didn't Spin?

How did scientists prove that Earth rotates?
What would happen if this rotation stopped?

Great minds such as Sir Isaac Newton and Robert Hooke tried to prove that Earth rotates. In 1679, Newton wrote that objects dropped from a tall tower swerved slightly to the east. Why? By the time they hit the ground, he reasoned, Earth would have already rotated to the east.

For years, scientists tried to find evidence that Newton was correct. Yet the change in a falling object's landing was too small to measure using the technology of the times. Finally, in 1851, a French scientist named Leon Foucault used a pendulum to show that Earth rotates. One of the great questions of science was answered!

The sun's movement across the sky was once cited as empirical evidence of the sun's revolution around Earth. New technology and additional observation was needed to demonstrate that Earth's rotation was the cause of the sun's apparent motion.

▶ Explain why finding evidence supporting Newton's hypothesis was difficult. Would an airplane have helped? Explain how.

_____

_____

_____

_____

_____

_____

_____

In 1851, Foucault performed a public demonstration. He used a pendulum that was 60 meters long. Each swing of the pendulum followed a slightly different path, providing evidence that the floor—and Earth beneath it—was moving.

Earth with No Rotation Some scientists wonder what would happen if Earth stopped rotating. Computer models show that Earth would be very different. In a spinless Earth, a single day and night cycle would last a whole year. For six months, half of Earth would be in daylight and the other half would be in darkness. The sunlit side of Earth would be very hot!

Earth's magnetic field, produced by its rotation, would disappear. This would allow more solar radiation to reach Earth's surface, causing health problems. Luckily, Earth's rotation shows no signs of stopping!

Spinless Earth

Part of North America, including the Great Lakes, would be swallowed up by the oceans.

The oceans would move to the poles.

One huge continent would form along the equator.

The ocean floor at the equator becomes a deep valley.

When you're done, use the answer key to check and revise your work.

Fill in the chart below to show how the sun and moon differ from Earth.

Compare sun, Earth, and moon		
	Similarities to Earth	Differences from Earth
sun	The sun has a(n) 1. _____ that extends far into space.	The sun produces 3. _____ _____on its surface that affect communications on Earth.
moon	The moon has a(n) 2. _____ surface and features that include mountains and plains.	Land features on the moon don't 4. _____ _____because there is no liquid water on the moon's surface.

Summarize

Fill in the missing words about the sun-Earth-moon system.

Earth 5. _____ around its axis once every 24 hours. This movement of Earth makes the

moon, stars, and 6. _____ appear to move across the sky. This movement also causes

the 7. _____ and 8. _____ cycle. Earth 9. _____ around the

sun once every 365 days. The time it takes Earth to go once around the sun is called a

10. _____. Earth's revolution and the tilt of its axis causes the 11. _____

to occur. 12. _____ keeps the moon in its orbit around Earth and Earth in its orbit

around the sun.

Name _____

Word Play

1 **Use the words in the box to complete the puzzle.**

1. has no solid surface and is made up of helium and hydrogen
2. the spinning of Earth around its axis causes this cycle
3. keeps Earth and the moon in orbit around the sun
4. Earth does this around its axis
5. Earth does this around the sun
6. an object in space that moves around the sun, has a round shape, and has cleared its path of most debris
7. the imaginary line that goes through Earth from pole to pole
8. Earth's path around the sun
9. short-term changes in climate caused by Earth's movement around the sun

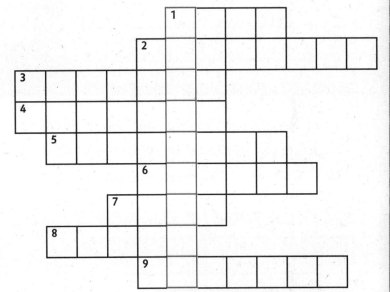

Read the letters going down the column with the red border. Use that word to complete the following riddle.

10. Sally Smith's spaceship goes around and around Earth, so it is a _____.

axis*	day/night	gravity	orbit*	planet	revolves*
rotates*	seasons	star			

* Key Lesson Vocabulary

Apply Concepts

2 Think about the characteristics of the moon. What would you need to survive there?

_____

_____

_____

3 Suppose east is to the left of the drawing. Draw the apparent path of the winter sun across the sky.

4 The data table shows information gathered by students over a year. Examine and evaluate the information on the second and third columns to infer the season for each observation period.

Observation Period	Shadows at Noon	Average Temperature	Season
1	getting shorter	18 °C	
2	shortest	28 °C	
3	getting longer	21 °C	
4	longest	7 °C	

5 Suppose Earth completes one rotation every 12 hours. How would this affect the cycle of day and night?

_____

Take It Home!

On a sunny day, face north and put a stick in the ground. Observe the shadow cast by the stick. Observe how the shadow changes throughout the day. Explain how these changes are related to Earth's rotation.

OHIO 5.ESS.1 The solar system includes the sun and all celestial bodies that orbit the sun. Each planet in the solar system has unique characteristics.

Lesson 2

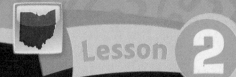

Essential Question

What Objects Are Part of the Solar System?

Engage Your Brain!

Find the answer to the following question in this lesson and record it here.

Which planets have rings, and what are the rings made of?

_____

_____

_____

Active Reading

Lesson Vocabulary

List the terms. As you learn about each one, make notes in the Interactive Glossary.

_____   _____

_____   _____

_____

Compare and Contrast

Many ideas in this lesson are connected because they explain comparisons and contrasts—how things are alike and different. Active readers stay focused on comparisons and contrasts when they ask themselves, How are these things alike? How are they different?

The Solar System

The sun, Earth, and its moon form a system in space. Earth revolves around the sun. That means Earth travels around the sun in a path called an orbit. The moon revolves around Earth. Read on to learn about other objects in space.

Active Reading As you read this page, underline two details that tell how all planets are alike.

Earth and its moon are part of a larger system in space called a solar system. A **solar system** is made up of a star and the planets and other space objects that revolve around it. A **planet** is a large, round body that revolves around a star. In our solar system, the planets and other objects revolve around a star we call the sun.

There are eight planets in our solar system. All of them rotate, or spin, about an axis. This is an imaginary line that goes through the center of a planet. Earth rotates on its axis once every 24 hours. This is the length of one day on Earth.

Unlike planets, some objects don't revolve directly around the sun. *Moons* are small natural objects that revolve around other objects. Many planets have moons. Earth has only one. It revolves once around Earth about every 27 days.

Earth is about 150 million kilometers from the sun!

Diagrams not to scale.

The planets in our solar system are very far from each other.

The orbits of the planets in our solar system are not perfect circles. They are oval-shaped, or elliptical [eh•LIP•tuh•kuhl].

Some planets have many moons. Earth has only one. Venus and Mercury have none!

Around and Around

Draw an orbit for the planet. Then draw a moon and its orbit.

sun

planet

At times, the brightest object in the night sky is not the moon or a star. It is Venus, one of Earth's closest neighbors in space.

Active Reading As you read this page, underline ways in which the inner planets are alike.

Mercury

Mercury, the smallest planet in our solar system, is less than half the size of Earth. Its surface is filled with craters, much like Earth's moon. Mercury is the closest planet to the sun. On Mercury, the sun would look three times as large as it does on Earth.

Planets in our solar system can be classified based on their distance from the sun. The four inner planets are the closest to the sun. In order from closest to farthest, the inner planets are Mercury, Venus, Earth, and Mars.

The inner planets are very dense and rocky. They have thin atmospheres and small diameters. A planet's diameter is the distance from one side of the planet, through its center, to the other side. The inner planets have large solid cores at their centers. They have few moons, and their revolution times are short compared to the other planets in the solar system.

Venus

Venus is so hot that lead would melt at its surface! Thick clouds surround Venus, and its atmosphere is made up mostly of carbon dioxide. Lava flows from more than 1,000 volcanoes on Venus's surface.

Planets not to scale.

sun

Earth

Earth is the third planet from the sun. It has an atmosphere made of mostly nitrogen, oxygen, and carbon dioxide. Earth is the only planet known to have abundant liquid water, which helps to keep Earth at temperatures that allow life.

No Home for Me

List three reasons why people could not live on Venus.

1. _____

_____

2. _____

_____

3. _____

_____

Mars

Sometimes you can see Mars in the night sky. Mars is known as the "Red Planet" because of its red, rocky surface. Giant dust storms often cover the entire planet, forming huge sand dunes. Mars, like the other inner planets, has many volcanoes.

The Outer Planets

On a clear night, Jupiter might appear to be a large, bright star in the night sky. But in fact, Jupiter is one of the outer planets in our solar system.

Great Red Spot

Active Reading As you read this page, underline ways in which the outer planets are alike.

Jupiter

Jupiter is the largest planet in the solar system. In fact, all of the other planets would fit inside Jupiter! Its Great Red Spot is about as wide as three Earths. The red spots are massive, spinning storms. Jupiter's faint rings were discovered by the *Voyager 1* space probe in 1979.

Jupiter, Saturn, Uranus, and Neptune are the outer planets. In that order, they are the farthest planets from the sun. The outer planets are also called the gas giants, because they are huge and made up mostly of gases. They don't have a solid surface, and their cores are very small.

Because the gas giants are so far away from the sun, their surfaces are much colder than the inner planets. All of the outer planets have many moons and ring systems. Saturn's ring system is more visible than those of the other outer planets.

Planets not to scale.

Saturn

Saturn, the second largest planet, has thousands of rings around it. The rings are made up of ice and chunks of rock. Some of Saturn's moons are found inside these rings. Like Jupiter, Saturn has large storms.

What Makes Them Unique?

Write one thing that is unique about each of the outer planets.

Jupiter

_____

_____

Saturn

_____

_____

Uranus

_____

_____

Neptune

_____

_____

Uranus

The axis of Uranus is tilted so far that, compared to other planets, it rotates on its side. This makes seasons on Uranus last more than 20 years! Deep inside Uranus, heated gases bubble and burst onto the surface, causing bright clouds to form. Uranus has a system of at least 13 faint rings.

sun

Neptune

Neptune is the windiest planet in our solar system. Its winds move at speeds of about 2,000 km/hr (1,243 mi/hr). These winds blow Neptune's Great Dark Spot around the planet. This spot is a storm, about the size of Earth, known to vanish and reform! Neptune has nine rings around it.

127

Compare Inner and Outer Planets

Size, surface features, and distance from the sun are just some differences between the inner and outer planets. Look at this chart to learn about other differences.

Planet	Period of Revolution (in Earth days and years)	Period of Rotation (in Earth hours and days)	Temperature (°C) (inner planets: surface range; outer planets: top of the clouds)	Number of Moons	Density (g/cm³)	Diameter
INNER PLANETS						
Mercury	88 days	59 days	−173 to 427	0	5.43	4,878 km (3,031mi)
Venus	225 days	243 days	462	0	5.24	12,104 km (7,521 mi)
Earth	365 days	1 day	−88 to 58	1	5.52	12,756 km (7,926 mi)
Mars	687 days	about 1 day	−87 to −5	2	3.94	6,794 km (4,222 mi)
OUTER PLANETS						
Jupiter	12 years	about 10 hours	−148	63	1.33	142,984 km (88,846 mi)
Saturn	29 years	about 10 hours	−178	61	0.70	120,536 km (74,898 mi)
Uranus	84 years	about 17 hours	−216	27	1.30	51,118 km (31,763 mi)
Neptune	165 years	about 16 hours	−214	13	1.76	49,528 km (30,775 mi)

Do the Math!
Find an Average

In the space below, find the average density of the four inner planets. Repeat for the four outer planets.

Inner planets:

Outer planets:

How do the average densities compare?

_____

_____

_____

The density of water is 1 gram per cubic centimeter (g/cm³). Saturn would float because its density is less than the density of water. Earth would sink.

Patterns in Data

Look at the data table on the previous page. Describe two trends in the data between the inner and outer planets.

_____

_____

_____

_____

_____

The Flying Objects

Besides planets, there are many other bodies that orbit the sun. Let's find out more about some of them.

Active Reading As you read these two pages, find and underline two facts about asteroids.

Moons

Other moons are very different from Earth's moon. Europa, one of Jupiter's moons, may have a liquid ocean under a layer of ice. Another of Jupiter's moons, Io [EYE•oh], has the most active volcanoes of any body in the solar system.

Io

Dwarf Planets

Pluto was once called a planet. But in 2006, it was reclassified as a dwarf planet. **Dwarf planets** are nearly round bodies whose orbits cross the orbits of other bodies. Most are found in a region of the solar system beyond Neptune's orbit called the Kuiper belt. These objects are far away and hard to study. Quaoar, shown above, was discovered in 2002.

Asteroids

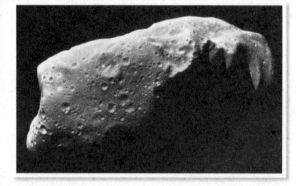

Asteroids are rock and iron objects that orbit the sun. Millions of them are found in the wide region between Mars and Jupiter known as the *asteroid belt*. Some asteroids are as small as a city block. Others could fill up an ocean. Some asteroids even have their own moons!

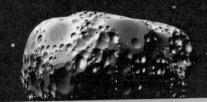

Meteoroids, Meteors, and Meteorites

Each day, tons of meteoroids hit Earth's atmosphere. *Meteoroids* are pieces of rock that break off of asteroids and travel through space. Most meteoroids burn up in Earth's atmosphere, causing a streak of light called a *meteor*. Meteoroids that reach Earth's surface are called *meteorites*.

Where's the Sun?

In the drawing of a comet, put an *S* to indicate the direction toward the sun. Put a *T* over each tail.

Comets

A **comet** is a chunk of frozen gases, rock, ice, and dust. Comets have long orbits around the sun. As comets pass close to the sun, part of their frozen surface begins to break away and turn into gases and dust. These particles reflect the sun's light and become visible as long tails. A comet's tails always point away from the sun.

Space Watch

Some objects in space cross each others' orbits. Often, nothing happens. But sometimes the objects hit each other. Scientists look out for objects that may cross Earth's orbit.

Pictures of the surface of the moon tell a story. Over millions of years, space objects such as comets, meteoroids, and asteroids have impacted, or hit, the moon. Impact craters of all sizes can be found on the moon's surface.

Space objects have also hit other bodies in the solar system. A comet named Shoemaker-Levy 9 impacted Jupiter in 1994. Pictures of the impact were taken by the *Galileo* space probe.

Scientists know that large objects have also hit Earth. In fact, a huge one impacted Earth about 65 million years ago. Many scientists think it caused changes in the environment that killed all the dinosaurs. Luckily, impacts like that one do not happen often.

Scientists use telescopes to scan space for near-Earth asteroids. These are objects that may cross Earth's orbit. Scientists keep track of their size, position, and motion. They analyze this data to determine if the objects could impact Earth.

The impact of Shoemaker-Levy 9 caused bubbles of hot gas to rise into Jupiter's atmosphere, as well as dark spots to form on its surface.

The Barringer Meteor Crater, in Arizona, was formed by a meteorite that struck Earth about 50,000 years ago.

Impacts can happen anywhere on Earth! This map shows some impact crater sites from around the world.

Impact Crater Diameter

- · 10–25 km
- · 25–50 km
- ● greater than 50 km

▶ On these pages, underline effects of impacts. Then circle a picture that shows evidence of an impact on Earth.

Observatories have powerful telescopes that enable scientists to track the movement of objects in space.

When you're done, use the answer key to check and revise your work.

Read the summary, and then place the information in the list into the correct box below.

The sun is at the center of the solar system. Planets, dwarf planets, moons, and other smaller objects make up the solar system. The eight planets in the solar system can be divided into inner planets and outer planets. Each group has different characteristics.

small and dense	longer revolutions	many moons	few moons
giant size	closest to sun	gaseous surface	low density
rings	rocky surface		

1 **Inner Planets**

2 **Outer Planets**

Fill in the missing information to describe the object shown below.

3

Io

a. Object Type: _____

b. Space Neighbors: _____

c. Key Feature: _____

d. How It's Different from Earth: _____

_____

_____

Word Play

1

Use each of the terms in the box to label the objects in the diagram below.

planet	comet	asteroid	solar system	dwarf planet
moon	orbit	gas giant	sun	* Key Lesson Vocabulary

(x 1) • ● **Pluto**

9._____

1._____

(x 27) • **Uranus**

Neptune

• (x 13)

8._____

7._____

Jupiter

• (x 63)

(x 61) •

Saturn

5._____

6._____

← 4._____

Mercury **Earth**

Mars

2._____

3._____

Venus

Apply Concepts

2 In the space below, draw pictures to show the key physical characteristics of an inner planet and an outer planet. Then describe your drawings.

_____   _____

_____   _____

_____   _____

_____   _____

3 Describe the features of a comet.

_____

_____

_____

_____

4 What is a meteoroid, and how does it become a meteorite?

_____

_____

_____

_____

5 Identify each of the following large objects in the solar system. Write how you are able to identify each one.

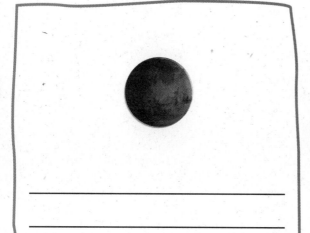

_____
_____

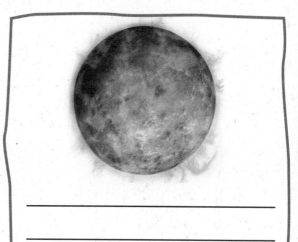

_____
_____

_____
_____

_____
_____

6 A scientist discovers an object in the solar system. She describes it as bigger than an asteroid, smaller than Mercury, and farther from the sun than Neptune. What kind of object could it be? Explain.

_____
_____

7 Complete the Venn diagram in order to compare and contrast an asteroid and a comet.

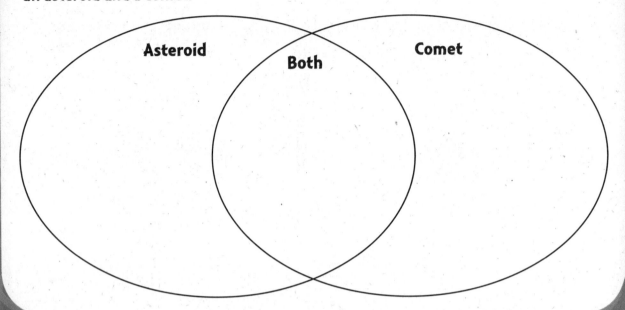

Asteroid   Both   Comet

8 Draw a picture of an object that might impact a planet. Label and describe the object. What evidence is there that these objects collide with planets and moons?

_____

_____

_____

Take It Home!

Many newspapers give the location of Venus, Mars, and Jupiter in the sky. Find out where in the sky these planets may appear. See if you can find them. They are among the brightest objects in the night sky.

Meet Two Space Explorers

On her first mission, Kalpana Chawla traveled more than six million miles in 15 days!

Kalpana Chawla

As a little girl in India, Kalpana Chawla dreamed about flying airplanes. She came to the United States and studied hard. She soon earned her degree as an aerospace engineer. Kalpana Chawla could fly many kinds of airplanes. Her dreams had come true! But she kept dreaming. She wanted to fly in space. She went to work for NASA and became an astronaut. Soon, Kalpana Chawla became the first Indian-born woman in space!

Claudia Alexander

Claudia Alexander explores outer space, too. But she never leaves Earth! She studies the moons of the planet Jupiter. She was in charge of NASA's *Galileo* mission. The mission sent an unmanned spacecraft to Jupiter. The spacecraft left Earth in 1989. It took six long years to reach Jupiter. Claudia Alexander directed it over 385 million miles! Under her command, *Galileo* was the first spacecraft to take detailed photos of Jupiter and its moons.

Galileo space probe

Two Ways to Study Space

Kalpana Chawla and Claudia Alexander study space in different ways. Write the statements that apply to each scientist in the correct circle.

Kalpana Chawla

_____
_____
_____
_____
_____

The Hubble Space Telescope sends scientists pictures of space from its orbit high above Earth.

- I lead space missions without leaving Earth.
- I traveled on the space shuttle.
- I study the moons of Jupiter.
- I grew up in India and learned to fly many types of airplanes.
- I study objects in space.

Claudia Alexander

_____
_____
_____
_____
_____

Many scientists study space from Earth by using a telescope, such as this one, in an observatory.

© Houghton Mifflin Harcourt Publishing Company   (t) ©JPL-Caltech/NASA; (b) ©Joe McNally/Getty Images

Lesson 3
INQUIRY

OHIO 5.ESS.1 The solar system includes the sun and all celestial bodies that orbit the sun. Each planet in the solar system has unique characteristics. **5.SIA.1** Identify questions that can be answered through scientific investigations. **5.SIA.2** Design and conduct a scientific investigation. **5.SIA.3** Use appropriate mathematics, tools and techniques to gather data and information. **5.SIA.4** Analyze and interpret data. **5.SIA.6** Think critically and logically to connect evidence and explanations. **5.SIA.8** Communicate scientific procedures and explanations.

Name _____

Essential Question

How Can We Model the Sun and Planets?

Set a Purpose

What do you think you will learn from this activity?

_____

_____

_____

Think About the Procedure

The word *scale* has several meanings. What does it mean to make a *scale model* of the sun and planets?

_____

_____

You know that diameter is any line that passes through the center of a circle and connects two points on its circumference. Based on Step 1 of the activity, how would you define *radius*?

_____

_____

Record Your Data

Complete the chart below. To find the missing values, divide the scale diameter of each object by 2.

Object	Actual Diameter (km)	Scale Diameter (cm)	Scale Radius (cm)
Sun	1,391,900	300.0	
Mercury	4,880	1.0	
Venus	12,104	2.6	1.3
Earth	12,756	2.8	
Mars	6,794	1.5	0.75
Jupiter	142,984	32.0	
Saturn	120,536	25.0	12.5
Uranus	51,118	10.0	
Neptune	49,532	9.8	4.9

Draw Conclusions

Which planet has the smallest diameter?

_____

Earth is the largest inner planet. What is Earth's diameter? How does it compare to the diameter of the outer planets?

_____

_____

_____

Jupiter is the largest planet in the solar system. How does Jupiter's diameter compare to the sun's diameter?

_____

_____

Analyze and Extend

1. Why would a scientist want to model the size of the sun and planets?

_____

_____

_____

_____

2. A section of the circumference of a circle is called an *arc*. In this investigation, why did you use an arc to model the sun and not the planets?

_____

_____

_____

3. In the space below, use your compass to draw an arc for a circle with a diameter of 8.6 cm.

4. If the circle in item 3 were a model of a new planet in the solar system, based on its size alone, to which group of planets would it belong? Explain.

_____

_____

_____

5. Think of other questions you would like to ask about objects in the solar system. Write your questions here.

_____

_____

_____

_____

OHIO **5.ESS.2** The sun is one of many stars that exist in the universe.

Lesson 4

Essential Question

What Are Stars and Galaxies?

Engage Your Brain!

Find the answer to the following question in this lesson and record it here.

• Space is not completely empty. There are small particles in space. What happens when these particles come together?

_____

_____

_____

A nebula, such as the Pelican Nebula shown here, is a giant cloud of gas and dust.

Active Reading

Lesson Vocabulary

List the terms. As you learn about each one, make notes in the Interactive Glossary.

_____

_____

_____

_____

Signal Words: Details

Signal words show connections between ideas. *For example, for instance,* and *such as* signal examples of an idea. *Also* and *in fact* signal added facts. Active readers remember what they read because they are alert to signal words that identify examples and facts about a topic.

TWINKLING STARS

You see stars as tiny points of white light in the night sky. Stars are not tiny, and they are not all white. Find out how scientists study stars.

Active Reading As you read these two pages, draw boxes around words or phrases that signal a detail or an added fact.

People have always looked at objects in the sky. **Astronomy** is the study of objects in space and their characteristics. *Astronomers* are scientists who study space and everything in it. They use many types of telescopes to observe objects in space, such as stars and planets.

Stars are huge balls of hot, glowing gases that produce their own heat and light. The sun is the star you know the most about. It seems much larger than other stars only because it is much closer to Earth.

Do the Math!
Dividing by 3-digit Numbers

A small telescope magnifies objects 150 times. A large observatory telescope magnifies an object 3,300 times. How many times as great is the magnification of the observatory telescope than the small telescope?

_____

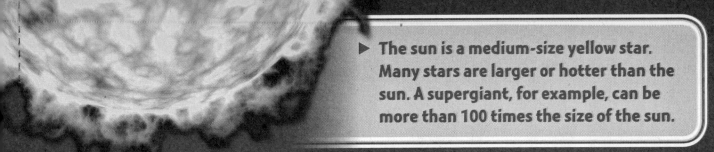

A STAR IS BORN

Stars form when gravity causes gas and dust particles found in space to pull together. These particles are squeezed together under great pressure. Eventually, energy stored in the particles is released as heat and light. A star is born.

Stars are classified by their color, temperature, brightness, and size. The color of a star can tell us about its temperature.

For example, blue stars are the hottest. A blue star's average temperature is about 15,000 °C.

Stars have a wide range of sizes. White dwarf stars, for instance, can be as small as a planet. Giant and supergiant stars are many times bigger than the average-size star. The largest stars are also usually the brightest. A star's brightness is related to the amount of visible light it gives off.

Super Hot and Just Hot

Draw a rectangle around the hottest stars in the diagram. Draw a circle around the brightest stars.

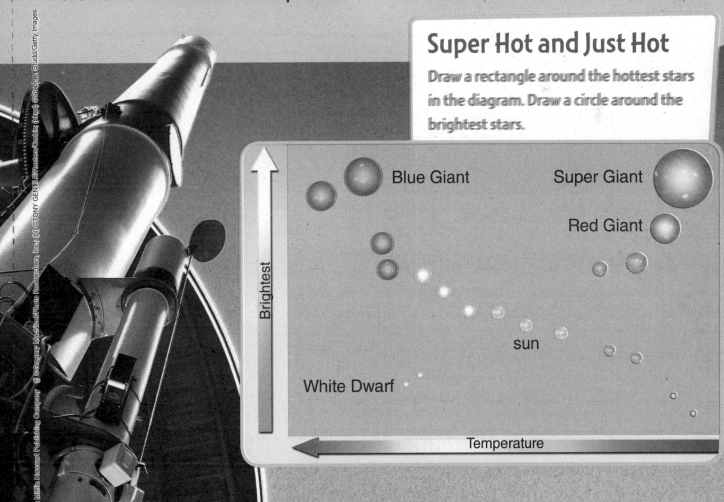

Blue Giant · Super Giant · Red Giant · Brightest · sun · White Dwarf · Temperature

GOING GALACTIC

Our solar system is huge. Yet it is only a tiny part of a much larger system in space. Our sun is one star in a group of billions of stars found in the Milky Way galaxy.

Active Reading As you read the next four pages, circle details about the ages of stars in each type of galaxy.

Milky Way Galaxy

YOU ARE HERE

Once, people thought Earth was at the center of the universe. The universe is everything that exists. Now we know that we are not even at the center of our own galaxy!

▶ In the space below, describe the position of the solar system within the Milky Way.

_____

_____

_____

_____

FEATURES OF GALAXIES

A **galaxy** is a group of billions of stars, the objects that orbit the stars, gas, and dust. A galaxy is held together by gravity. There are billions of galaxies in the universe. Galaxies are separated by large distances. On a cloudless night, you might see what looks like a faint band of clouds among the stars. This is a part of our home galaxy, the Milky Way. Most other galaxies can be seen only by using powerful telescopes.

TYPES OF GALAXIES

In the 1920s, astronomer Edwin Hubble was the first to study galaxies. He classified them by shape. Through his telescope, Hubble observed pinwheel-like groups of stars that he called *spiral galaxies*.

Some spiral galaxies, called *barred spiral galaxies*, have a center shaped like a long bar. Recent evidence suggests that the Milky Way is a barred spiral galaxy.

SPIRAL **GALAXIES**

Spiral galaxies consist of a rotating disk of young stars, gas, and dust and a central bulge made of older stars.

BARRED SPIRAL **GALAXIES**

Barred spiral galaxies may have two or more spiral arms. Unlike regular spirals, there are young stars at the center of barred spiral galaxies.

MORE TYPES OF GALAXIES

Most of the brightest galaxies in the universe have spiral shapes. But spiral galaxies are not the only type of galaxy. In fact, they make up only about 20 percent of all galaxies. The dimmer *irregular galaxies* and *elliptical galaxies* make up about 80 percent of all galaxies in the universe.

IRREGULAR GALAXIES

Irregular galaxies do not have any particular shape. The stars are randomly scattered. There is lots of gas and dust to form new stars. About 20 percent of all galaxies are irregular. Some astronomers think that gravity from nearby galaxies causes irregular galaxies to form.

ELLIPTICAL GALAXIES

Elliptical galaxies are brightest at their center. About 60 percent of all galaxies in the universe are elliptical. They can be shaped like a perfect sphere or a flattened globe. Large ellipticals are made up of old stars and have too little dust or gas to form new ones.

COSMIC **CRASHES**

Sometimes galaxies collide, or crash together, in space! Why? Gravity pulls galaxies toward each other. Although galaxies may collide, single stars and planets almost never do.

Many things can happen when galaxies collide. Often, large amounts of dust and gas are pressed together. This causes a starburst, or rapid formation of many new stars. Sometimes, a smaller galaxy becomes part of a larger galaxy. A collision of galaxies can also form a large, irregular galaxy. Scientists believe that many irregular galaxies were once spiral or elliptical galaxies that were involved in a cosmic crash.

Galaxies do not stand still. They are always moving. Galaxies can move away from each other or toward each other.

▶ Look at pictures 1–5. Draw a picture to show what you think will happen next to these two galaxies. Write a sentence to describe it.

_____

_____

Sum It Up!

When you're done, use the answer key to check and revise your work.

The universe is composed of billions of galaxies. Dust, gas, and billions of stars make up a galaxy. The idea web below summarizes information about stars and galaxies. Complete it using the words and phrases from the box.

Types of Galaxies	Elliptical	Temperature
Spiral	Characteristics of Stars	Size
Color	Irregular	

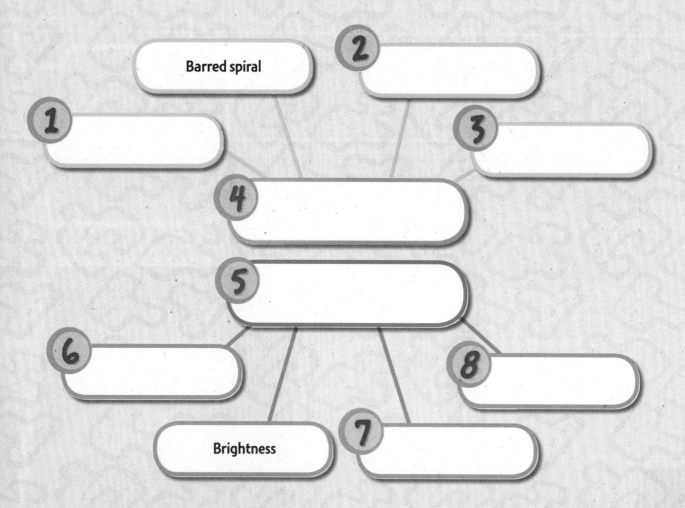

Barred spiral

2

1

3

4

5

6

8

Brightness

7

Answer Key: 1–3 (in any order): Spiral; Elliptical; Irregular   4. Types of Galaxies   5. Characteristics of Stars
6–9 (in any order): Color; Size; Temperature

Name _____

Word Play

1 Complete the puzzle. If you need help, use the words in the box below the clues.

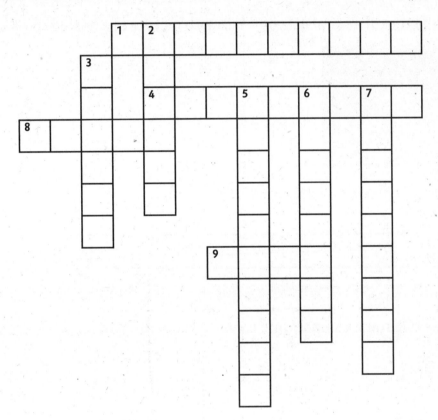

Across

1. A person who studies the universe
4. A galaxy with no particular shape
8. Characteristic that is related to a star's temperature
9. A ball of hot, glowing gases

Down

2. A pinwheel-like galaxy
3. A group of stars, dust, and gases
5. A galaxy shaped like a flattened globe
6. Everything that exists—planets, stars, dust, and gases
7. The study of the objects in space and their properties

| spiral | elliptical | astronomy* | irregular | galaxy* | star* |
| astronomer | color | universe* | * Key Lesson Vocabulary | | |

Apply Concepts

2 What are some ways in which galaxies differ?

_____

_____

3 Look at this picture of a spiral galaxy.

Draw a picture of a barred spiral galaxy.

Tell how the two galaxies are alike and different.

_____

_____

4 Look at these two stars. Compare and contrast them using at least two properties.

red
giant  blue
star

_____

_____

_____

5 How do these stars compare to the sun?

_____

_____

Take It
Home!

Find out which are the brightest stars that are visible this time of year in your area. With an adult, observe the stars. Make a diagram of the night sky showing where to find the brightest stars.

S.T.E.M.
Engineering & Technology

Tools in Space

An astronaut often has to use screwdrivers or drills to fix things in space. The astronaut's tools are specially designed for a person wearing bulky gloves and floating in orbit. Hand tools must work in the extreme cold vacuum of space and be tethered so they don't float away. A robotic arm helps the astronaut move around outside. However, the astronaut's most important tool is the space suit that maintains an environment in which the astronaut can breathe.

Troubleshooting

Find the astronaut's drill. How is it similar to a drill used on Earth? How is it different?

_____

_____

_____

You are used to doing everything under the pull of Earth's gravity. That's what makes it possible for you to feel motions such as up, down, and side-to-side. There is no "right side up" in space! It is harder than you might think to work in such an unfamiliar environment.

Turn your book so that the top of this page is closest to you.

_____

Hold your pencil near the eraser. Write your name on the line below so that it reads properly when you turn the page right side up again.

What made this task difficult?

_____

_____

How do engineers account for microgravity when designing the inside of a space station?

_____

_____

Build On It!

Rise to the engineering design challenge—complete **Improvise It: How High is That Star?** in the Inquiry Flipchart.

Name _____

Vocabulary Review

Use the terms in the box to complete the sentences.

asteroid
comet
galaxy
orbit
planet
rotate
solar system
star

1. Together, a star and all the planets and other objects orbiting it

   form a(n) _____.

2. A chunk of rock or iron that is less than 1,000 km (621 mi) in diameter and that orbits the sun is called

   a(n) _____.

3. A huge ball of very hot, glowing gases in space that can produce

   its own heat and light is called a(n) _____.

4. A group of solar systems that are held together by gravity and

   classified by shape is called a(n) _____.

5. The picture shows an example of a(n)
   _____.

6. The path Earth takes around the sun is called a(n)

   _____.

7. It takes Earth 24 hours to _____ once around its axis.

8. Earth moves around the sun, has a nearly round shape, and has cleared its path of most debris, so it is called a(n)

   _____.

Science Concepts

Fill in the letter of the choice that best answers the question.

9. Astronomers use the term *brightness* to describe the amount of light a star produces, not how bright a star appears from Earth. The diagram below compares the color, temperature, and brightness of some stars that can be seen from Earth.

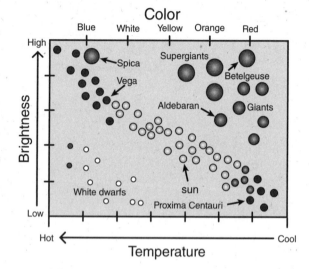

Which of these stars produces the **most** light?

(A) Betelgeuse

(B) Proxima Centauri

(C) our sun

(D) Vega

10. During a school field trip to an observatory, Smita used a telescope to observe stars of different colors. Based on the diagram in Question 9, which factor determines a star's color?

(A) its size

(B) its brightness

(C) its temperature

(D) its distance from Earth

11. Ming is doing a project on planets in other solar systems. She learns about a planet called Planet Z. Planet Z is very large and has a thick atmosphere and a low density. Which planet is Planet Z most similar to?

(A) Earth

(C) Mercury

(B) Mars

(D) Saturn

12. The diagram below shows planets orbiting a star.

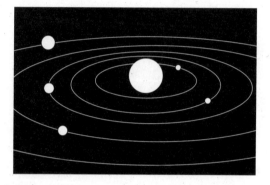

What type of group is the diagram illustrating?

(A) a constellation

(C) a solar system

(B) the Milky Way

(D) a universe

13. Some elliptical galaxies appear to be perfect spheres. How are the stars distributed within this kind of galaxy?

(A) The stars are evenly distributed throughout the galaxy.

(B) The center is very dense with many stars, and density decreases farther out.

(C) Most of the stars are near the outside of the sphere with dust clouds in the center.

(D) The stars are spread throughout the sphere in bands that look like the arms of spiral galaxies.

14. There are many types of stars. Each picture below shows two stars of the **same** color. Which picture and statement is true?

(A)

The larger star must be brighter.

(B)

The smaller star must be hotter.

(C)

The smaller star must be closer to Earth.

(D)

Stars that are the same color are usuallly the same size.

15. Scientists use models to represent or explain things in the natural world. Why are models useful for the study of the solar system?

(A) because models cannot be proved wrong

(B) because models are always accepted by all scientists

(C) because models describe the way things actually are

(D) because models can be used to describe how things work

16. The diagram below shows the orbit of Earth and the orbit of Borrelly.

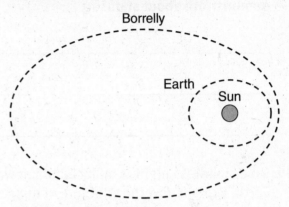

Which of these types of space objects is Borrelly **most** likely to be?

(A) an asteroid

(B) a comet

(C) a moon

(D) a planet

17. When Galileo observed Jupiter, he saw four objects in line with the planet. These four objects moved from night to night and sometimes disappeared in front of or behind the planet. What kind of space object was Galileo observing?

(A) dwarf planets

(B) solar systems

(C) meteoroids

(D) moons

Apply Inquiry and Review the Big Idea

Write the answers to these questions.

18. When Galileo used his telescope to observe the Milky Way, the stars appeared as small points of light. What did Galileo's observations demonstrate about stars?

_____

_____

_____

19. On a cloudless night, a milky band known as the Milky Way is visible from Earth. Explain how the structure of our galaxy and the position of our solar system within our galaxy relate to this observation.

_____

_____

_____

20. Sofia observes an object in the night sky. What questions and observations can she use to determine whether the object is a planet or a star?

Questions _____

_____

Observations _____

_____

21. People have developed models of the universe for thousands of years. Identify two observations that a model of the universe would need to explain in order to be useful.

a. _____

_____

b. _____

_____

UNIT 4
Ecosystems

Big Idea

Organisms perform a variety of roles in an ecosystem.

OHIO 5.LS.1, 5.SIA.1, 5.SIA.2, 5.SIA.4, 5.SIA.6, 5.SIA.8

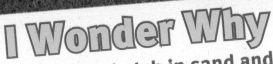

I Wonder Why

Sea turtles hatch in sand and make their way to the ocean. Why should sea turtle nests be protected? *Turn the page to find out.*

SAVE OUR SEA TURTLES

PROTECTED ENDANGERED SPECIES
NESTING SEASON MAY–OCTOBER
REPORT NESTING TURTLES

CLEARWATER
MARINE SCIENCE CENTER

Here's Why Human activities, such as accidentally walking on nests, can harm turtle eggs. Turtle nests are protected so that the young turtles can safely hatch and reach the ocean.

In this unit, you will explore the Big Idea, the Essential Questions, and the Investigations on the Inquiry Flipchart.

SAVE OUR SEA TURTLES
PROTECTED ENDANGERED SPECIES
NESTING SEASON MAY–OCTOBER
REPORT NESTING TURTLES
CLEARWATER
MARINE SCIENCE CENTER

Levels of Inquiry Key ■ DIRECTED ■ GUIDED ■ INDEPENDENT

Track Your Progress

Big Idea Organisms perform a variety of roles in an ecosystem.

Essential Questions

○ **Now I Get the Big Idea!**

Science Notebook

Before you begin each lesson, be sure to write your thoughts about the Essential Question.

OHIO **5.LS.1** Organisms perform a variety of roles in an ecosystem.

Lesson **1**

Essential Question

What Is an Ecosystem?

Engage Your Brain!

Find the answers to the following questions in this lesson and record them here.

The three organisms seen here share the same living space. How are their needs similar? How are they different?

_____

_____

_____

_____

Active Reading

Lesson Vocabulary
List the terms. As you learn about each one, make notes in the Interactive Glossary.

_____ _____

_____ _____

_____ _____

Main Ideas
The main idea of a paragraph is the most important idea. The main idea may be stated in the first sentence, or it may be stated elsewhere. Active readers look for main ideas by asking themselves, What is this section mostly about?

What Is an ECOSYSTEM?

A frog that lives in a pond couldn't survive in a desert or on a mountaintop. Could you live in a swamp?

Active Reading As you read these two pages, **circle** the biotic parts of environments. Draw a box around each abiotic part.

An organism's **environment** is all the living and nonliving things that surround and affect the organism. You are surrounded by many things that make your environment suitable for you to live in. Would that be true if you lived in a swamp? Environments include biotic parts and abiotic parts. *Biotic* parts are the living things in an environment: plants, animals, and other organisms. *Abiotic* parts are the nonliving things. Abiotic parts of an environment include climate, water, soil, light, air, and nutrients.

This swamp environment is made up of both living and nonliving things. The climate, abundance of water, moist air, muddy soils, and shady areas are all abiotic parts that make swamps different from other environments.

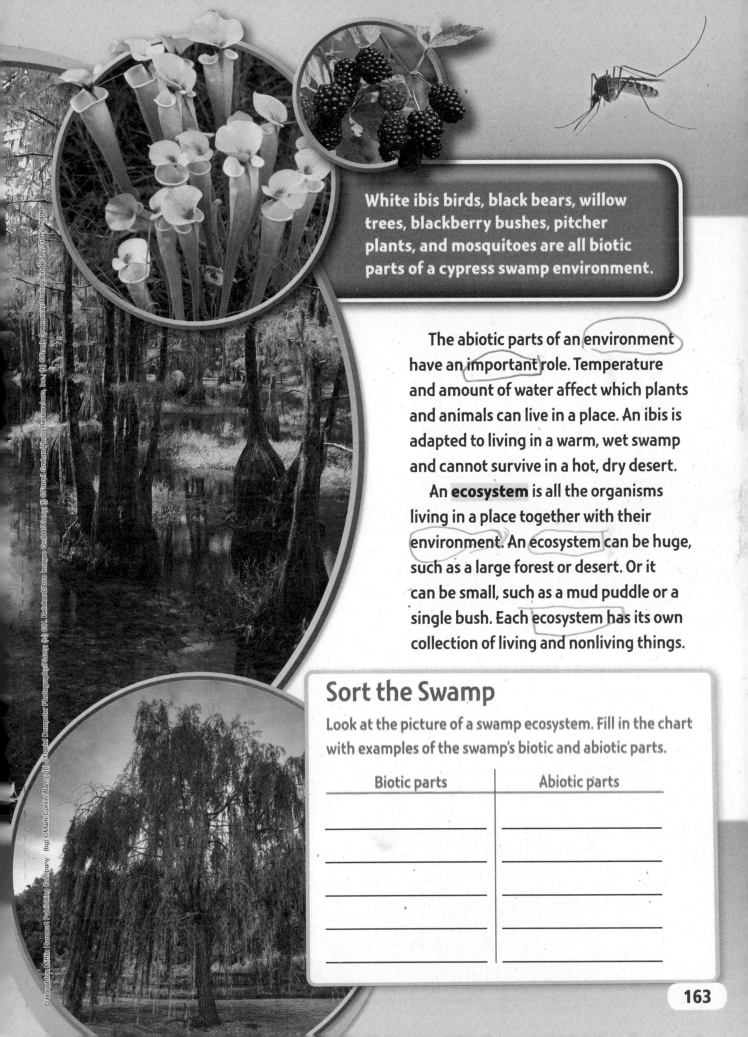

White ibis birds, black bears, willow trees, blackberry bushes, pitcher plants, and mosquitoes are all biotic parts of a cypress swamp environment.

The abiotic parts of an environment have an important role. Temperature and amount of water affect which plants and animals can live in a place. An ibis is adapted to living in a warm, wet swamp and cannot survive in a hot, dry desert.

An **ecosystem** is all the organisms living in a place together with their environment. An ecosystem can be huge, such as a large forest or desert. Or it can be small, such as a mud puddle or a single bush. Each ecosystem has its own collection of living and nonliving things.

Sort the Swamp

Look at the picture of a swamp ecosystem. Fill in the chart with examples of the swamp's biotic and abiotic parts.

Biotic parts	Abiotic parts

Populations and Communities

You are part of a group of students in your classroom. There are other classes in your school, too, and other groups of people, such as teachers. Together, you make up your school's community. Other organisms live in communities, too.

Each ecosystem contains different groups of living things. The big picture shows several species of animals sharing water in a savanna ecosystem. A group of organisms of the same species in an ecosystem is called a **population**. For example, a savanna ecosystem may contain a population of zebras as well as populations of gazelles and lions. It also contains populations of grasses and trees.

The different populations that share an ecosystem make up a community. A **community** consists of all the populations that live and interact in an area.

These moray eels are part of a population of eels sharing the same living space. The crack in the rock will hold only so many eels. At a certain point the eels must compete for this living space.

These plants and animals are part of the community that lives in an ecosystem. Each population competes with other populations for the resources in the ecosystem.

Do the Math!
Calculate Area

Bison graze on grass. It takes 5 acres of grass to feed 2 bison for a season. How much land would be needed to support 100 bison for a season?

200

In winter, a population of bison must work to find food. As resources become scarce, bison within the population compete with each other.

Populations in every ecosystem need food, water, shelter, and space to live. The interaction between populations to meet needs is called *competition*. Populations that compete and obtain enough resources will survive. Those that cannot compete will not survive in the ecosystem. Because there is only enough food, water, shelter, and space to support a certain number of organisms, these resources are called *limiting factors*.

Competition also occurs within populations. The stronger individuals in a population are the ones that get the most food and take the best shelter for themselves. Weaker individuals may not survive.

Find Your Niche

Maybe you have to share your room, your clothes, or snacks with your family members. Organisms that live in the same ecosystem often compete for available resources.

Active Reading As you read these two pages, draw boxes around the clue words that compare and contrast habitat and niche.

Organisms perform a variety of roles in an ecosystem. An organism's **habitat** is the place where it lives within an ecosystem. Several populations often live in a single habitat. For example, barred owls and red-shouldered hawks live in habitats with woods, nearby open country, and bodies of water.

An organism's **niche** [NICH] is its complete role, or function, in its ecosystem. A niche is different from a habitat because it includes all the ways the organism survives. An organism's niche includes how it finds food as well as the climate it thrives in.

The panda has a narrow niche in terms of food. Its diet consists mainly of bamboo, so pandas cannot survive in habitats where bamboo does not grow.

Red-shouldered hawks and barred owls share a habitat but have different niches. How is this so?

_____

_____

Every organism has a niche. Having different niches allows organisms to survive in the same habitat. When an organism has a very specific way of living, it has a narrow niche. For example, a bird that eats just one type of insect or lives only in one kind of tree has a narrow niche, while an animal that can eat many kinds of food has a broad niche. Organisms with a narrow niche tend to live in specific places, while those with a broad niche often move around large areas.

Populations can share a habitat but not the same niche. Red-shouldered hawks and barred owls, for example, share a habitat, but they have different niches. Hawks hunt by day and owls hunt at night, hunting different prey. If two populations of organisms share a niche, they must compete for resources.

Nice Niche

Suppose a bird is the only animal in a habitat that eats a certain type of berry. The berries are the bird's only food. Describe how this narrow niche could be both good and bad for the bird.

_____

_____

_____

_____

Sharks have a broad niche in terms of food. They are able to eat many different foods.

Diversity

Suppose all the shelves in your grocery store held only one kind of food. You couldn't stay healthy for long. Ecosystems need diversity, too.

Active Reading As you read these two pages, draw a star next to the most important sentence.

This coral reef is a diverse ecosystem. Many populations live closely together here.

The word *diverse* means "different in kind." *Diversity* is the variety of different species that live in an ecosystem. An ecosystem that is diverse contains a lot of species. Ecosystems without much diversity are inhabited by only a few species.

Why is diversity important? All organisms rely on other organisms. Their relationships are connected in a large, complex web. The more types of organisms in an ecosystem, the larger the web, and the more resources available.

A rain forest is a diverse ecosystem. The warm temperatures and high rainfall support many different populations.

Why are some ecosystems very diverse while others have only a small number of species? Climate and location affect the amount and types of resources that are available for organisms. Locations of high diversity make a pattern on the map. In general, very diverse ecosystems such as coral reefs and rain forests are found near the equator. The farther away from the equator, the less diverse environments tend to be.

Other things can affect diversity as well. Humans can damage ecosystems and reduce the number of species living in them. Activities such as overhunting may lower the numbers of important species. In some areas, humans have destroyed forests or other environments in order to build cities and other structures. Species in those environments have lost their habitats, and diversity has decreased.

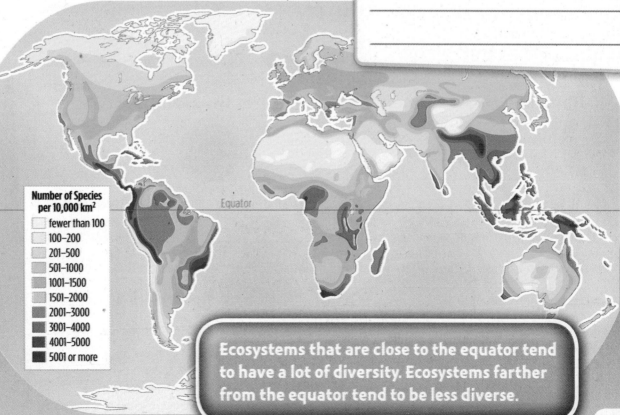

The cold arctic is a less diverse ecosystem. The polar bear is one of a small number of large organisms that can survive there.

Habitat Change

Describe how you think building a large shopping mall and parking lot might affect the diversity of a forest.

everything will die

Number of Species per 10,000 km²

- fewer than 100
- 100–200
- 201–500
- 501–1000
- 1001–1500
- 1501–2000
- 2001–3000
- 3001–4000
- 4001–5000
- 5001 or more

Equator

Ecosystems that are close to the equator tend to have a lot of diversity. Ecosystems farther from the equator tend to be less diverse.

When you're done, use the answer key to check and revise your work.

1

The words in the ovals describe parts of a desert ecosystem. Draw lines to show whether each part is a *biotic* or *abiotic* part.

Cactus

Sandy soil

Biotic

Lizard

Rattlesnake

Little water

Sunlight

Abiotic

Summarize

2 Fill in the blanks with words from the word box. Use each word once.

community	ecosystem	environment
habitat	niche	population

An organism's 1. _____ includes all the living and nonliving things that

surround and affect the organism. Each different 2. _____ is an area made

up of biotic and abiotic factors where organisms interact. Within these areas, groups of the same

species of organisms, or 3. _____, interact with other organisms, forming

a large 4. _____. The place where an organism normally lives is called its

5. _____. The way the organism lives there is called its specific 6. _____.

Answer Key: Biotic: Cactus, Rattlesnake, Lizard; Abiotic: Sunlight, Sandy soil, Little water; 1. environment
2. ecosystem 3. populations 4. community 5. habitat 6. niche

Name _____

Word Play

1 Use the words in the box to complete the puzzle.

Across

3. The average weather in an area over time
5. The variety of species in an ecosystem
6. Nonliving

Down

1. Living
2. The struggle for resources in an ecosystem
4. The type of factor that determines the size of a population

abiotic

biotic

climate

competition

diversity

limiting

Use the three across words to write a sentence.

_____

_____

_____

_____

Apply Concepts

2 Draw an organism and its habitat.

3 List three abiotic factors that are in your environment right now.

_____

_____

_____

4 Explain why two species of organisms can share a habitat but not a niche.

_____

_____

_____

5 Draw a line from the organism to the ecosystem it would most likely live in.

1. A warm, wet swamp

2. A grassy prairie

3. A snowy arctic ocean area

Take It Home! Your neighborhood is an environment that supports plants and animals. With your family, list as many organisms living in your neighborhood as you can. Compare lists with your classmates.

Quest for the Serpent Eagle

Jane Juniper is a wildlife surveyor. She is deep in the forest of Madagascar, an island off the coast of Africa, observing birds.

What's that sound? Jane hears a loud, screeching bird call that she never expected to hear. It sounds like... But could it be?

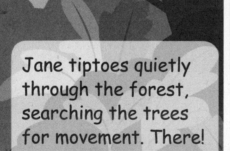

Jane tiptoes quietly through the forest, searching the trees for movement. There!

Jane stands perfectly still. The bird has a dark back and a striped chest. It has yellow eyes, and sharp talons. But it's not supposed to exist!

Jane Juniper has studied all about African birds. It takes her just a moment to be sure. But she is still amazed! With her camera she collects evidence of her find.

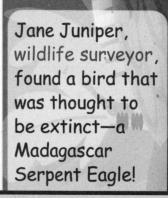

Jane Juniper, wildlife surveyor, found a bird that was thought to be extinct—a Madagascar Serpent Eagle!

Now You Be the Surveyor

Imagine you're a wildlife surveyor. Survey the forest below.
Write the kinds of animals you find and the number of each kind.

OHIO **5.LS.1** Organisms perform a variety of roles in an ecosystem. **5.SIA.1** Identify questions that can be answered through scientific investigations. **5.SIA.2** Design and conduct a scientific investigation. **5.SIA.4** Analyze and interpret data. **5.SIA.6** Think critically and logically to connect evidence and explanations. **5.SIA.8** Communicate scientific procedures and explanations.

Name _____

Essential Question

What Makes Up a Land Ecosystem?

Set a Purpose
What do you think you will learn in this activity?

_____

_____

_____

_____

Think About the Procedure
Why do you think your sample site should have a variety of plants and soil coverings?

_____

_____

_____

_____

_____

Why did you measure and mark your sample area?

_____

_____

_____

Record Your Data
In the space below, make a table to record the different living things found in your sample site and their role in the ecosystem.

Draw Conclusions

How did you determine the roles that each organism played in their ecosystem?

_____

_____

_____

_____

Compare your results with the results of other groups. Explain any differences or similarities.

_____

_____

_____

_____

Analyze and Extend

1. What kind of living things did you find in your sample area?

_____

_____

2. Which role in the ecosystem had the greatest amount of living things?

_____

_____

3. Which role in the ecosystem had the greatest variety of living things?

_____

_____

4. In the space below, draw a picture of your sample area. Make sure to include an example of a producer and a consumer that you found living in it.

5. Think of other questions you would like to ask about how living things interact in the ecosystem.

_____

_____

_____

© Houghton Mifflin Harcourt Publishing Company

OHIO **5.LS.1** Organisms perform a variety of roles in an ecosystem.

Lesson **3**

Essential Question

What Are Physical and Behavioral Adaptations?

Engage Your Brain!

Find the answer to the following question in this lesson and record it here.

Watch out! Don't get bitten by that ... caterpillar? What type of adaptation does this caterpillar have?

_____

_____

_____

Active Reading

Lesson Vocabulary

List the terms. As you learn about each one, make notes in the Interactive Glossary.

_____

_____

Signal Words: Details

This lesson gives details about how living things are suited to where they live. Signal words link main topics to added details. *For example* and *for instance* are often used as signal words. Active readers look for signal words that link a topic to its details.

Adaptations

Living things have many similarities. They also have many interesting differences.

Active Reading As you read this page, underline the definition of *adaptation*.

Deserts are home to many kinds of snakes. This is because snakes have characteristics that help them survive in a desert. For example, snakes have tough, scaly skin that keeps them from drying out.

A characteristic that helps a living thing survive is called an **adaptation**. Suppose an animal is born with a new characteristic. If this characteristic helps the animal survive, the animal is likely to reproduce and pass on the characteristic to its young. As long as the animal's habitat doesn't change, the young that have this characteristic are also likely to survive and reproduce. Over time, the adaptation becomes more common in the population. In this way, populations of plants and animals become adapted to their habitats.

These hares live in very different habitats. Because of this, they have different adaptations.

An arctic hare lives in a cold habitat. It has thick fur to keep it warm and small ears that prevent heat from being lost.

A jackrabbit lives in a hot habitat. Jackrabbits have large ears that help keep their blood cool.

Ostriches, rheas, and emus all live on different continents. Even though they live very far from each other, they look almost the same! Their habitats are very similar, and so they share similar adaptations. These birds are all adapted for running fast. Ostriches are the fastest flightless birds on Earth. They can reach speeds of 72 km/hr (45 mi/hr)!

ostrich

emu

rhea

▶ Vines and trees are both plants, but they are very different from each other. What adaptations can you see in these plants, and how do you think these adaptations help them survive?

_____

_____

_____

_____

_____

_____

Form and Function

Why can penguins live in the Antarctic while most other birds can't? They have a layer of blubber to keep them warm!

Active Reading As you read these two pages, underline the words and phrases that describe animal and plant adaptations.

Some adaptations are differences in the bodies of organisms. These are called physical adaptations. Organisms have physical adaptations that help them live and survive in different environments. When a plant or animal has a characteristic that enables it to survive in a way that other plants or animals cannot, the organism with the adaptation has an advantage. Consider how some of the organisms shown on these two pages are better able to survive in their environments than organisms that do not have these adaptations.

The eyes of this bird are covered with a thin, transparent eyelid that keeps the eye moist when the bird flies.

A penguin has many adaptations that allow it to live in an icy, wet environment. A layer of blubber under waterproof feathers keeps penguins warm. They also have wings shaped like flippers and webbed feet for swimming.

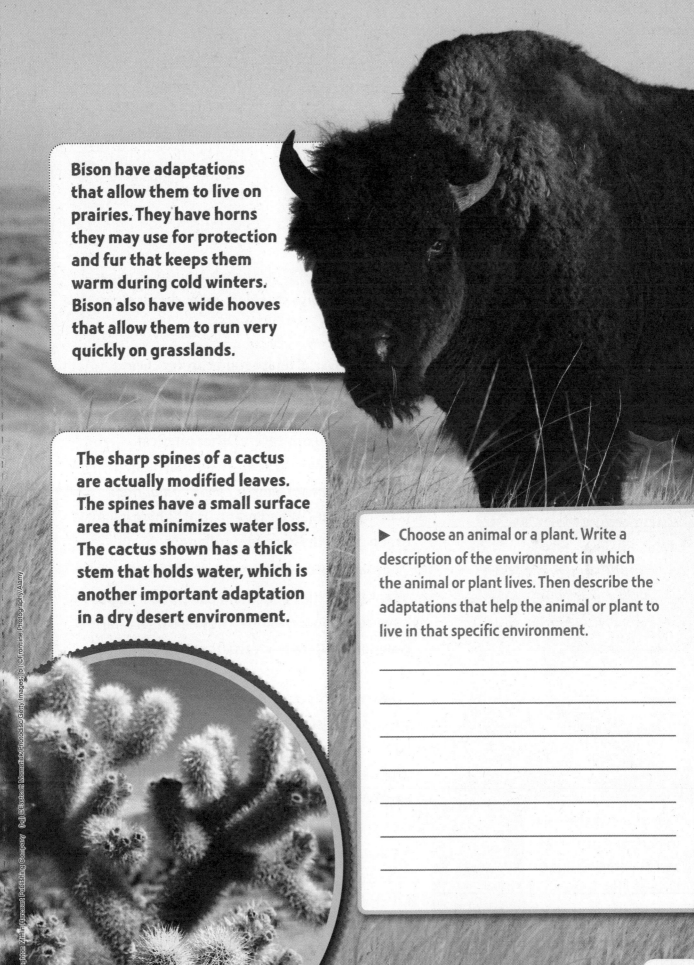

Bison have adaptations that allow them to live on prairies. They have horns they may use for protection and fur that keeps them warm during cold winters. Bison also have wide hooves that allow them to run very quickly on grasslands.

The sharp spines of a cactus are actually modified leaves. The spines have a small surface area that minimizes water loss. The cactus shown has a thick stem that holds water, which is another important adaptation in a dry desert environment.

▶ Choose an animal or a plant. Write a description of the environment in which the animal or plant lives. Then describe the adaptations that help the animal or plant to live in that specific environment.

_____

_____

_____

_____

_____

_____

_____

Eat or Be Eaten

Whether blending in or standing out, physical adaptations help organisms survive.

Some physical adaptations protect living things from being eaten. For example, roses have sharp thorns that help keep their stems from being eaten. Other physical adaptations help to keep an animal hidden. This type of adaptation is called *camouflage* [KAM•uh•flazh]. When green lizards hide in green grass, they are camouflaged.

Animals that hunt, such as eagles, have adaptations that help them catch food. Eagles have very good eyesight. They also have sharp claws on their feet, which they use to capture their food.

Many plants have adaptations that help spread their seeds. Some seeds can be carried by the wind. Other seeds are inside berries. When the berries are eaten, the seeds are carried to a new location.

Can you see the owl in this picture? The owl is camouflaged to look like bark.

The bright color of this rose attracts pollinators, but the thorns keep plant-eating animals away.

Catching Flies

Bright coloring on an animal is often a warning that the animal is dangerous. Many animals know that paper wasps, like the one shown below, have a painful sting. The black and yellow hoverfly doesn't have a stinger. It is completely harmless. But because the hoverfly looks like a wasp, animals will think twice before trying to eat it. This adaptation is called *mimicry*.

► Draw a line from the chameleon's tongue to the insect it would most likely eat.

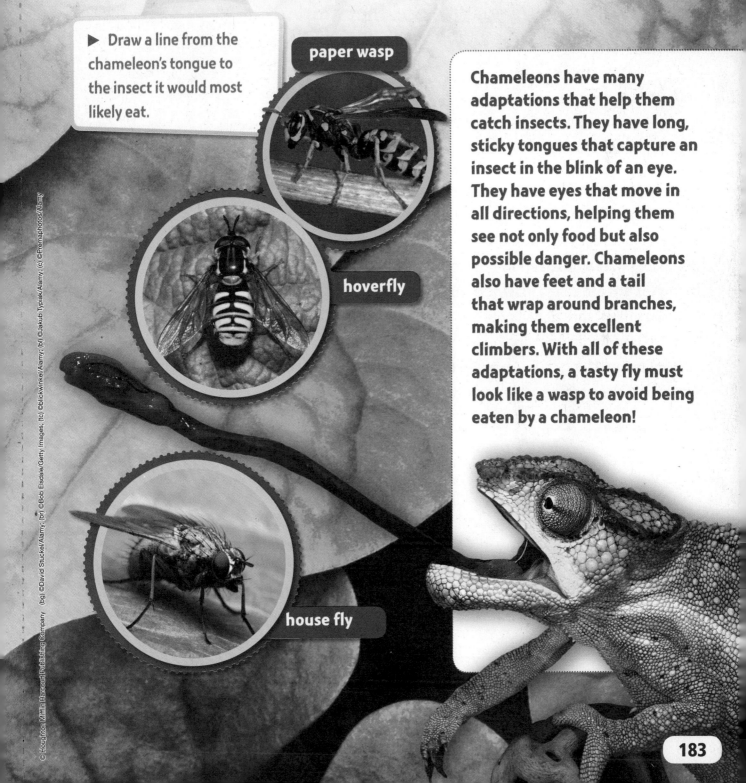

paper wasp

hoverfly

house fly

Chameleons have many adaptations that help them catch insects. They have long, sticky tongues that capture an insect in the blink of an eye. They have eyes that move in all directions, helping them see not only food but also possible danger. Chameleons also have feet and a tail that wrap around branches, making them excellent climbers. With all of these adaptations, a tasty fly must look like a wasp to avoid being eaten by a chameleon!

On Your Best Behavior

The way living things act is called behavior. Some behaviors are adaptations that help animals survive.

Active Reading As you read the paragraph below, circle examples of instinctive behavior and underline examples of learned behavior.

Some things that animals do seem to come naturally. Babies do not have to be taught how to cry. Spiders are not taught how to spin webs. Behaviors that animals know how to do without being taught are called **instincts**. Animals have to learn other types of behaviors. For example, a lion cub is not born knowing how to hunt. It learns to hunt by watching its mother. Raccoons learn to wash food by watching other raccoons.

Some bats are *nocturnal*. This means they are active at night and sleep during the day. This allows bats to hunt insects that are active only at night.

Many animals have behaviors that help protect them from predators. When an octopus is frightened, it releases ink into the water. If the octopus is being attacked, the animal attacking it will not be able to see, and the octopus can escape.

Each year, millions of snow geese migrate south in autumn and north in spring.

Some animals move to different locations at certain times of the year to find food, reproduce, or escape very cold weather. This instinctive behavior is called *migration*. Many birds, butterflies, and some bats migrate long distances.

Some animals hibernate. *Hibernation* is a long period of inactivity that is like sleeping. But hibernation is not the same as sleeping. When an animal hibernates, its body processes slow down and it stays inactive for months. Can you imagine taking a three-month nap?

The way that animals act toward other animals of the same type is called *social behavior*. Honeybees have very complex social behavior. They communicate using movements called the "waggle dance." A bee that finds food will return to the hive and do a waggle dance. The pattern of the dance gives other bees a lot of information! The dance communicates which way to go, how far away the food is, how much food there is, and even what kind of food it is!

Do the Math!
Interpret Data in a Bar Graph

Ground squirrels hibernate. They must eat a lot during the spring, summer, and fall to store up enough energy to survive hibernation. Study the graph below.

Ground Squirrel Body Mass

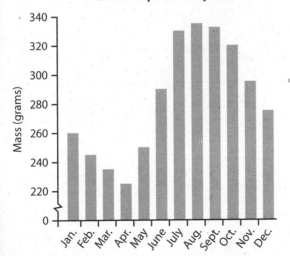

About how much mass does a ground squirrel have in March?

_____

During which month do ground squirrels start to hibernate? How do you know?

_____

_____

185

The Circle of Life

All living things grow and develop. The way that living things develop can be an adaptation.

Active Reading Circle two different examples of organisms whose life cycles keep adults and young from competing for food.

Living things go through stages of growth and development called a *life cycle*. A living thing's life cycle is related to its habitat. Because of this, differences in life cycles are a type of adaptation.

Most frogs are adapted to live near water. A frog's life cycle starts when its eggs are laid in water. When the eggs hatch, tadpoles emerge. Tadpoles live in water until they grow legs and lungs. At this point, they are frogs and ready to live on land. In places where water dries quickly, tadpoles develop more quickly. This variation in frog life cycles helps tadpoles survive.

Tadpoles and frogs live in different places, and eat different foods. This is another kind of adaptation. Frogs and tadpoles don't compete with each other for food, allowing for more frogs to survive. Many other organisms have similar adaptations. For example, caterpillars eat plant leaves and most butterflies sip nectar from flowers.

adult luna moth

luna moth caterpillar

salmon eggs

Adult salmon live in the ocean, which is a dangerous place for young salmon. Adults migrate from the ocean to shallow rivers to lay eggs. More young salmon are able to survive in rivers.

© Houghton Mifflin Harcourt Publishing Company (tc) ©George H.H. Huey/Corbis (c) ©medicaid/Corbis (r) ©James Urbach/SuperStock (r) ©Natural Visions/Alamy

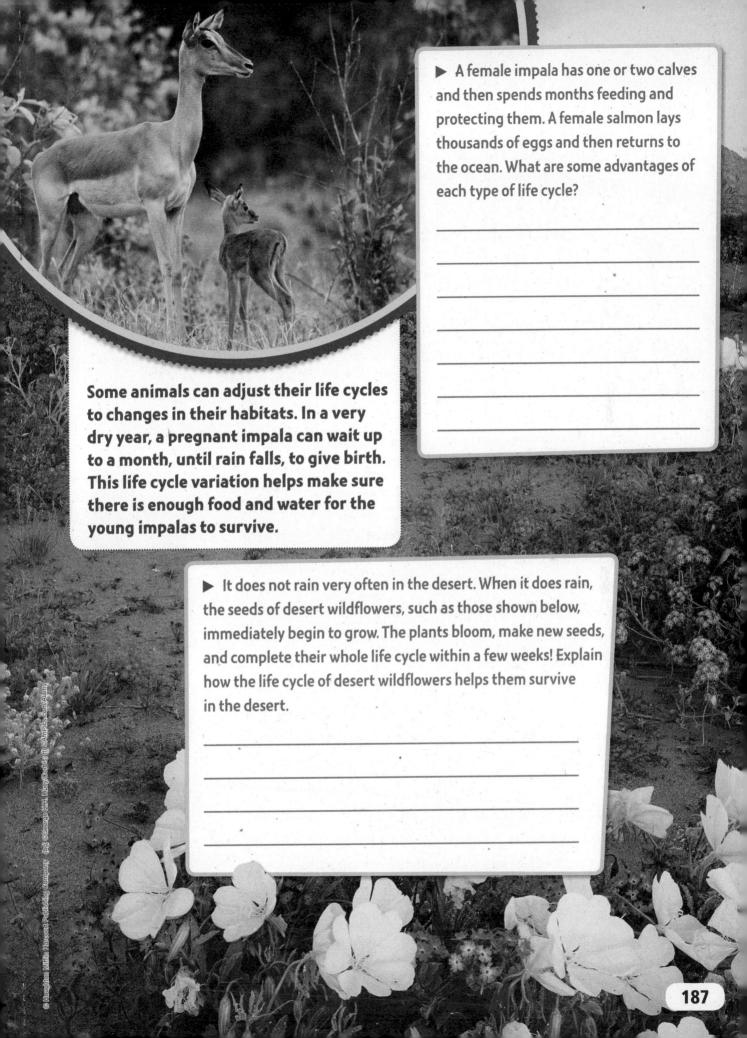

▶ A female impala has one or two calves and then spends months feeding and protecting them. A female salmon lays thousands of eggs and then returns to the ocean. What are some advantages of each type of life cycle?

_____
_____
_____
_____
_____
_____
_____

Some animals can adjust their life cycles to changes in their habitats. In a very dry year, a pregnant impala can wait up to a month, until rain falls, to give birth. This life cycle variation helps make sure there is enough food and water for the young impalas to survive.

▶ It does not rain very often in the desert. When it does rain, the seeds of desert wildflowers, such as those shown below, immediately begin to grow. The plants bloom, make new seeds, and complete their whole life cycle within a few weeks! Explain how the life cycle of desert wildflowers helps them survive in the desert.

_____
_____
_____
_____

Living Things Change

Look at the snakes slithering on this page. Each snake looks different, but they are all the same kind of snake. Why don't they look the same?

As you read these two pages, circle the clue word or phrase that signals a detail such as an example or an added fact.

You don't look exactly like your parents. You have many similarities, but there are also small differences that make you unique. Every organism is slightly different from every other organism. Sometimes these differences can be very important.

Corn snakes, like the ones shown here, come in many colors and patterns. Some are very light colored, some are golden brown, and some are bright orange. Suppose a hawk is flying over a wheat field, looking for a snack. Which of these snakes is least likely to become lunch? If you guessed the golden brown snake, you are correct. Why? Its color would blend in with the wheat. The hawk would not see it, and the snake would survive. The snake would reproduce and pass on its coloring to its offspring. Its golden brown offspring would have a better chance of surviving in the wheat field and would also produce more offspring. Eventually, most of the snakes living in the wheat field would be golden brown.

© Houghton Mifflin Harcourt Publishing Company (cr) ©David Stuckel/Alamy; ©Dan Suzio/Photo Researchers, Inc.

Sometimes living things change because their environment changes. For example, bacteria have changed as a result of their changing environment. Since the discovery of antibiotics, people have learned how to kill bacteria. The first antibiotic, penicillin, saved many lives by killing bacteria that cause disease.

But in a very large population of bacteria, a few are not affected by penicillin. These bacteria survive and multiply. Over time, they produce large populations of bacteria that are not affected by penicillin.

Researchers have had to find new antibiotics to kill these bacteria. But, again, some bacteria are not killed. These bacteria continue to multiply.

While different types of antibiotics have been developed, bacteria have become resistant to many of them. Now there are bacteria that are resistant to almost all known types of antibiotics. These bacteria are extremely difficult to kill.

Do the Math!
Find Median and Mean

Length of Corn Snakes	
Snake 1	3.5 m
Snake 2	5.5 m
Snake 3	4.6 m
Snake 4	5.1 m
Snake 5	4.8 m
Snake 6	3.9 m
Snake 7	5.3 m

Adult corn snakes vary not only in color, but also in length. The table shows the lengths of several adult corn snakes. Study the data, and then answer the questions.

1. The median is the middle number of a data set when the numbers are placed in numerical order. Find the median of the data set. _____

2. The mean is the average of a data set. Find the mean of the data set. _____

Antibiotics in soaps and cleaners kill many bacteria. However, when not all of the bacteria are killed, the ones that survive multiply. Little by little, bacteria are becoming resistant to antibacterial soap and cleaners.

When you're done, use the answer key to check and revise your work.

The outline below is a summary of the lesson. Complete the outline.

Summarize

I. Instincts: A behavior that a living thing does without being
   taught to do.
   A. Example: _bee thes_
   tr bnt

   B. Example: _____
   _____

II. Adaptations: A characteristic that helps a living thing survive is
    called an adaptation. Kinds of adaptations include:

   A. Physical Adaptations
      1. Example: _____
      the bes is
      2. Example: _misk_
      _____

   B. Behavioral Adaptations
      1. Example: _____
      istraxt
      2. Example: _gc l_
      _____

   C. Life Cycle Adaptations
      1. Example: _____
      astrige
      2. Example: _are fast_
      _____

Name _____

Word Play

1 Use words from the lesson to complete the puzzle.

Across

1. What type of adaptation helps a living thing hide in its environment?
6. An animal that is active at night is described as being _____.
7. Stages that living things go through as they develop are called life _____.

Down

2. An example of _____ is birds flying south in winter.
3. What are characteristics that help an animal survive?
4. What behavior causes an animal to be inactive for a long period of time?
5. A behavior that an animal doesn't need to learn is a(n) _____.

Apply Concepts

2 Draw a picture of a cactus. Next to the cactus, draw a plant that is found in a non-desert environment. Label three adaptations and their functions that help the cactus plant live and survive in a desert.

3 Circle the camouflaged animal.

4 In winter, ground squirrels retreat into burrows and do not come out until spring. Circle the term that best describes this behavior.

Communication   Hibernation

Migration   Nocturnal hunting

5 A narrow-mouthed frog's eggs hatch directly into tiny frogs. The environment where narrow-mouthed frogs live is very dry. How is this adaptation helpful?

_____

_____

_____

_____

Take It Home! Go for a walk through your neighborhood or a local park with your family. Look at different plants and animals, and point out different adaptations that the plants or animals have.

International Space Station

S.T.E.M.
Engineering & Technology

How It Works:
Life in a Box

How are an aquarium, a terrarium, and the International Space Station similar? In each contained space, habitats and organisms can be observed, and different parts of the environment must be controlled to make it possible for organisms to live there. Some of these parts include light, heat, water, and oxygen.

Terrarium

Aquarium

Troubleshooting

An aquarium is usually outfitted with a filter, a pump, a heater, an aerator (to add oxygen to the water), and a light. Choose one of these devices, and tell what might happen to the living things in the aquarium if it failed and explain why.

_____

_____

Artificial environments must have all of the things that the organisms living inside them need.

Draw an organism in an artificial environment. Explain how the environment is designed to supply what the organism needs.

Research Biosphere 2. What is it?

_____

_____

What was one problem people living in such a closed system would have?

_____

_____

How could they solve it?

_____

_____

Biosphere 2

Build On It!

Rise to the engineering design challenge—complete **Design It: Mobile Ecosystems Lab** in the Inquiry Flipchart.

Unit 4 Review

Vocabulary Review

Use the terms in the box to complete the sentences.

> adaptation
> community
> ecosystem
> environment
> habitat
> instincts
> niche
> population

1. A community of organisms and the environment in which they live is called a(n) _____.

2. A scientist would look at a group of rabbits that live in a meadow and call them a(n) _____.

3. All of the living and nonliving things that surround you make up your _____.

4. A scientist who is describing the place where an organism lives is defining the organism's _____.

5. The role a plant or animal plays in its habitat is its _____.

6. Behaviors that animals know how to do without being taught are called _____.

7. A characteristic that helps an animal live and survive is considered to be a(n) _____.

8. A group of plants and animals that live in the same area and interact with each other is called a(n) _____.

Science Concepts

Fill in the letter of the choice that best answers the question.

9. The organisms that live around a pond interact with biotic and abiotic factors. Which of the following is a biotic factor of the pond environment?

   Ⓐ cattail plants

   Ⓑ muddy soil

   Ⓒ slowly flowing water

   Ⓓ warm temperature

10. The diagram below shows how an antlion gets food.

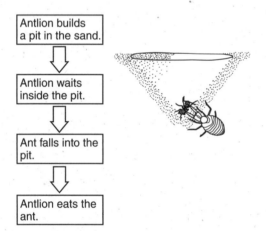

What does the diagram suggest about the antlion?

   Ⓐ The antlion uses mimicry to catch prey.

   Ⓑ The antlion is not adapted to its environment.

   Ⓒ The antlion lives on a diet of both plants and animals.

   Ⓓ The antlion uses a behavioral adaptation to catch prey.

11. Alejandra wants to identify an ecosystem to research. She starts by looking at the globe below.

Where on the globe should she look to identify the most areas with high biodiversity?

   Ⓐ near water

   Ⓑ near mountains

   Ⓒ near the equator

   Ⓓ near the north or south pole

12. The coloring of the rough green snake allows it to blend in with its background. What type of adaptation is the rough green snake's color?

   Ⓐ behavioral adaptation

   Ⓑ life-cycle adaptation

   Ⓒ physical adaptation

   Ⓓ reproductive adaptation

13. A coral reef has many different kinds of species. An area near the arctic has few species. Which term describes the variety of species that live in an ecosystem?

   Ⓐ community   Ⓒ niche

   Ⓑ diversity   Ⓓ population

14. A new shopping center was built on a vacant lot. The table shows the numbers of plants before and after construction.

Plants	Before	After
flowers	500	1,000
grass	1,000	0
shrubs	260	50
trees	26	3

Which of these statements is **true** based on these data?

Ⓐ Humans did not change the environment.

Ⓑ There were fewer total plants before the shopping center was built.

Ⓒ There were more kinds of plants before the shopping center was built.

Ⓓ There were more kinds of plants after the shopping center was built.

15. The picture below shows organisms that live in a land ecosystem.

1   **2**

3   **4**

Which organism is the producer?

Ⓐ organism 1

Ⓑ organism 2

Ⓒ organism 3

Ⓓ organism 4

16. The diagram shows a polar bear in its natural habitat.

Which of the following helps the polar bear live and survive in its habitat?

Ⓐ thick fur   Ⓒ large ears

Ⓑ long tail   Ⓓ wide hooves

17. Tropical rain forests are ecosystems that have a great deal of diversity. Many different organisms live there because of the abundance of resources. Which factors affect the amount of resources and the diversity of an ecosystem?

Ⓐ age and altitude

Ⓑ motion and humans

Ⓒ climate and location

Ⓓ minerals and sunshine

Apply Inquiry and Review the Big Idea

Write the answers to these questions.

18. Leo is exploring a small creek near his home. Identify two biotic and two abiotic factors that the frogs living in the creek are likely to interact with.

_____

_____

_____

19. Eli's class takes a field trip to a grassy meadow. He sees several field mice scurrying through the grass. He records ways that the mice both <u>use</u> resources and <u>are</u> resources in the meadow. What is it likely that Eli recorded?

a. How mice use resources: _____

_____

b. How mice are resources: _____

_____

20. The table shows different bird adaptations.

Use the table to draw a model bird that is adapted to swimming and eating fish.

Beak and Feet Adaptations			
Type of beak	Adapted for	Type of foot	Adapted for
	eating seeds		perching
	eating insects		wading
	probing for food		preying
	preying on animals		swimming
	straining food from water		climbing
	eating fish		

UNIT 5

Energy and Ecosystems

Big Idea

Organisms require energy in order to perform their roles in an ecosystem.

OHIO 5.LS.1, 5.LS.2, 5.SIA.1, 5.SIA.2, 5.SIA.4, 5.SIA.5, 5.SIA.6, 5.SIA.8

I Wonder Why

Polar bears and gray whales live in the Arctic. Polar bears eat seals and fish. Why are polar bears eating a whale? *Turn the page to find out.*

Here's why While polar bears are mainly carnivores that hunt seals and fish for food, they will also scavenge the blubber from dead whales that they find.

In this unit, you will explore the Big Idea, the Essential Questions, and the Investigations on the Inquiry Flipchart.

Levels of Inquiry Key ■ DIRECTED ■ GUIDED ■ INDEPENDENT

Track Your Progress

Big Idea Organisms require energy in order to perform their roles in an ecosystem.

Essential Questions

Now I Get the Big Idea!

Science Notebook
Before you begin each lesson, be sure to write your thoughts about the Essential Question.

Lesson **1**

Essential Question

What Are Roles of Organisms in Ecosystems?

Engage Your Brain!

Find the answer to the following question in the lesson and record it here.

Giraffes eat tree leaves to get the energy they need to live and grow. Where do trees get their energy?

_____

_____

_____

_____

Active Reading

Lesson Vocabulary

List the terms. As you learn about each one, make notes in the Interactive Glossary.

_____   _____

_____   _____

_____   _____

Signal Words: Details

Signal words show connections between ideas. *For example* and *for instance* signal examples of an idea. *Also* and *in fact* signal added facts. Active readers remember what they read because they are alert to signal words that identify examples and facts about a topic.

Green Machines

You know that animals depend on plants for food. Did you know that animals depend on the oxygen plants produce, too?

Active Reading As you read, underline three things plants need in order to make their own food.

The movement of gases back and forth between plants and animals is called the carbon dioxide–oxygen cycle.

The Carbon Dioxide–Oxygen Cycle

Plants use carbon dioxide to make the food that most living things need to live.

1. Plants take in carbon dioxide. Plants need carbon dioxide and energy from sunlight to make sugars they use for food. As a byproduct, plants give off oxygen.

2. When animals breathe in, they take in oxygen. When animals breathe out, they give off carbon dioxide.

3. Most plants take in some oxygen. Plants use oxygen to process the sugars they make. As plants do so, they give off carbon dioxide.

Photosynthesis

Chloroplast

1. Carbon dioxide enters a plant through tiny holes in its leaves.

2. Water from the soil enters the plant through its roots.

3. Chloroplasts inside cells found in leaves and other green parts of the plant capture energy from sunlight.

4. Chlorophyll helps change carbon dioxide, water, and solar energy into sugar and oxygen.

The process by which plants and plantlike organisms make food is **photosynthesis** [foh•toh•SIN•thuh•sis]. Photosynthesis takes place with the help of a green molecule called **chlorophyll** [KLAWR•uh•fil]. Chlorophyll is found in structures within a plant's cell called chloroplasts. During photosynthesis, plants use the energy in sunlight to change water and carbon dioxide into sugars and oxygen. The oxygen is released from tiny holes called stomata on the plants' leaves. All of the oxygen we breathe comes from plants and plantlike organisms.

The Carbon Dioxide-Oxygen Cycle

Write the missing terms to complete the cycle.

carbon dioxide

give off ↗   ↘ used by

_____   _____

used by ↖   ↙ give off

oxygen

Eat Your Vegetables!

Have you ever heard these words? You may think that you can live without plants. But even if you skip the spinach, you still depend on plants for food.

As you read these two pages, circle the clue words or phrases that signal a detail such as an example or an added fact.

All organisms need energy to live and grow. That energy comes from food. **Producers** are organisms that make their own food. Plants are producers. Tiny plantlike organisms called phytoplankton that live in oceans and other bodies of water are also producers.

This hippopotamus is a consumer that eats plants.

Humans are consumers. Most people eat both producers and other consumers.

Squirrels are consumers that eat mostly producers.

Organisms that cannot make their own food are called **consumers**. Consumers eat other living things in order to get the energy they need to live and grow. Some consumers eat only plants. Some eat only animals. Others eat both plants and animals.

No matter what kind of consumer an organism is, it cannot survive without producers. For example, mice and rabbits eat only plants. Hawks eat the mice and rabbits. If there were no plants, then the mice and rabbits would die. The hawks that eat the mice and rabbits would also die. Living things depend on the food made by plants.

Consumer or Producer?

Write which are producers and consumers.

You Are What You Eat

Some people eat only foods made from plants. Others eat a mix of meat and plant foods. Just like people, different kinds of consumers eat different types of food.

Active Reading As you read this page and the next, underline the definitions of herbivore, carnivore, and omnivore.

Consumers are classified into three main groups based on what they eat. *Herbivores* eat only producers. Common herbivores are mice, rabbits, and deer. Pandas, koalas, elephants, and many insects, including butterflies, are also herbivores.

Meat-eating consumers are called *carnivores*. When you think of a carnivore, you might think of the lion shown here. But not all carnivores are mammals. Penguins are birds that eat only fish. Ladybugs are beetles that eat other insects.

This snake is a carnivore. It eats other animals for food.

Lions are carnivores that eat other animals such as zebras and antelopes.

Consumers that eat both plants and animals are called *omnivores*. Forest-dwelling box turtles, for example, eat strawberries, blackberries, and mushrooms. The box turtles also eat insects and spiders.

Carnivores and omnivores that hunt and eat other animals are also called *predators*. The animals that predators hunt are called *prey*. The numbers of predators and prey are linked. As a predator population increases, it consumes more and more prey. Eventually the predators consume so much prey that the prey animals become scarce. The predators have trouble finding food. Some predators may move away. Others die. With fewer predators to eat them, prey animals have a chance to increase in number again.

A toucan is an omnivore. It will eat fruit, insects, snakes, and just about anything else it can find.

Do the Math!
Interpret a Line Graph

The graph shows the number of gazelles and cheetahs in an area over time.

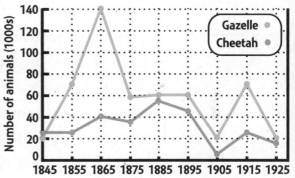

How many of the following were there?

	in 1865	in 1905
gazelles	_____	_____
cheetahs	_____	_____

What do you notice about the relationship of predators to prey?

_____

_____

_____

Break It Down, Clean It Up

Just as garbage collectors remove the garbage people throw away, nature has its own cleanup crew.

Active Reading As you read these two pages, underline the main roles of scavengers and decomposers.

Have you ever thought about what happens to the bodies of dead plants and animals? When plants and animals die, some organisms in the environment eat them for food. These organisms are called *scavengers*. Vultures are well-known scavengers. These birds are famous for eating the bodies of dead animals. Some carnivores are also scavengers. Polar bears, sharks, and leopards both hunt for food and eat dead animals that they find. Scavengers play an important role in cleaning up the environment.

Millipedes are scavengers. They eat dead plant matter that they find in the soil.

Crabs scavenge algae, fungus, and decaying matter from the ocean floor.

Many vultures don't have feathers on their heads. This helps these birds keep clean when they stick their heads inside the dead animals they scavenge.

▶ Explain what you think an ecosystem would look like without scavengers and decomposers.

_____

_____

_____

_____

_____

_____

_____

_____

Scavengers aren't the only living things that clean up dead organisms. **Decomposers** are organisms that break down, or decompose, wastes and the remains of dead organisms. This process returns nutrients to the soil, air, and water. Bacteria are microscopic decomposers that use chemicals called enzymes [EHN•zymz] to break down the last remains of plants and animals and animal wastes. In so doing, they obtain the energy they need to carry out their life processes.

Fungi are decomposers that release enzymes. These enzymes break down dead matter, releasing nutrients that enrich the soil.

A Starring Role

Every organism plays an important part in its ecosystem.

Scientists study living things in their environment to better understand how these organisms relate to one another. Some species cannot survive if their habitat changes even in small ways. Tiger salamanders, for example, live in wetlands. Scientists know that if the number of salamanders in a wetland goes down, it is a sign that the wetland has been polluted or damaged.

Some species, such as the Bengal tiger of South Asia, are in danger of dying out. Governments work to protect these species as well as their habitats. When a species' habitat is protected, all the organisms within it are protected, too. Kelp forests are rich ocean habitats where many fish have their young. Kelp forests are found throughout the world in cold, coastal waters. Protecting these forests helps protect the organisms that depend on them, in the same way that protecting the animals that live in the kelp forests helps protect the forests themselves.

▶ Think of a species that is common in your area. What might happen if this species suddenly disappeared?

_____

_____

_____

_____

_____

Tiger salamander

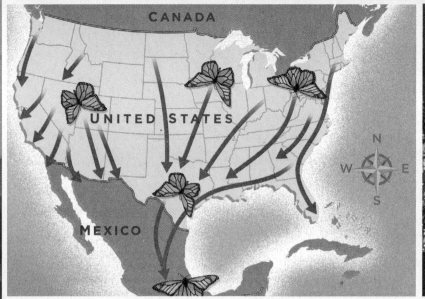

Monarch butterflies migrate south to warm climates for the winter. Over their lifetime, monarchs live in many different ecosystems. Conservationists have worked to protect the areas where these insects live. Doing so also protects other organisms that share the same area with the monarchs.

Sea turtles eat small animals that they find floating in seaweed. Conservationists have focused on protecting sea turtles. That in turn helps protect both their habitats and the organisms that live there.

Sea urchins feed on kelp. If there are too many urchins, they can completely destroy the forest. Sea otters eat sea urchins and help keep kelp beds healthy.

Sum It Up!

When you're done, use the answer key to check and revise your work.

Match each picture to its description.

1

2

3

A Omnivores are consumers that eat both plants and animals.

B Carnivores and omnivores that hunt and eat other animals are also called predators.

C Plants make food through the process of photosynthesis.

Summarize

The idea web below summarizes the lesson. Complete the web.

Roles of Organisms

A 4. _____ makes food for itself and other animals.

Bacteria are 5. _____ that break down dead matter and wastes.

Carnivores are consumers that 7. _____ .

The number of predators tends to rise when there is a rise in the number of 6. _____ .

Answer Key: 1. C 2. B 3. A 4. producer 5. decomposers 6. prey 7. eat other animals

Name _____

Word Play

1 Unscramble each group of letters to spell an important term from the lesson. Use the clues to help you.

1. breehivor

 _ _ _ _ _ _ _ _ _

 An animal that eats only producers

2. toradrep

 _ _ _ _ _ _ _ _

 A living thing that hunts and eats other animals

3. reyp

 _ _ _ _

 An animal that is hunted by other animals

4. pocodemser

 _ _ _ _ _ _ _ _ _ _

 An organism that breaks down wastes and plant and animal remains and returns their nutrients to the soil

5. evormoni

 _ _ _ _ _ _ _ _

 An animal that eats plants and other animals

6. vengescra

 _ _ _ _ _ _ _ _ _

 An organism that eats dead plants or animals

7. clyophohlrl

 _ _ _ _ _ _ _ _ _ _ _

 A green molecule that enables plants to turn water, carbon dioxide, and sunlight into sugars

8. rumcosne

 _ _ _ _ _ _ _ _

 An organism that cannot make its own food

Bonus: List five omnivores.

_____

_____

_____

_____

_____

Apply Concepts

2 Complete the sentences to identify two roles of decomposers in an ecosystem.

a. Decomposers break down the remains of _____ and the wastes of

_____ .

b. Decomposers return

_____ to the soil.

3 All scavengers are consumers, but not all consumers are scavengers. True or false?

_____

Explain your answer.

_____

_____

_____

_____

4 Circle the activity that occurs when plants make sugars for food.

Plants take in oxygen and give off carbon dioxide.

Animals take in oxygen and give off carbon dioxide.

Plants take in carbon dioxide and give off oxygen.

5 Label the consumers and producers.

_____ _____ _____ _____

Take It Home! List all the plants and animals your family eats today in a two-column chart. Don't forget to count the plant materials that make up bread and pasta! Are the members of your family herbivores, carnivores, or omnivores?

Meet the Environment Detectives

Erika Zavaleta

Erika Zavaleta is an ecologist in California. She studies the links between the environment and people. Cities grow and climates change. These changes make it hard for some plants and animals to survive. Part of Erika Zavaleta's job is figuring out good ways for people, plants, and animals to live in harmony.

Recently, Erika Zavaleta has studied oak trees. Fires and other disasters can kill a whole forest of these trees. She is studying the best ways to help new trees grow after such a disaster.

Peter & Rosemary Grant

Peter and Rosemary Grant study animal adaptation. On the Galápagos Islands off the coast of South America, they study how birds called finches change over time. They are most interested in changes in the birds' beaks. The Grants have found that beak shape and size change when the environment changes.

During severe droughts many birds die of starvation. When the only seeds remaining on the ground are large, hard seeds, only the birds with the biggest beaks can crack them. They survive and the small-beaked birds die. The next year, the big-beaked birds produce big-beaked young like themselves.

215

Now You Look For Clues

Answer the questions below about the scientists you just read about.

What kind of problems in the environment does Erika Zavaleta study?

_____

_____

_____

_____

What measurements do you think the Grants made as part of their studies?

_____

_____

_____

_____

What have these scientists learned about plant and animal adaptation?

_____

_____

_____

_____

_____

Essential Question

How Does Energy Move Through Ecosystems?

Engage Your Brain!

Find the answer to the following question in the lesson and record it here.

There are many kinds of animals at this watering hole. Why aren't they running away from each other?

_____

_____

_____

_____

Active Reading

Lesson Vocabulary

List the terms. As you learn about each one, make notes in the Interactive Glossary.

_____

_____

_____

Using Diagrams

Diagrams add information to text that appears on the page with them. Active readers pause their reading to review diagrams and decide how the information in them adds to what is provided in the running text.

Food Chains

From producers to consumers to decomposers, the food chain never stops.

Active Reading As you read these two pages, underline all the important members of a food chain.

Tundra Food Chain

The tundra is the coldest, driest ecosystem on Earth. Short summers mean little plant life grows here. Many animals either migrate or hibernate during the long, cold winters.

Reindeer moss uses energy from the sun to make and store sugars. Producers, such as reindeer moss, form the base of tundra food chains.

Caribou are first-level consumers. These herbivores eat reindeer moss and other producers to get energy for their life functions.

Wolves are second-level consumers. They are predators. Animals, such as caribou, are their prey.

The transfer of food energy from one organism to the next in an ecological community is called a **food chain**. Almost every food chain begins when producers capture energy from the sun. Through photosynthesis, producers convert this light energy into chemical energy in sugars, which they use for food. Food not used for life processes is stored in the tissues of the producers and then passed on to herbivores that eat the producers. Herbivores are first-level consumers.

Next in the food chain are carnivores and omnivores, the second-level consumers. Second-level consumers eat herbivores and receive the food energy stored in their bodies. Third-level consumers eat second-level consumers. Scavengers may be second- or third-level consumers, as they eat organisms that have died.

Decomposers are the final link in any food chain. They get energy as they break down the remains of dead plants and animals and return nutrients to the soil.

Scavengers, such as this Arctic gull, feed on the dead bodies of caribou, wolves, and other animals. Fungi and bacteria do the final cleanup work as they decompose the final remains of tundra organisms.

▶ Number the pictures to show their position in a food chain.

Food Webs

Like a spiderweb held together by many connecting threads, the paths in a food web show the feeding relationships among species in a community.

Active Reading As you read, underline the information that helps you understand the food web diagram.

You don't eat just one kind of food, and neither do organisms in food chains. Each consumer has a variety of choices when it comes to its next meal. A **food web** shows how food chains overlap. In other words, it shows what eats what. Look at the forest food web on the next page. Both the mouse and the insect eat parts of the pine tree or its seeds. A snake can eat a mouse or a salamander. All of these living things eventually become food for decomposers. Decomposers return nutrients to soil. These nutrients, in turn, are used by producers to make food.

Arrows in the web point in the direction that energy moves. Find the acorns and the mouse. Which way does the arrow point?

It points from the acorns to the mouse. Energy moves from producer to consumer when the mouse eats the acorns.

Predators limit the number of animals below them in a food web. If snakes were removed from this forest food web, the number of mice would increase. More mice mean that more plants would be eaten. Eventually, the mice might run out of food and begin to die off. This would affect the hawks and other living things that eat mice. All of the organisms in a food web are interdependent.

▶ In the forest food web, trace two overlapping food chains that include the snake. Make the path of each food chain a different color.

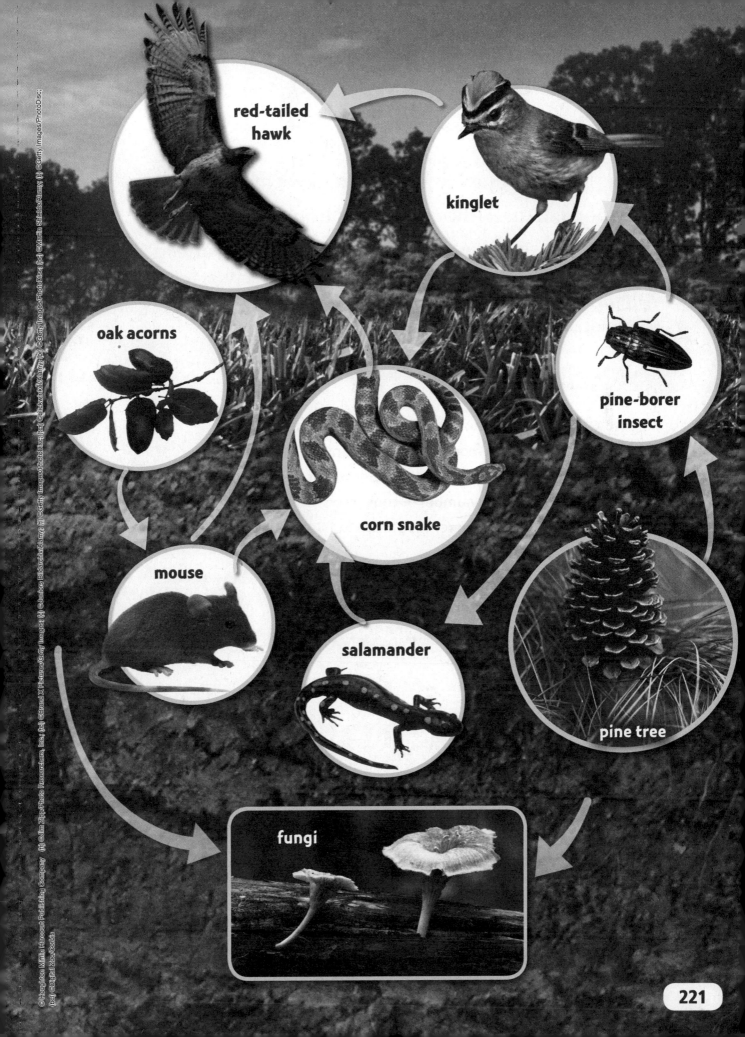

red-tailed hawk

kinglet

oak acorns

pine-borer insect

corn snake

mouse

salamander

pine tree

fungi

At the Top

It takes a lot of grass to support a hawk at the top of a food chain. Although hawks don't eat grass, the energy they use comes from the grass at the bottom.

Active Reading As you read, circle the lesson vocabulary each time it is used.

An **energy pyramid** shows how much energy passes from one organism to another up a food chain. The organisms in a layer of the pyramid feed on those in a lower layer. Because it takes many producers to support a smaller number of consumers, producers in the bottom layer are the most numerous group.

Third-level consumers like the leopard seal, a predator at the top of this energy pyramid, have the least amount of energy available to them. That is why their population is small.

Second-level consumers, such as octopuses and salmon, feed on first-level consumers below them in the pyramid. Because less energy is available to them, they are fewer.

Krill, clams, and herring are first-level consumers. They consume phytoplankton. Some first-level consumers eat millions of tiny phytoplankton every day.

Producers called phytoplankton are the base of this ocean energy pyramid.

Do the Math!
Calculate Units

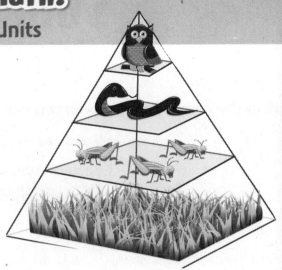

At each level of an energy pyramid, 90% of the energy received from the lower level is used for life processes. Only 10% is available to be passed upward.

If the grasses have 100 units of energy, how much can be passed to the grasshoppers?

_____

Why do the snakes only get 1 unit of energy?

_____

_____

BONUS How much energy is available to the owls that eat the snakes? Show your work.

_____

Environmental changes can affect energy flow in an energy pyramid. Suppose the number of salmon is reduced because of overfishing. Seals that eat the salmon may go hungry. They may even starve. Without salmon to eat them, the krill population could increase at a rapid rate. Such a large number of krill could then eat up its own food source as well as that of other species. One change in the flow of energy through an ecosystem affects every species in the ecosystem. Whatever happens at one level affects the energy available in the rest of the pyramid.

Sum It Up!

When you're done, use the answer key to check and revise your work.

Fill in the missing words to summarize the main ideas of the lesson.

Energy Moves Through Ecosystems

Food Chains

The first organisms in a food chain are

1. _____.

Herbivores are the

2. _____-level consumers, and

3. _____

and 4. _____ are the second- and third-level consumers.

5. _____

are the final organisms in all food chains. They recycle materials by breaking down plant and animal remains, thereby returning nutrients to the environment.

Food Webs

A food web shows how food chains

6. _____.

Arrows show the direction of

7. _____

transfer through the web.

Energy Pyramids

Most of the energy in an ecosystem is present in the

8. _____.

At each level, organisms use

9. _____ percent of the available energy for life processes. Only

10. _____ percent of the energy is passed from one level to the next level above.

Answer Key: 1. producers 2. first 3. carnivores 4. omnivores 5. Decomposers 6. overlap 7. energy 8. producers 9. 90 10. 10

Name _____

Word Play

1 Unscramble the terms. The first letter of each term is in the center of the target. Use the definitions to help you.

1.  _____ A diagram that shows overlapping food chains (2 words)

2.  _____ Plants and some plantlike microorganisms

3. 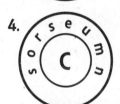 _____ A single path that shows how food energy moves from one organism to the next in an ecosystem (2 words)

4. 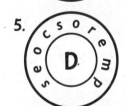 _____ Animals that eat plants and animals

5.  _____ Organisms that break down the nutrient remains of dead things

6. _____ A diagram that shows how energy is used, stored, and passed on in each level of a food chain (2 words)

Apply Concepts

2 This food chain is scrambled. Rewrite the links in the correct order.

hawk ➡ bacteria ➡ corn ➡ mouse

_____ ➡ _____ ➡ _____ ➡ _____

3 Complete the facts about the energy pyramid below.

a. The shrubs use _____ percent of their energy and pass on _____ percent to the deer that eat them.

b. Which organisms get the least amount of energy?

_____

c. Which organisms must be the most plentiful to support this food chain?

_____

4 Many food chains used the sun's energy to produce the food in this sandwich. The cheese came from milk from a cow that ate grass that took energy from the sun, for example. Fill in the other chains.

sun _____ ➡ you

sun _____ ➡ you

sun _____ ➡ you

5 Label the role of each organism. Some have more than one role.
Use these terms: *producer, herbivore, carnivore, first-level consumer, second-level consumer, decomposer.*

_____   _____   _____   _____

_____   _____   _____   _____

6 A drought has affected an ecosystem. Many plants have died for lack of water. What do you think will happen to the other organisms in the area?

_____

_____

_____

_____

_____

_____

_____

_____

_____

7

Draw arrows to show what the hawk would eat.

Identify one complete food chain in this food web in the correct order.

_____

_____

Explain what might happen if the grass in this food web were to disappear.

_____

_____

_____

_____

Take It Home!

At your next meal, make a game with your family to identify the food chains that led to the different foods you are eating. What is the longest chain? The shortest chain?

OHIO 5.SIA.4 Analyze and interpret data. 5.SIA.6 Think critically and logically to connect evidence and explanations.

S.T.E.M.
Engineering & Technology

Designing a New Dog

People modify animals for a variety of reasons. Selective breeding is the process of breeding animals so their offspring inherit certain desired traits. People have selectively bred dogs for many centuries. Now there are more than 200 breeds of dogs, each with its own characteristics.

The dog's primary ancestor is the wolf.

It's uncertain whether ancient people started keeping dogs for companionship or as work animals. But we know dogs and people have shared a bond for thousands of years.

Working dogs were historically bred to do certain jobs, such as hunt, haul things, or herd livestock.

Today dogs are bred mainly for companionship and sport.

Critical Thinking

How has selective breeding of dogs changed over time?

_____

_____

_____

In nature, an animal's environment determines whether it survives to breed successfully. People control the environments of the dogs they breed, so people can choose to keep traits that might not have been passed on in nature.

Draw a dog that might lead a visually impaired person.

How do this dog's physical and behavioral characteristics help it do its job?

_____

_____

Draw a dog that might help to locate people after an earthquake.

How do this dog's physical features help it do its job?

_____

_____

Dogs have been bred for many reasons. What kind of new dog breed would you like to develop? What traits would your new dog need? What skills would you teach it?

_____

_____

Build On It!

Rise to the engineering design challenge—complete **Improvise It: Measuring Decomposer Activity** in the Inquiry Flipchart.

OHIO 5.LS.1 Organisms perform a variety of roles in an ecosystem. 5.LS.2 All of the processes that take place within organisms require energy. 5.SIA.1 Identify questions that can be answered through scientific investigations. 5.SIA.2 Design and conduct a scientific investigation. 5.SIA.4 Analyze and interpret data. 5.SIA.5 Develop descriptions, models, explanations and predictions. 5.SIA.6 Think critically and logically to connect evidence and explanations. 5.SIA.8 Communicate scientific procedures and explanations.

Name _____

Essential Question

What Role Do Decomposers Play?

Set a Purpose

How do you think decomposers change materials?

_____

_____

_____

_____

Write a statement summarizing how you think mold changes the food it grows on.

_____

_____

_____

_____

Think About the Procedure

What are different observations you can make about the appearance of the bread?

_____

_____

_____

Why do we spray one of the bread slices with water and not the other?

_____

_____

_____

Record Your Data

In the space below, make a table in which you record your observations.

Draw Conclusions

In the space below, draw a picture of the appearance of breads *A* and *B* during the last day of your investigation.

[drawing space]

Did your observations indicate that mold is a decomposer? Explain.

_____

_____

_____

_____

Analyze and Extend

1. How did the mold change the bread?

_____

_____

2. Where do you think mold gets its nutrients from?

_____

_____

3. Did spraying the bread with water have any effect on how fast the mold grew? Explain.

_____

_____

_____

_____

4. What do you think would happen to the bread if you continued to let the mold grow on it?

_____

_____

_____

_____

5. Use your observations to describe the role of decomposers in the environment.

_____

_____

_____

6. Think of other questions you would like to ask about decomposers.

_____

_____

_____

_____

_____

Name _____

Vocabulary Review

Use the terms in the box to complete the sentences.

> chlorophyll
> consumers
> decomposers
> energy pyramid
> food chain
> food web
> photosynthesis
> producers

1. A diagram that shows that energy is lost at each level in a food

   chain is called a(n) _____.

2. Organisms that break down wastes and the remains of dead

   organisms are called _____.

3. Organisms that do not make their own food are

   called _____.

4. A network of overlapping food chains is called

   a(n) _____.

5. Organisms that make their own food are

   called _____.

6. Most plants contain a green, food-producing molecule

   called _____.

7. The transfer of food energy from one organism to the next is

   called a(n) _____.

8. Plants make their own food through a process

   called _____.

Science Concepts

Fill in the letter of the choice that best answers the question.

9. Renata was studying mountain lions like this one.

She made a list of the ways she could classify this animal. Which is Renata's correct list?

(A) omnivore, prey, consumer

(B) carnivore, predator, consumer

(C) herbivore, predator, producer

(D) carnivore, prey, consumer

10. Marc gets a pet rabbit for his birthday. He looks online and learns that rabbits are herbivores. Which of the following foods might he feed his new pet?

(A) lettuce

(B) bacteria

(C) meat scraps

(D) dead insects

11. Which of these is the final link in every food chain?

(A) producers

(B) decomposers

(C) first-level consumers

(D) second-level consumers

12. This diagram shows the movement of food energy through an ecosystem.

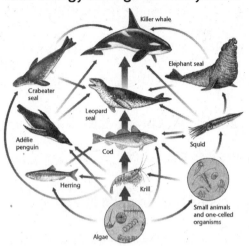

Which statement is the **best** description of this diagram?

(A) It is an energy pyramid.

(B) It is a forest food chain.

(C) It is an ocean food web.

(D) It is a chart of third-level consumers.

13. Which is the initial source of energy in most ecosystems?

(A) sunlight

(B) decomposers

(C) nutrients in soil

(D) oxygen in the air

14. Pablo has a hamburger and a salad for lunch. What does this tell you about him?

(A) He is a producer.

(B) He is a scavenger.

(C) He is a herbivore.

(D) He is an omnivore.

234   Unit 5

15. Plants and animals are interdependent. Plants rely on animals to produce carbon dioxide. What do plants produce for animals?

(A) food and oxygen

(B) sunshine and rain

(C) carbon dioxide and food

(D) herbivores and carnivores

16. An ecosystem includes this food chain.

pine seed → mouse → snake → hawk

What would happen if all the mice died from a disease?

(A) The snakes would eat pine seeds instead of mice.

(B) The producers would stop making food.

(C) The population of snakes would increase.

(D) The population of snakes would decrease.

17. A shark is preparing to eat a fish swimming in front of it. What is the **best** way to describe these two animals?

(A) predator and prey

(B) producer and consumer

(C) herbivore and omnivore

(D) scavenger and producer

18. Some animals are known for their specific food-gathering behaviors. Vultures are examples of which of the following?

(A) predator

(B) producer

(C) scavenger

(D) decomposer

19. Halie is doing a report on photosynthesis. She draws a diagram to represent the materials used by plants to make food and the byproducts that this process produces. Which is the correct diagram?

(A) sunlight + carbon dioxide + water → sugar + oxygen

(B) sunlight + oxygen + water → sugar + carbon dioxide

(C) sunlight + carbon dioxide + sugar → water + oxygen

(D) sunlight + oxygen + sugar → carbon dioxide + water

20. Terrell notices that a tree in his backyard has fungi growing on one side. What is the role of fungi, and what are these organisms doing?

(A) Fungi are producers. They are making their own food.

(B) Fungi are scavengers. They are eating the dead parts of the tree.

(C) Fungi are producers. They are providing the tree with food.

(D) Fungi are decomposers. They are decomposing a part of the tree.

Apply Inquiry and Review the Big Idea

Write the answers to these questions.

21. This diagram shows various organisms that live in the same ecosystem.

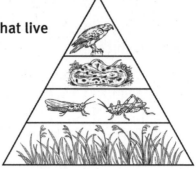

   a. What is this diagram called, and what is its purpose? _____

_____

   b. Describe a food-chain relationship between the four organisms shown. _____

_____

   c. Suppose all the organisms on the third level died out. What would be the effect on the organisms on the levels above and below? _____

_____

_____

22. This diagram shows the carbon dioxide–oxygen cycle.

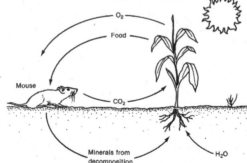

Explain the cycle, the gases involved, how they are used, and how they move in the cycle.

   a. Plants in sunlight: _____

_____

   b. Animals at any time: _____

_____

   c. Plants at any time: _____

_____

236   Unit 5

Motion

Big Idea

A change in the motion of an object is based on the mass of the object and the amount of force exerted.

OHIO 5.PS.1, 5.SIA.1, 5.SIA.2, 5.SIA.3, 5.SIA.4, 5.SIA.5, 5.SIA.6, 5.SIA.8

I Wonder Why

Why does a pit crew need to replace the racecar's tires several times during the race? *Turn the page to find out.*

Here's why Friction gives the racecar traction and allows it to grip the track, but it also produces a lot of heat. The high speed and forceful turns of a race wear tires out quickly.

In this unit, you will explore the Big Idea, the Essential Questions, and the Investigations on the Inquiry Flipchart.

Levels of Inquiry Key ■ DIRECTED ■ GUIDED ■ INDEPENDENT

Track Your Progress

Big Idea A change in the motion of an object is based on the mass of the object and the amount of force exerted.

Essential Questions

Now I Get the Big Idea!

Science Notebook
Before you begin each lesson, be sure to write your thoughts about the Essential Question.

Essential Question

What Is Motion?

Engage Your Brain!

As you read the lesson, figure out the answer to the following question. Write the answer here.

How would you describe the motion of the hummingbird in this picture?

_____

_____

_____

_____

_____

_____

Active Reading

Lesson Vocabulary

List the terms. As you learn about each one, make notes in the Interactive Glossary.

_____   _____

_____   _____

_____

Main Idea and Details

Detail sentences give information about a main idea. The details may be examples, features, characteristics, or facts. Active readers stay focused on the topic when they ask, What fact or other information does this detail add to the main idea?

Twisting and Turning

What tells you that the person in the picture is moving? Is it possible for a person to move in more than one direction at a time? You can find out!

Active Reading

As you read the next page, find and circle details about how this girl can move.

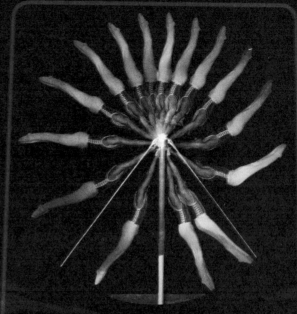

Curve

The boy's body moves in a curved path around the bar.

The blurry lines show you the directions in which the girl is moving.

Straight Line

As the girl flips down the balance beam, she moves in a straight line.

How would you describe where your left hand is right now? Is it on top of this book, or is it touching your chin? Can you describe where it is without naming something else that is close by? No! **Position** is the location of an object in relation to a nearby object or place. The second object or place is called the *reference point*.

Now put your left hand in a different place. This change in position is **motion**. To describe your hand's motion, you'd tell in what direction it moved from its earlier position as well as how fast it moved.

The girl in the picture is in motion. Parts of her body move up and down, back and forth, in circles, and in a straight line. Her feet move in a straight line down the beam and then up and down as she flips forward.

Back and Forth

Draw a picture of something that vibrates, or moves back and forth.

▶ Name a part of the girl's body that is moving in several ways as she flips.

_____

Where Is It?

10

How can you tell that the penguin is moving?

Active Reading As you read the next page, underline the words that describe specific reference points.

1. The penguin has just jumped from the top of the ice.

2. The penguin is between the top of the ice and the water.

3. The penguin is entering the water.

You know something is moving if its position changes against a background. The background is called the *frame of reference*.

The picture of the penguin shows three images taken as the penguin jumped off the ice. Notice that each image of the penguin has the same frame of reference. You can choose any part of that background as a reference point. The words *top of the ice* describe the reference point for Image 1. Both *top of the ice* and *the water* describe reference points for Image 2. Only *the water* describes a reference point for Image 3.

What if the images of the penguin had been in the wrong order? Could you put them in the correct order? Sure! You know that things don't fall up, so you could use the water as the reference point for each image. The image of the penguin highest above the water must be first. The image of the penguin closest to the water is last.

Look at the pictures of the horse race. In the pictures, what can you use for reference points? How can you use the reference points to put the pictures in order?

▶ Put these pictures in order by writing numbers in the circles. Then explain how you decided on the order.

_____

_____

_____

_____

5
meters

| 0 | 5 | 10 | 15 | 20 | 25 | 30 | 35 | 40 | 45 |

Ready! Set! Go!   `00:00` → `00:10`

The turtle, cat, and rabbit start running at the same time. How far does each of them go in 10 seconds?

Fast or Slow?

Could a turtle beat a rabbit in a race? It depends on each animal's speed.

Active Reading As you read this page, underline the definitions of *speed* and *velocity*.

One way to describe motion is to find speed, or how fast or slow something is moving. **Speed** tells you how the position of an object changes during a certain amount of time. You can measure time in hours (hr), minutes (min), or seconds (sec).

To find an object's speed, you divide how far it goes by the time it takes to get there. So if you walk 30 meters (m) in 15 seconds (sec), your speed is 2 m/sec.

$$30 \text{ m} \div 15 \text{ sec} = 2 \text{ m/sec}$$

How is velocity different from speed? **Velocity** is the speed of an object in a particular direction. Suppose you walk toward the east. If your speed is 2 m/sec, then your velocity is 2 m/sec, east.

In a race on a straight track, all the runners move in the same direction. Their velocities differ only because their speeds differ. Could a turtle win a race against a rabbit? Sure! The rabbit might run at a very slow speed—or in the wrong direction!

80 meters

100 meters

| 50 | 55 | 60 | 65 | 70 | 75 | 80 | 85 | 90 | 95 | 100 |

Do the Math!
Calculate Speed

1. What is the speed of the rabbit during the race?

_____

2. What is the speed of the turtle during the race?

_____

3. A chicken joins the race and runs at 4 m/sec. On the distance line, draw the chicken where it would be after 10 seconds.

_____

_____

_____

_____

Changing It Up

The gas pedal on a car is called an accelerator. Did you know that the brakes and steering wheel are also accelerators?

Active Reading As you read these pages, circle three phrases that tell how an object can accelerate.

You may hear people say that a car is accelerating when it speeds up. That's only partly correct. **Acceleration** is any change in velocity. Remember that velocity tells both the speed and the direction of motion. So matter accelerates if it speeds up, slows down, or changes direction.

Acceleration of any kind is caused by forces. Forces can push and pull on matter from all directions. If a force pushing against an object in one direction is greater than a force pushing in the opposite direction, the object will accelerate.

Look at the path of the fly. The fly accelerates each time it changes either its speed or its direction. Sometimes it changes both its speed and its direction at the same time!

Turn and Speed Up
In this section, the fly accelerates because it changes both its direction and its speed.

Slow Down
Here, the fly is traveling in a straight line while slowing down. This is also acceleration.

Speed Up
In this section of its path, the fly travels in a straight line. It accelerates because it is speeding up.

Stop and Start

The fly lands on the wall and stops moving. Its body doesn't accelerate. When it starts moving again, it speeds up. So it accelerates.

Change Direction

The fly's speed stays the same as it changes direction. Because its velocity changes, it accelerates.

▶ Fill in the missing parts of the table.

Item	Speed	What happens?	Acceleration?
Mouse	1 m/sec	suddenly chased by a cat	
Runner	8 m/sec	runs at the same speed around a circular track	
Train	80 km/hr	moves along a straight track	
Jet plane	300 km/hr		Yes, slows down.

Sum It Up!

When you're done, use the answer key to check and revise your work.

Read the summary statements below. Each statement is incorrect.
Change the part of the statement in blue to make it correct.

1 You know that something is in motion when it speeds up.

_____

_____

2 Before you describe how an object in a picture moved, you have to choose a type of motion.

_____

3 To measure the speed of an object, you need to know how far it traveled and in what direction it traveled.

_____

_____

4 An object accelerates when it moves left or moves right.

_____

_____

248

Answer Key: 1. changes its position 2. reference point 3. how long it took 4. speeds up, slows down, or changes direction

Name _____

Word Play

1 Important words from this lesson are scrambled in the following box.
Unscramble the words. Place each word in a set of squares.

| lcaoeciranet | despe | eerrfcnee | oitmon |
| hapt | crefo | ritcidnoe | ovltyiec |

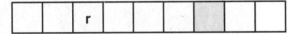

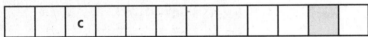

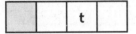

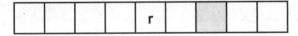

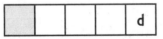

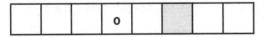

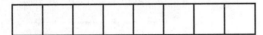

Rearrange the letters in the colored boxes to form
a word that describes the location of an object.

Put a star next to two words that describe
how fast something moves.

Apply Concepts

2 Describe the motion and path of the diver. Use the words *position, speed, velocity,* and *acceleration* in your description.

_____

_____

_____

_____

_____

_____

_____

_____

_____

_____

_____

_____

3 You are riding in a bus. Your friend is standing on the street corner as the bus goes by. How would you describe the way your friend seems to move? How would your friend describe your motion? Why do the descriptions differ?

_____

_____

_____

_____

_____

Name _____

4

0 seconds   1 second   2 seconds   3 seconds   4 seconds   5 seconds

0 meters   2 meters   4 meters   6 meters   8 meters   10 meters

The diagram represents the motion of a cow walking in a straight line across a field. Use it to answer these questions.

a. Is the cow accelerating? Why or why not?

_____

_____

_____

_____

_____

b. Calculate the speed of the cow.

_____

_____

_____

_____

c. How long will it take the cow to travel 24 meters? Describe how you found the correct answer.

_____

_____

_____

_____

_____

d. How far will the cow travel in 35 seconds? Describe how you found the correct answer.

_____

_____

_____

_____

_____

5 The student in the image below is walking to class. Describe the student's position in relation to a reference point. Describe how the boy's body could move as he walks to class.

_____

_____

_____

_____

_____

_____

6 In each box, draw a picture that shows an object moving in the way described by the label at the top of the box.

curve

back and forth and curve

Take It Home!

Choose three places in your community. With a family member, visit each place and look for things that move. Record what you observe in a chart. Can you identify the forces causing the motion?

252

OHIO **5.PS.1** The amount of change in movement of an object is based on the mass of the object and the amount of force exerted.

Lesson **2**

Essential Question
What Are Forces?

Engage Your Brain!

As you read the lesson, figure out the answer to the following question. Write the answer here.

What forces are acting on this cyclist? Are all the forces balanced?

_____

_____

_____

_____

_____

_____

Active Reading

Lesson Vocabulary

List the terms. As you learn about each one, make notes in the Interactive Glossary.

_____   _____

_____   _____

_____

Cause and Effect

Some ideas in this lesson are connected by a cause-and-effect relationship. Why something happens is a cause. What happens as a result of something else is an effect. Active readers look for effects by asking themselves, What happened? They look for causes by asking, Why did it happen?

© Houghton Mifflin Harcourt Publishing Company © Larry Kasperek/NewSport/Corbis

Inquiry Flipchart p. 31 — On a Roll/Make It Easier

PUSHING and Pulling

You pull on a door to open it. You lift up a backpack. You push on the pedals of a bike to go faster. What is the relationship between force and motion?

The horse and the road it is on both exert a force on the cart.

▶ **Draw an arrow that shows the direction of the force applied to the cart by the horse.**

Changes in motion all have one thing in common. They require a **force**, which is a push or a pull. Forces can cause an object at rest to move. They can cause a moving object to speed up, slow down, change direction, or stop. Forces can also change an object's shape.

Forces are measured with a spring scale in units called newtons (N). The larger the force, the greater the change it can cause to the motion of an object. Smaller forces cause smaller changes. Sometimes more than one force can act together in a way that does not cause a change in motion.

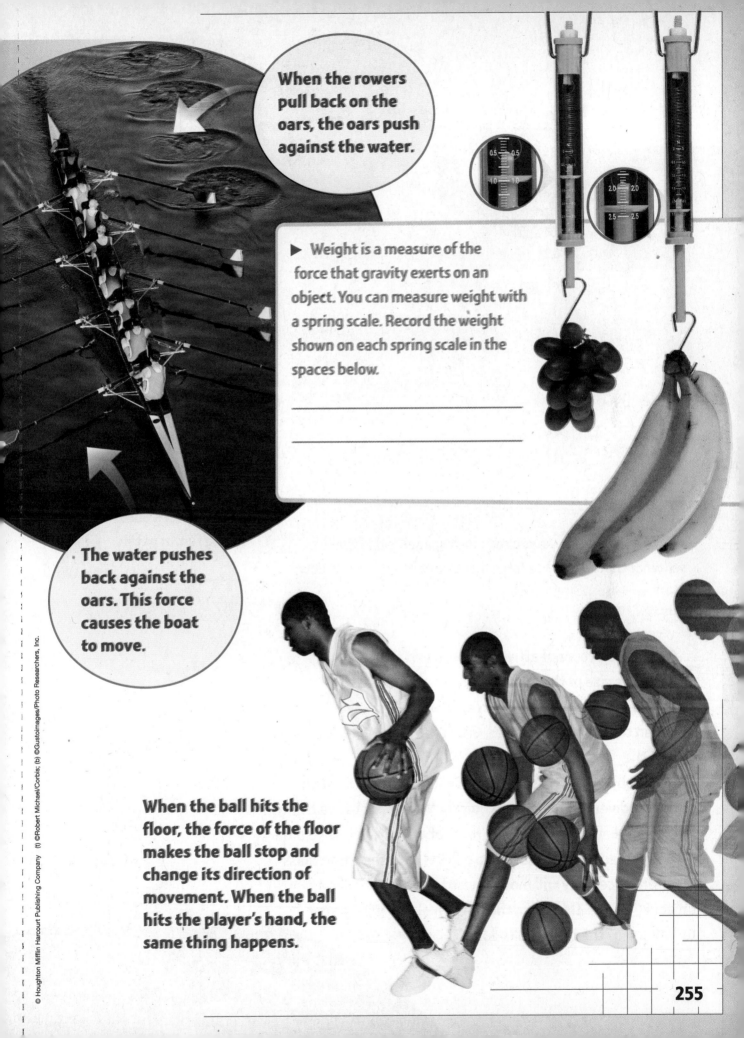

When the rowers pull back on the oars, the oars push against the water.

▶ Weight is a measure of the force that gravity exerts on an object. You can measure weight with a spring scale. Record the weight shown on each spring scale in the spaces below.

_____

_____

The water pushes back against the oars. This force causes the boat to move.

When the ball hits the floor, the force of the floor makes the ball stop and change its direction of movement. When the ball hits the player's hand, the same thing happens.

TWO COMMON
Forces

What do the skydivers and some of the flower petals have in common? They are both falling! What causes this?

▶ Draw an arrow showing the direction of the gravitational force between Earth and the falling flower petals.

→ Gravity

Gravity is a force of attraction between two objects. The size of this force increases as the mass of the objects increases. It decreases as the distance between the objects increases. Gravity acts on objects even if they are not touching.

Large objects such as Earth cause smaller objects, such as the skydivers, to accelerate quickly. We expect to see things fall toward Earth. However, the force of attraction is the same on both objects. If you place two objects with the same mass in outer space, they will move toward one another. If one object is "above" the other, the bottom object will appear to "fall up" as the other "falls down"!

256

© Houghton Mifflin Harcourt Publishing Company (t) ©blickwinkel/Alamy; (b) ©Peter Casolino/Alamy

→ Friction

Is it easier to ride your bike on a smooth road or on a muddy trail? Why?

Friction is a force that opposes motion. Friction acts between two objects that are touching, such as the bike tires and the road. Friction can also exist between air and a moving object. This is called air resistance.

It is easy to slide across smooth ice because it doesn't have much friction. Pulling something across rough sandpaper is a lot harder because there is lots of friction.

An air hockey table blows air upward. This layer of air reduces the surface friction, so the pieces move quickly.

▶ In the pictures on this page, circle the places where there is friction between two objects. In the small boxes, write *Inc* if the object is designed to increase friction and *Dec* if the object is designed to decrease friction.

The tires on this bike are designed to keep the rider from slipping. You have to pedal harder on a rough surface to overcome the force of friction.

BALANCED
or Unbalanced?

The tug-of-war teams are both applying forces. So why isn't anyone moving?

Draw a circle around a sentence that explains why objects don't always move when a force is applied.

When you sit on a chair, the force of gravity pulls you down. The chair pushes you up. You stay in one place because the forces on you are balanced. **Balanced forces** are forces on an object that are equal in size and opposite in direction. They cancel each other out.

The tug-of-war teams in the picture don't move because the forces are balanced. Friction keeps them from sliding. They won't move until one side exerts a larger force. Then, the forces are no longer balanced. **Unbalanced forces** are forces that cause a change in motion. A force must also overcome the force of friction before an object will move.

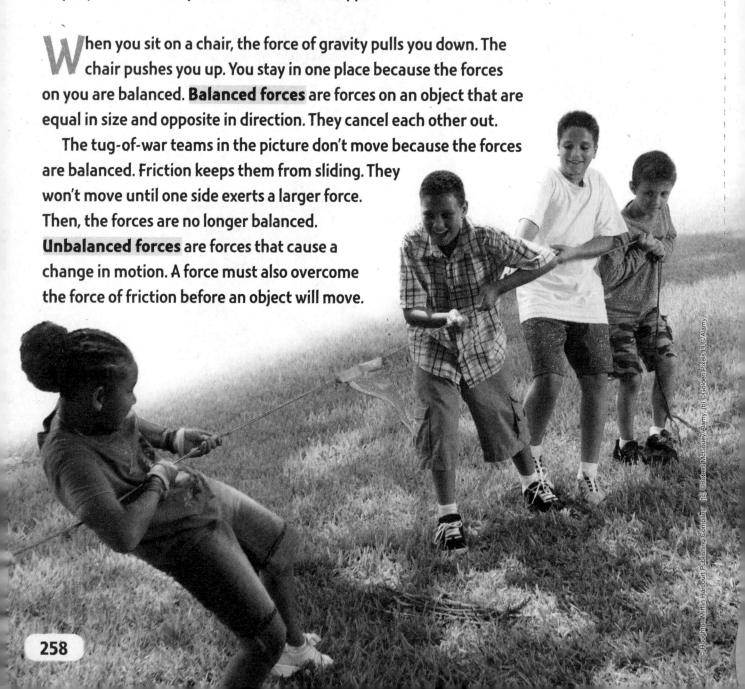

258

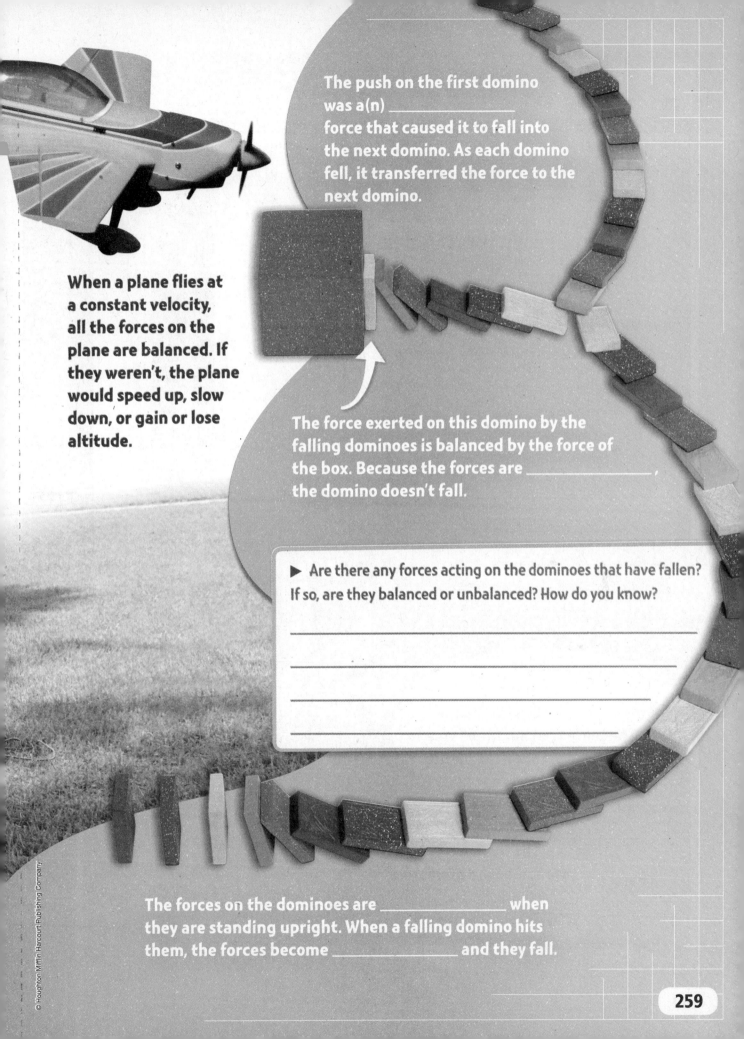

The push on the first domino was a(n) _____ force that caused it to fall into the next domino. As each domino fell, it transferred the force to the next domino.

When a plane flies at a constant velocity, all the forces on the plane are balanced. If they weren't, the plane would speed up, slow down, or gain or lose altitude.

The force exerted on this domino by the falling dominoes is balanced by the force of the box. Because the forces are _____, the domino doesn't fall.

▶ Are there any forces acting on the dominoes that have fallen? If so, are they balanced or unbalanced? How do you know?

_____

_____

_____

_____

The forces on the dominoes are _____ when they are standing upright. When a falling domino hits them, the forces become _____ and they fall.

PULL (or Push) Harder!

Would you expect a bunt in baseball to go out of the park? Why or why not?

Active Reading As you read, circle the sentences that explain the relationship between the size of a force and motion.

▶ Use forces to explain why the boy can't ring the bell.

_____

_____

_____

When the man swings the hammer, he exerts a force on a plate. The plate transfers the force to a piece of metal that rises up the column and rings the bell.

The boy swings the same kind of hammer at the same kind of machine. Why doesn't the metal hit the bell?

TEST YOUR STRENGTH

TEST YOUR STRENGTH

If you want to make the cue ball knock another ball into a pocket, you hit the cue ball with a lot of force. This large force makes the cue ball change its velocity, or accelerate, quickly. It has lots of energy to transfer to the other ball. The energy causes the other ball to accelerate.

The greater the force applied to the cue ball, the more force it can transfer to the other ball. A large force will cause a large change in the motion of the other ball. A small force will cause little change. Changes in velocity can also include changes in direction.

Do the Math!
Display Data in a Graph

Use the data in the table to make a graph that shows the relationship between the force applied to an object and its acceleration.

Force (N)	Acceleration (m/sec^2)
1	0.5
2	1.0
5	2.5
8	4.0
10	5.0

I'M NOT Moving!

It's easy to lift your empty backpack off the ground. Could you use the same force to lift it when it's full of books?

Active Reading As you read these pages, circle cause-and-effect signal words, such as *because*, *so*, or *therefore*.

The springs in the pictures all exert the same force on the balls, causing them to roll across the page. The ball with the least mass accelerates the fastest. Therefore, it travels the farthest. The same force has a greater effect on an object with a small mass than an object with a larger mass.

▶ Rank the balls by writing *greatest*, *middle*, or *least* in the six blanks.

Foam Ball

mass: _____

acceleration: _____

Baseball

mass: _____

acceleration: _____

▶ Both drivers began to brake at the same time. The brakes applied the same force to the trucks. Why did one truck take longer to stop?

_____

_____

_____

An object's acceleration depends on the object's mass and the force applied to it. The larger the force, the greater is the acceleration. Suppose you push a wagon gently. The wagon speeds up slowly. If you use more strength to push, then the wagon's speed changes quickly.

The less an object's mass is, the less force is needed to change its motion. It's easier to push an empty shopping cart than a full one. Light cars are used in drag races because a car with less mass speeds up faster than a car with more mass.

If you want to slide a heavy box across the floor faster, you have two options. You could take some items out of the box, which decreases its mass. Or you could have a friend help you, which increases the force you apply.

Steel Ball

mass: _____

acceleration: _____

How did I get to Mars?

LET'S GO to Mars!

How did an understanding of forces help to send a rover to Mars and safely land it there?

1 The first force you need is an unbalanced force to oppose Earth's gravity. A huge booster rocket produces nearly 900,000 N of force that accelerates the rocket upward.

USAF
BOEING
Guardrop
SGS
DELTA
MER-A

2 After the booster rocket falls away, smaller rockets in the second stage fire. The rockets change the direction of the vehicle's motion and put it in orbit around Earth.

3 The third-stage rocket firing produces enough force to reach "escape velocity." Earth's gravity can no longer pull it back down. We're on our way!

▶ What forces act on the rocket while it's at rest on Earth's surface? Are they balanced or unbalanced?

_____

_____

_____

_____

_____

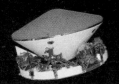

Balanced

▶ At what points during the Rover's trip to Mars are the forces on it balanced?

_____

_____

_____

Unbalanced

▶ What unbalanced forces are acting on the Rover as it lands on Mars?

_____

_____

_____

Gravity

▶ Use forces to explain why the Rover required a parachute and "air bags."

_____

_____

_____

During much of the time it takes the spacecraft to travel to Mars, it travels at a constant velocity. The forces acting on the spacecraft are balanced, so its motion does not change.

Tiny rockets occasionally fire to keep the spacecraft on course. During these times, the forces are unbalanced.

As the spacecraft approaches Mars, gravitational attraction begins to accelerate it toward the surface. Like a person jumping from a plane, the Rover detaches from the spacecraft. Parachutes open to slow its fall. Then a big ball inflates around the Rover. When the Rover hits the surface of Mars, it bounces around until it comes safely to rest.

Mars Rover air bag testing

Sum It Up!

When you're done, use the answer key to check and revise your work.

Change the part of the summary in blue to make it correct.

1. Forces are pushes and pulls that increase the speed of objects.

_____
_____

2. Gravity is the force of attraction between a planet and another object.

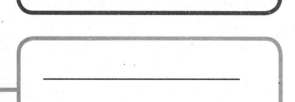

3. An object moving through the air slows down because it is affected by the force of gravity.

_____
_____

4. When balanced forces act on an object, the object falls.

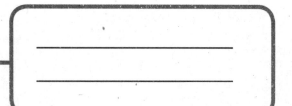

5. In order for an object to change its speed or direction, someone has to push it.

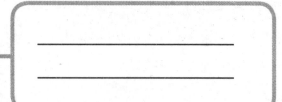

© Houghton Mifflin Harcourt Publishing Company

Answer Key: 1. can change the motion or shape of objects 2. any two objects 3. the force of friction 4. doesn't change its motion 5. an unbalanced force must act on it

Name _____

Word Play

1 A foreign-language teacher placed words from other languages into the following sentences. For each sentence, write the English word that means the same as the foreign word. Then use the circled letters to complete the riddle.

1. **Italian** — A push is an example of a forza. Another example is a pull.

   _ ◯ _ ◯ _
     11 3

2. **French** — The force of attraction between Earth and objects on its surface is pesanteur.

   _ ◯ _ _ _ _
     8

3. **Russian** — The force between two moving objects that are touching is Трение.

   ◯ _ _ _ _ ◯ _
   4   7

4. **German** — Two forces that are equal in size but opposite in direction are ausgeglichene Kräfte.

   _ _ _ _ _ ◯ _ _ _ _ ◯ _ _ ◯ _
         10   5   9

5. **Portuguese** — Two forces that are not equal in size are Forças desequilibradas.

   ◯ _ _ _ _ _ _ _ _ _ _ ◯ _
   2   6

6. **Chinese** — A 彈簧秤 is a tool that can be used to measure the size of a force.

   ◯ _ _ _ _ _ ◯ _ _ ◯
   1   12 13

Riddle: What conclusion did the student draw?

The _ _ o _ r _ e of the _ _ o _ c _ is the h _ _ _ _ _ e, of _ _ _ u r _ _ _ .
  1 2 3   4 5 6   7 8 9   10 11 12 13

Try saying that five times fast!

Apply Concepts

2 Draw pictures of two activities that you might do. In the first, draw a pushing force. In the second, draw a pulling force.

pushing force

pulling force

3 The golfer applied a force when he hit the ball. Describe at least two forces acting on the ball as it rolls. Draw arrows to show the forces.

_____
_____
_____

4 Two students are using a catapult to try and hit a target. The catapult has only one setting. The first time they tried, they used Rock B. Which of the remaining rocks is likely to come closer to the target? Why?

_____
_____
_____

5 Use the words *balanced* and *unbalanced* as you name and describe the forces acting in each of these pictures.

a.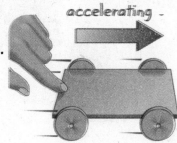

accelerating

b.

c.

_____   _____   _____

_____   _____   _____

_____   _____   _____

_____   _____   _____

6 Draw what will happen to a ball that you throw straight up into the air. Explain why this happens.

_____

_____

_____

_____

7 Explain why it is easy to slip on a floor that is wet.

_____

_____

_____

_____

8 Look at the drawings to the right. Mary measured the distance each ball traveled. Draw lines to match the ball with the distance it traveled.

Explain why each ball traveled a different distance.

_____

_____

_____

25 cm

15 cm

20 cm

9 Give an example of each of the following.

a. A force is applied but nothing happens.

_____

b. A force causes an object to change shape.

_____

c. A force causes an object to change position.

_____

d. A force causes an object to stop moving.

_____

10 Circle the object(s) whose velocities are not changing. Draw an up arrow next to the object(s) whose speeds are increasing. Draw a down arrow next to the object(s) whose speeds are decreasing.

A car travels 35 miles per hour around a bend in the road.

A car comes to a stop when a traffic light turns red.

A race car accelerates when a race begins.

A car is driving 45 miles per hour down a straight road.

Take It Home!

Discuss with your family what you've learned about forces. Together, identify five forces that you use to change the motion of objects in your everyday life. Consider forces that weren't discussed in the lesson.

S.T.E.M.
Engineering & Technology

Football Safety Gear

Football is a rough sport. In order to protect players from injury, designers have developed protective gear.

The first helmets were custom made out of leather by horse harness makers. Later, ear holes and padding were added. These helmets had little padding and no face guards.

Hard plastic shells, fitted foam linings, and metal facemasks now make helmets more protective. Some helmets even contain sensors that transmit signals to warn if a player's head has been hit hard enough to cause a serious injury.

Critical Thinking

How do modern materials make it possible to build a better helmet than one made of just leather?

_____

_____

When engineers develop new materials, it can spark new and improved designs of all sorts of familiar objects.

Choose two pieces of safety gear from your favorite sport or activity. Draw each piece of gear. Do research to find out what material makes up each piece. Label the materials. Explain how one material's properties made it a good design choice.

List three features of this bicycle helmet. Draw arrows to the feature(s) that are for safety. Circle the feature(s) that are for comfort.

_____

_____

_____

_____

Build On It!

Rise to the engineering design challenge—complete **Design It: Balloon Racer** in the Inquiry Flipchart.

OHIO **5.PS.1** The amount of change in movement of an object is based on the mass of the object and the amount of force exerted. **5.SIA.1** Identify questions that can be answered through scientific investigations. **5.SIA.2** Design and conduct a scientific investigation. **5.SIA.3** Use appropriate mathematics, tools and techniques to gather data and information. **5.SIA.4** Analyze and interpret data. **5.SIA.5** Develop descriptions, models, explanations and predictions. **5.SIA.6** Think critically and logically to connect evidence and explanations. **5.SIA.8** Communicate scientific procedures and explanations.

Name _____

Essential Question

How Do Forces Affect Motion?

Set a Purpose
What will you learn from this experiment?

_____

_____

_____

State Your Hypothesis
Write your hypothesis, or testable statement.

_____

_____

_____

_____

Think About the Procedure
Why do you use a rubber band to start the toy truck rather than your hand?

_____

_____

_____

Why do you add bolts to the truck?

_____

_____

_____

Record Your Data
In the table below, record the data you gathered.

How Forces Affect Motion			
Part I:	Distance rubber band was stretched		
	1 cm	3 cm	5 cm
Distance traveled (cm)			
Part II:	Rubber band stretched to 3 cm		
	Empty truck	Truck with 4 bolts	Truck with 8 bolts
Distance traveled (cm) Trial 1			
Distance traveled (cm) Trial 2			
Distance traveled (cm) Trial 3			

Draw Conclusions

Each time you changed a variable and launched the truck, you ran three trials. Calculate the average distance traveled by the truck in each experimental setting.

Experimental settings	Average distance traveled (cm)
Rubber band at 1 cm	
Rubber band at 3 cm	
Rubber band at 5 cm	
Truck with 0 bolts	
Truck with 4 bolts	
Truck with 8 bolts	

Draw two bar graphs to display your data.

Analyze and Extend

1. Interpret your data. How is an object's mass related to its change in motion when acted on by a force?

_____

_____

_____

2. How does the size of the force applied to an object affect its motion?

_____

_____

_____

3. Why is it important to repeat an experiment several times or to have several people perform the same experiment?

_____

_____

_____

_____

4. Write another question you could ask about using forces and motion. What experiment could you do to answer your question?

_____

_____

_____

_____

_____

Inquiry Flipchart page 34

OHIO **5.PS.1** The amount of change in movement of an object is based on the mass of the object and the amount of force exerted. **5.SIA.1** Identify questions... investigations. **5.SIA.2** Design and conduct a scientific investigation. **5.SIA.3** Use appropriate mathematics... to gather data and information. **5.SIA.4** Analyze and interpret data. **5.SIA.5** Develop... predictions. **5.SIA.6** Think critically... explanations. **5.SIA.8** Communicate scientific procedures and explanations.

Name _____

Essential Question

How Do Gravity and Friction Affect Motion?

Set a Purpose

What will you learn from this investigation?

_____

_____

_____

Think About the Procedure

Which forces act on the blocks when they are sitting on the table?

_____

_____

_____

Why will you pull the block across several different surfaces?

_____

_____

_____

Record Your Data

After you observe and measure, record your data in the table below.

Forces and Motion	
Action	**Force (N)**
Lift one block	
Lift two blocks	
Lift three blocks	
Pull block on sandpaper	
Pull block on waxed paper	
Pull block on oiled paper	

Draw Conclusions

How did you use the spring scale?

_____

_____

_____

Analyze and Extend

1. The block below is being pulled to the right. Draw arrows to show the forces acting on the object. Label each arrow.

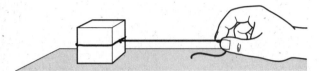

2. Scientists often perform repeated investigations. Why did you repeat your force measurements three times for each surface?

_____

_____

_____

_____

_____

3. How is an object's mass related to the upward force needed to oppose the pull of gravity in order to lift the object?

_____

_____

_____

4. Which forces acted on the block as you tried to pull it horizontally?

_____

_____

_____

_____

_____

_____

5. Why did the blocks require a different force to begin moving on the three different surfaces?

_____

_____

_____

_____

6. Which other questions would you like to ask about how gravity and friction affect motion? Which investigations could you do to answer the questions?

_____

_____

_____

_____

_____

_____

276

1. A safety engineer helps design and test devices to make them safer.

2. Safety engineers make changes to designs to avoid possible dangers.

3. I'm a crash test dummy. Some safety engineers use me as a model.

10

THINGS TO KNOW ABOUT
Safety Engineers

4. Safety engineers can make machines, such as cars, safer to use.

5. Safety engineers make cars safer with inventions such as seat belts and air bags.

6. Some safety engineers focus on stopping specific dangers, such as fires.

7. Safety engineers help society have fewer injuries and illnesses.

8. Some keep germs from spreading into our food and making us sick.

9. They may focus on protecting workers from getting hurt on the job.

10. To do their jobs, safety engineers need to study physics, chemistry, math, and human behavior.

Careers in Science *continued*

Now You Be the Engineer!

1. What do you think is the best thing about being a safety engineer?

2. How do safety engineers help society?

3. What safety features in cars have safety engineers helped to develop?

4. What question would you like to ask a safety engineer?

1. _____
_____
_____
_____

2. _____
_____
_____
_____

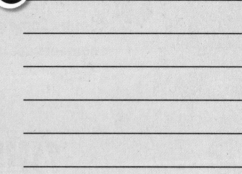

3. _____
_____

4. _____
_____
_____
_____

Unit 6 Review

Name _____

Vocabulary Review

Use the terms in the box to complete the sentences.

> acceleration
> balanced forces
> force
> friction
> gravity
> position
> unbalanced forces
> velocity

1. Forces that cause a change in motion are

   _____.

2. A force of attraction between two objects, even if they are not

   touching, is _____.

3. A measure of an object/s change in position during a certain

   amount of time is _____.

4. A push or a pull, which causes movement or change in an

   object's movement or shape, is a(n) _____.

5. Forces on an object that are equal in size and opposite in

   direction are _____.

6. A force that opposes motion and acts between two objects that

   are touching is _____.

7. A change in velocity is _____.

8. The location of an object in relation to another object or place

   describes _____.

Science Concepts

Fill in the letter of the choice that best answers the question.

9. Suri places magnets on three identical toy cars, as shown below. Then she measures how far each car rolls when she launches it from the same starting point using the same stretched rubber band.

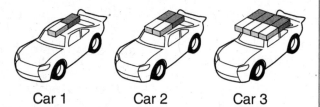

Car 1   Car 2   Car 3

How will the force of the rubber band affect the cars?

(A) Car 3 will travel the longest distance.

(B) Car 1 will travel the shortest distance.

(C) Car 1 will be the least affected by the force acting upon it.

(D) Car 3 will be the least affected by the force acting upon it.

10. The line graph records the measurement of an object's speed over time.

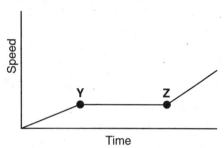

Analyze the line graph. What happens to the object between Point Y and Point Z?

(A) The object is speeding up.

(B) The object has no velocity.

(C) The object is slowing down.

(D) The object's acceleration is zero.

11. This table shows the masses of several different objects.

Object	Metal washer	Plastic disk	Rock	Wooden block
Mass (g)	1.5	34	16	22

Which object will require the most force to toss it 2 meters?

(A) rock

(B) plastic disk

(C) metal washer

(D) wooden block

12. Which of these is an example of a force being applied?

(A) watching TV

(B) reading a book

(C) pulling a wagon

(D) standing at the top of a hill

13. A spring scale measures force.

What is the force that causes the reading on the spring scale shown in the illustration?

(A) mass

(B) weight

(C) gravity

(D) friction

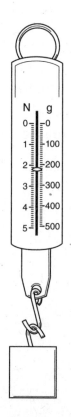

14. Four forces are acting on the block shown in the following illustration:

- F is the applied force.
- F_f is friction.
- F_g is the gravitational force.
- F_n is the normal force—the upward push of the table on the block.

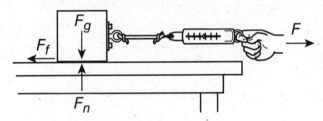

The block is not moving. Which of the following statements is **true**?

Ⓐ F and F_f are equal.

Ⓑ F and F_g are equal.

Ⓒ F_f is greater than F.

Ⓓ F_g is greater than F.

15. Jared wants to test the effect of friction on an object. Which would be the best experiment for him to test this effect?

Ⓐ Use a pulley to lift several blocks.

Ⓑ Drop a ball from different heights.

Ⓒ Roll a toy car across different surfaces.

Ⓓ Use a balance to find the mass of objects.

16. This table shows the masses of four blocks and the forces that are being applied to each one.

Block color	Mass (g)	Pushing force (N)	Friction (N)
Red	50	24	6
Green	100	24	6
Blue	40	24	6
Yellow	75	24	6

Which block will have the greatest change in motion?

Ⓐ red block

Ⓑ blue block

Ⓒ green block

Ⓓ yellow block

17. The following illustration shows all the forces that are acting on a box.

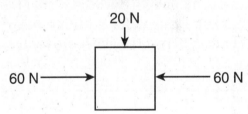

What type of motion will the forces cause?

Ⓐ The box will remain in its current position.

Ⓑ The box will move downward in a straight line.

Ⓒ The box will move to the right in a straight line.

Ⓓ The box will move back and forth from the left to the right.

Apply Inquiry and Review the Big Idea

Write the answers to these questions.

18. Jermaine wondered if a heavy ball rolls down a ramp faster than a light ball. Use the space below to describe an investigation he could conduct in order to find out.

_____

_____

_____

_____

19. This worker is pushing a box with a force, which is shown by the arrow. The box does not move.

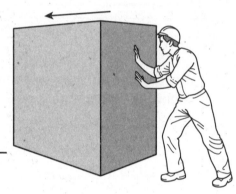

What keeps the box from moving even though the worker is pushing on it?

_____

20. Lui and Simone want to test the effects of gravity on speed. They have two equal-length tracks that start from raised platforms and then flatten out into straight, flat sections. Design an experiment Lui and Simone can conduct to test the effect of gravity.

_____

_____

_____

21. The spring scale shown has a weight attached to it. When the weight was attached, the pointer on the scale moved downward.

What will happen if a second weight is added to the spring scale? Explain your answer.

_____

_____

Forms of Energy

Big Idea

Energy occurs in many forms and can be observed in cycles, patterns, and systems.

OHIO 5.PS.2, 5.SIA.1, 5.SIA.2, 5.SIA.3, 5.SIA.4, 5.SIA.5, 5.SIA.6, 5.SIA.8

I Wonder Why

The image shows a "solar farm." Why is it called a farm? What do you think is being "harvested"? *Turn the page to find out.*

Here's why A solar farm collects energy from the sun and converts it to electricity, which is carried by transmission lines to wherever it is needed. The electricity is then used in homes, businesses, and industries.

In this unit, you will explore the Big Idea, the Essential Questions, and the Investigations on the Inquiry Flipchart.

Levels of Inquiry Key ■ DIRECTED ■ GUIDED ■ INDEPENDENT

Track Your Progress

Big Idea Energy occurs in many forms and can be observed in cycles, patterns, and systems.

Essential Questions

Now I Get the Big Idea!

Science Notebook

Before you begin each lesson, be sure to write your thoughts about the Essential Question.

OHIO **5.PS.2** Light and sound are forms of energy that behave in predictable ways.

Lesson **1**

Essential Question

What Is Energy?

Engage Your Brain!

As you read the lesson, figure out the answer to the following question. Write the answer here.

What kinds of energy are represented in this picture?

_____

_____

_____

_____

Active Reading

Lesson Vocabulary
List the terms. As you learn about each one, make notes in the Interactive Glossary.

_____   _____

_____   _____

_____   _____

Compare and Contrast
Many ideas in this lesson are about ways that things are alike or different. Active readers stay focused on comparisons and contrasts by asking how things are alike and how they are different.

Energy
All Around
· · · · ·

What does a melting scoop of ice cream have in common with a kicked soccer ball? The ice cream and the ball both change in some way. What causes these changes?

Active Reading As you read this page, underline important details about energy.

▶ A soccer ball won't move unless something gives it energy. Energy changes the ball's motion. Circle the thing in the picture that gave the ball energy.

Think about all the ways that you use energy. **Energy** is the ability to cause changes in matter. Energy is involved when matter moves or changes its shape. A change in temperature also involves energy.

Energy can transform, or change, from one form into another. The boy in the picture is using energy to run. The energy came from food that he ate.

When the boy kicks the ball, his foot transfers energy to the ball. The moving ball transfers energy again. Energy moves to particles in the air and on the ground. These tiny particles begin to move faster.

The ball stops moving after it has transferred all its energy. Energy is never used up. It just changes from one form to another.

The tiny particles that make up solid ice cream move slowly. Energy from the sun causes a change in their motion. The particles move faster. The ice cream melts and becomes a liquid.

▶ What caused this ice cream to melt?

_____

_____

_____

▶ For each statement, write *T* for true or *F* for false.

◯ 1. Energy can cause a change in matter.

◯ 2. Energy can change from one form to another.

◯ 3. Energy can be used up and destroyed.

◯ 4. Energy can be transferred from one object to another.

The Ups and Downs of Energy

Does an object that is not moving have any energy? Let's find out!

Does a book sitting on a shelf have energy? Yes! Someone gave it energy by lifting the book to the shelf. The energy is now stored in the book. The energy an object has because of its position or condition is called **potential energy** (PE).

If the book falls off the shelf, it begins moving. Its potential energy changes to the energy of motion. The energy an object has because of its motion is called **kinetic energy** (KE).

When the roller coaster car is at the top of a hill, most of its energy is potential energy due to its position. Gravity will change this PE to KE as the car starts downhill.

288

When you compress a spring or stretch a rubber band, your energy is stored in the object as potential energy. The potential energy changes to kinetic energy when you release the spring or rubber band.

Position isn't the only way that energy can be stored. A match head has potential energy stored in chemical bonds between its particles. Striking the match releases the stored energy as heat and light. A charged battery also contains potential energy. A battery dies when all of its potential energy has been transformed to electrical energy.

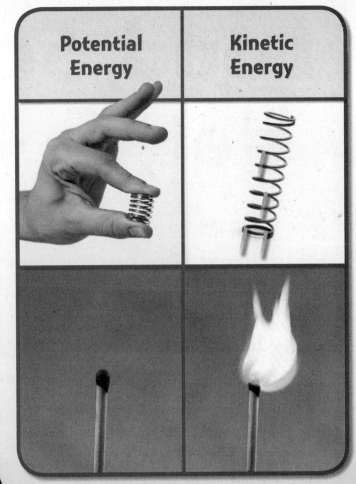

Potential Energy	Kinetic Energy

As the car moves downhill, its PE changes to kinetic, or moving, energy. At the bottom of the hill, the car's energy is kinetic. This KE becomes PE as the roller coaster car travels up the next hill.

▶ Fill in the three bubbles on the roller coaster track. Write *KE* if a coaster car at that position would have mostly kinetic energy. Write *PE* if it would have mostly potential energy.

▶ When does a roller coaster car have the most kinetic energy?

_____

_____

_____

_____

Loud, Soft, Hot, Cold

The kinetic energy of a moving roller coaster car is easy to see. How can you sense energy in tiny particles of matter that are too small to see?

Active Reading As you read these two pages, underline the sentences that tell you how sound energy and thermal energy are alike.

When a trumpet makes noise, it vibrates, or moves back and forth. The trumpet transfers energy to tiny particles of air. Each particle of air moves back and forth, bumping into other particles. The sound travels outward.

▶ Draw an arrow to show the direction that sound waves are traveling.

If someone knocks on your door, the particles in the door vibrate. They bump into particles in the air on your side of the door. The sound travels through the door and through the air to you as a sound wave.

Sound energy is —

- a form of energy that is carried as waves in vibrating matter.

- a type of kinetic energy, because particles of matter are moving.

- the cause of all the sounds you hear.

Another type of energy that involves moving particles is thermal energy. *Thermal energy* is the total kinetic energy of the particles that make up a substance.

Thermometers measure thermal energy. You sense thermal energy as temperature. The more thermal energy an object has, the greater its temperature. Thermal energy helps you to stay warm, to cook your food, and to heat water for washing or bathing.

▶ In a hot-air balloon, the burning of propane produces thermal energy. This energy raises the temperature of the air particles inside the balloon to _____ °C.

▶ This thermometer shows normal body temperature, which is _____ °C (98.6 °F).

▶ The air at the top of this icy mountain has very little thermal energy. Its temperature is _____ °C.

Do the Math!
Use Number Lines

Draw a number line. On the line, place the three temperatures (in °C) shown in the pictures on this page. Then add a point for normal room temperature, 22 °C.

See a Sea of Energy

The sun is the source of the light energy entering the cave.

Your ears use sound energy to hear. What kind of energy allows your eyes to see?

Active Reading As you read, draw boxes around the descriptions of light energy and electrical energy.

Suppose you are using a flashlight in a dark room. You drop the flashlight and it breaks. What can you see? Nothing! Your eyes need light energy to work.

Light energy is a form of energy that can travel through space. Light can also pass through some types of matter, such as air or glass. Light energy travels as waves.

You can see light energy. Some objects give off light. You see all other objects when light reflects, or bounces off, from them and enters your eyes.

▶ List three sources of light.

_____

_____

_____

You see the cave walls when light bounces off them and reaches your eyes.

Electrical energy changes to light energy in a flashlight.

Objects that give off light energy often give off heat. But the two types of energy are different. You can tell them apart by the way you sense the energy. Your skin senses heat, but it cannot sense light energy. Your eyes sense light energy.

Flashlights and television sets produce light. To do this, they use another type of energy, called electrical energy. **Electrical energy** is energy caused by the movement of electric charges. When you use electricity, you are using electrical energy.

Electrical energy can change to other types of energy you can use. Electrical energy changes to thermal energy in a toaster or a stove. Cell phones and stereo speakers use electrical energy to produce sound. In lamps and spotlights, electrical energy changes to light energy.

Computers and other devices that are plugged in use electrical energy.

▶ List three objects that use electrical energy.

_____

_____

_____

Energy in Machines and Food

You have learned about machines that use electrical energy. Some machines don't need to be plugged in. What forms of energy do they use?

Active Reading Draw one line under things that have mechanical energy. Draw two lines under things that have chemical energy.

Many objects, such as a ball thrown in the air, have both kinetic and potential energy. **Mechanical energy** (ME) is the total energy of motion and position of an object. As a ball drops, its potential energy decreases as its kinetic energy increases. Its mechanical energy, though, stays constant. The relationship among these forms of energy is shown by the following equation.

Mechanical Energy = Kinetic Energy + Potential Energy

A machine uses mechanical energy to do work. For example, a fan plugged into the wall uses electrical energy. It changes that energy into the mechanical energy of the spinning fan blades. The spinning fan uses the mechanical energy to do work—moving the air in a room.

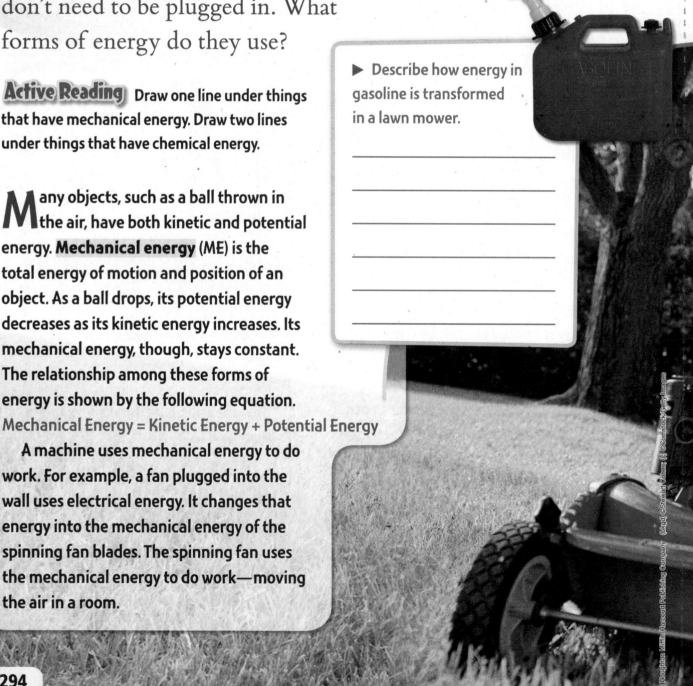

▶ Describe how energy in gasoline is transformed in a lawn mower.

_____

_____

_____

_____

_____

Have you ever felt as if you were going to "run out of energy"? The energy your body uses comes from the food you eat. Food contains a kind of potential energy called chemical energy. **Chemical energy** is energy that is stored in matter and that can be released by a chemical reaction.

When your body needs energy, it breaks down food and releases potential chemical energy from it. If you use that energy to run or jump, it changes into kinetic energy. Your body also uses chemical energy stored in food to produce thermal energy. This keeps your body at a steady temperature.

Cars use chemical energy in liquid fuel such as gasoline. A flashlight uses the chemical energy stored in a battery to produce light. Some stoves change chemical energy to thermal energy by burning a gas called propane.

▶ Winding the key on the toy increases the toy's _____ energy.

▶ Our bodies use the _____ energy in food to move and stay warm.

▶ These gears make the hands of this watch move because they have _____ energy.

Spotlight on Energy

A stage production requires different kinds of energy. How many are being used on this stage?

Active Reading As you read these pages, draw a box around each type of energy.

Some stage shows use fire, sparklers, and explosions. These elements turn stored chemical energy into light, heat, and sound energy.

These performers are high above the stage. They have a lot of potential energy due to their position.

Musicians use mechanical energy to play instruments. The instruments make sound energy that the audience hears as music.

► Write a caption about the energy shown in this part of the picture.

_____

_____

_____

► Write a caption about this performer. Describe at least one form of energy.

_____

_____

_____

_____

When you're done, use the answer key to check and revise your work.

Part I: Circle the word that completes each sentence.

A. Energy is the ability to cause motion or create (matter / change).

B. There are two main categories of energy—potential and (thermal / kinetic).

C. Energy can't be created or (destroyed / captured).

D. Energy can change from one form to another, which is called energy
(transformation / conservation).

Part II: Complete the graphic organizer below.

ENERGY

Potential energy is energy stored in an object because of its position or condition.

Kinetic energy is the energy of motion.

A. _____ energy is energy that can be released by a chemical reaction.

B. _____ energy is the total kinetic energy of the particles in matter.

C. _____ energy is the form of energy that you can see.

F. _____ energy is the combination of the potential and kinetic energy an object contains.

D. _____ energy travels as waves through vibrating matter.

E. _____ energy is energy caused by movement of electrical charges.

Brain Check

Lesson 1

Name _____

Word Play

1 Use the clues and the word bank to fill in the puzzle.

Across

2. Stored energy due to position or condition
6. A substance that contains useful chemical energy
7. Energy caused by the movement of electric charges
10. Energy of motion
11. To move back and forth
12. Energy of moving particles of matter

Down

1. Form of energy you can hear
3. Form of energy you can see
4. Total potential and kinetic energy of an object
5. Energy that can be released by a chemical reaction
8. Ability to cause changes in matter
9. What your body feels thermal energy as

| mechanical* | chemical* | electrical* | sound | light | energy* |
| potential* | kinetic* | thermal | vibrate | food | heat |

* Key Lesson Vocabulary

Apply Concepts

2 Complete the matching game. The first one is done for you.

Light Energy Ⓔ③	**A.** The total kinetic energy of the particles in matter
Thermal Energy ◯◯	**B.** Energy caused by motion of electric charges
Sound Energy ◯◯	**C.** Energy that is stored in matter and can be released during a chemical reaction
Electrical Energy ◯◯	**D.** Energy carried as waves of vibrating matter
Mechanical Energy ◯◯	**E.** Energy that travels as a wave and that you are able to see
Chemical Energy ◯◯	**F.** Sum of an object's potential and kinetic energy

3 Use the terms *potential energy* and *kinetic energy* to tell what is happening to the skier.

_____

_____

_____

_____

_____

4 Identify the types of energy present or produced in each lettered part of the picture.

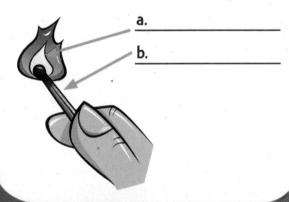

a. _____

b. _____

Take It Home! When you go home, ask your family to help you list all the kinds of energy you use around your house. Try to find at least one example of each type of energy you learned about in this lesson.

Ask a Windsmith

Q. What does a windsmith do?

A. A windsmith operates, maintains, and repairs the electrical and mechanical parts of wind turbines.

Q. What is a wind turbine?

A. A wind turbine is a modern windmill. It uses the energy of wind to do work and to generate electrical energy.

Q. How does a wind turbine work?

A. The wind's kinetic energy is transferred to the turbine's blades, causing them to spin. When the blades spin, a long shaft, or pole, also spins. The shaft is connected to a generator. In the generator, kinetic energy is transformed into electrical energy.

Q. Is it scary to climb a wind turbine?

A. If you are afraid of heights, it could be, but windsmiths are used to working high up. The first day a windsmith climbs a turbine is a day to celebrate.

Now It's Your Turn!

What fields of science do you think can help choose the location of a wind turbine?

_____

_____

_____

SHOW WHAT YOU KNOW ABOUT
Windsmiths

Answer these four questions
about windsmiths.

1

What part of a windsmith's work
do you find most interesting?

_____

_____

_____

2

How is energy transferred and
transformed by a wind turbine?

_____

_____

_____

_____

3

How do windsmiths help society?

_____

_____

_____

4

What questions do you have about
windsmiths?

_____

_____

_____

OHIO **5.PS.2** Light and sound are forms of energy that behave in predictable ways.

Lesson **2**

Essential Question

What Is Thermal Energy?

Engage Your Brain!

As you read the lesson, look for the answer to the following question and record it here.

The person in the picture uses energy from the fire to keep warm and cook food. How does the fire's energy reach the person and the food?

_____

_____

_____

Active Reading

Lesson Vocabulary
List each term. As you learn about each one, make notes in the Interactive Glossary.

_____

_____

_____

Compare and Contrast
Many ideas in this lesson are connected because they explain how things compare and contrast—how they are alike and different. Active readers stay focused on how things compare and contrast when they ask themselves, How are conduction, convection and radiation alike? How are they different?

Lively Particles!

Why do some substances feel cold while others feel hot? What causes this difference? Moving particles!

Active Reading As you read these two pages, underline the definitions of vocabulary terms.

Although you can't see them, the tiny particles that make up all matter are constantly moving. They buzz around like a swarm of bees, bouncing in every direction as they collide. These particles have *kinetic energy*, or energy of motion. **Thermal energy** is the total amount of kinetic energy of the particles in a substance.

The particles of the hot liquid in the cup move faster than the particles of cooler water in the pool. However, the water in the pool has more thermal energy because it has more particles.

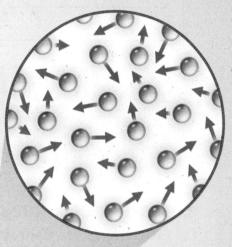

Temperature

Temperature is a measure of the average kinetic energy of the particles in a substance. A thermometer helps you compare the average kinetic energy of different substances. The faster the particles move in a substance, the higher its temperature. In a traditional liquid-filled thermometer, the height of the liquid in the tube increases as temperature increases. The thermometer in this beaker uses a heat sensitive metal.

Do the Math!
Use a Calculator

An average is the sum of the numbers in a set divided by the number of items in that set. Use a calculator to help you collect, record, and analyze the information in the table.

Student	Sit-ups /minute
A	30
B	25
C	40
D	33

What is the sum of the numbers in the set?

_____

What is the number of items in the set?

_____

What is the average number of sit-ups done by the four students in one minute?

_____

More Thermal Energy

Less Thermal Energy

The iceberg and ice cube have the same temperature. The iceberg contains more thermal energy because it has many more vibrating particles.

Move It Around

In order to use thermal energy, we must move it from place to place. How does it move?

E nergy is transferred between substances with different temperatures. We call this transfer of energy **heat**. Heat always moves from a substance with a higher temperature to one with a lower temperature.

Conduction

Conduction is the transfer of energy between particles that are in contact. When the girl holds the ice cube against her skin, fast-moving particles in her skin collide with slower moving particles in the ice cube. Heat flows from her skin to the ice cube by conduction. This lowers the temperature of her skin, so she feels cooler. What happens to the ice?

When cooking food over a campfire, heat transfers from the burning logs to the pot by conduction.

306

Analyze Energy Transfer

Label each type of energy transfer in the diagram. Draw arrows to show the direction of energy transfer.

_____

_____

_____

Radiation

Earth has thermal energy. Some of this energy is transferred outward to space. This color-enhanced image, taken by cameras in space, shows energy from Earth that has radiated to space. _Radiation_ is the transfer of energy in waves without matter to carry it. Heat from a campfire reaches the people sitting around it by radiation.

Convection

Convection is the transfer of energy by currents in a liquid or gas. When liquids or gases are heated, the particles move farther apart. The fluid expands and becomes less dense. In the lava lamp, the heating element at the bottom of the lamp transfers energy to the liquid above it. The liquid warms and becomes less dense. It rises, carrying the energy with it. The cooler liquid on top sinks to the bottom, where it is heated.

Going to the Source!

Where does the thermal energy that we use come from?

Active Reading As you read these two pages, draw a box around sources of thermal energy.

Most thermal energy used on Earth comes from the sun. We can use thermal energy directly, such as when we warm ourselves. We can also change it into other forms of energy, such as mechanical or electrical energy. Thermal energy can be "lost" when it changes form. Moving parts in machines produce friction, releasing heat to the environment that is not used.

Solar Radiation

The sun's energy reaches Earth by radiation. Solar radiation is the most important energy source on Earth. Only a tiny fraction of the sun's energy reaches Earth. Yet it enables life to exist on our planet. Solar radiation and Earth's atmosphere help keep Earth within the narrow range of temperatures needed for life to survive and thrive.

Combustion of Fuels

A *fuel* is a substance that can burn. *Combustion* occurs when a fuel rapidly combines with oxygen. This process produces light and thermal energy. Combustion of fuels is the second most important source of energy on Earth. The most common fuels are fossil fuels, such as petroleum, coal, and natural gas. Fuels made from living organisms, such as trees or corn plants, are called *biofuels*.

Natural Gas

Oil

Coal

Construct a Chart Using Technology

Use the chart to organize, examine, and evaluate information about two of the sources of thermal energy described on these pages.

Geothermal Energy

Geothermal energy is thermal energy naturally produced under Earth's surface. Below Earth's cool surface, there are regions so hot that rocks melt. In some places, we can directly observe geothermal energy. Volcanoes, geysers, and hot springs are visible examples of geothermal energy.

Uses of Energy

So much energy! But what can we do with it? Let's find out.

Active Reading As you read these two pages, put brackets [ ] around the detail sentences. Draw arrows from the details to the main idea being explained.

How many ways can you think of to use thermal energy? You might think of keeping warm, cooking your food, or ironing your clothes. That's just a start!

Examine the information in the simple circle graph. What percentage of energy use could come from solar panels? Explain.

_____

_____

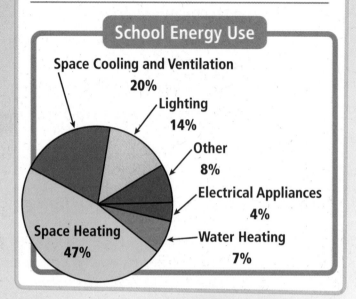

School Energy Use

Space Cooling and Ventilation 20%

Lighting 14%

Other 8%

Electrical Appliances 4%

Water Heating 7%

Space Heating 47%

Energy from the Sun

One way to use the sun's energy is to heat water for homes and businesses. Water runs through pipes in a solar panel, where it is heated by solar radiation. The hot water is then stored until it is needed. You have to pay for the panel, but the energy to heat the water is free!

During colder weather, solar radiation passing through windows warms a room. The energy makes the room warmer than the temperature outside. A plant nursery's greenhouse works in the same way.

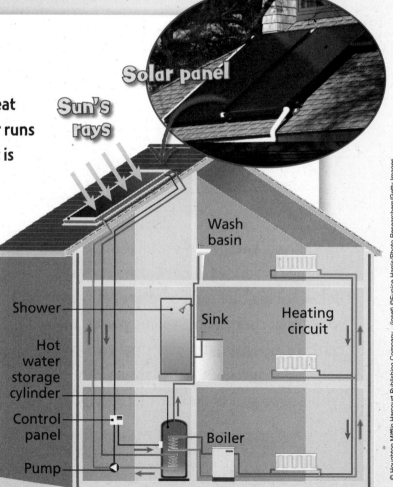

Solar panel

Sun's rays

Wash basin

Shower

Sink

Heating circuit

Hot water storage cylinder

Control panel

Boiler

Pump

310

Geothermal Energy

The diagram shows how geothermal energy is transformed into electrical energy. First, super-hot groundwater is pumped to the surface, where it changes into steam. The steam turns a fan-like device called a *turbine*. Then the steam loses energy and changes back to water, which is pumped back to the ground to be reheated. The turbine turns a *generator*—a machine that uses magnets to change mechanical energy into electricity. The electricity travels through wires to homes, businesses, factories, and other consumers.

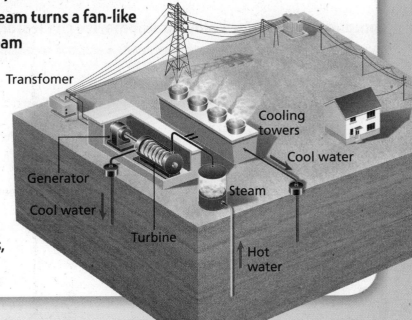

Transfomer

Cooling towers

Cool water

Generator

Cool water

Steam

Turbine

Hot water

Thermal Energy from Combustion

Thermal energy is used to process products such as foods, plastics, and metals. In many cities, fossil fuels are burned to produce the electricity used in factories. Thermal energy from combustion also is important in transportation. Engines in vehicles change the thermal energy of fossil fuels into motion. Some of this energy is wasted, though. It heats fluids that are then air-cooled to prevent the engine from overheating. Energy produced by the combustion of fossil fuels is used in many ways.

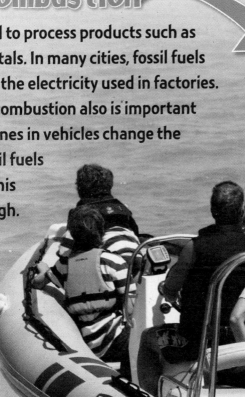

When you're done, use the answer key to check and revise your work.

Complete the outline below to summarize the lesson.

1

I. Thermal Energy

    A. Thermal energy is **1** _____

    _____

    _____

    B. **2** _____ is a measure of the

    average kinetic energy of the particles in

    a substance.

II. Transfer of Energy

    A. **3** _____ is the transfer

    of energy between substances at

    different temperatures.

    B. Energy travels from place to place by:

        1. **4** _____

        2. Convection

        3. **5** _____

III. Sources of Thermal Energy

    A. Solar Radiation

    B. **6** _____ of Fuels

    C. Geothermal Energy

IV. Uses of Thermal Energy

    A. Roof panels can use **7** _____

    to heat water.

    B. Geothermal energy can be changed to

    8 _____ .

    C. Engines in vehicles use combustion to

    produce energy of motion

Summarize

Fill in the missing words to tell what happens when heat moves from one substance to another.

9. Heat always travels from a substance with a _____ temperature to a substance with a lower temperature.

10. When particles are touching, heat moves by _____ .

11. Heat moves by convection in a _____ or gas.

12. Energy that can travel through empty space is called _____ .

Answer Key: 1. the total kinetic energy in the particles of a substance; **2.** temperature; **3.** heat; **4.** conduction; **5.** radiation; **6.** Combustion; **7.** solar radiation; **8.** electricity; **9.** higher; **10.** conduction; **11.** liquid; **12.** radiation

Name _____

Word Play

1 Use the clues to unscramble the science terms and solve the riddle below.

1. Total kinetic energy of the particles of a substance

RALTHEM GYENER

☐☐☐☐☐☐☐ ☐☐☐☐☐
15　　　　　　　5

2. Transfer of energy between substances with different temperatures

TAEH

☐☐☐☐
7　11

3. Measure of the average kinetic energy of the particles in a substance

PERMETRETUA

☐☐☐☐☐☐☐☐☐☐☐
9

4. Transfer of energy between solids

COUNONDITC

☐☐☐☐☐☐☐☐☐☐
14　　　　4

5. Makes up most of Earth's energy

OALRS DIATRIONA

☐☐☐☐☐ ☐☐☐☐☐☐☐☐
2　12　16

6. Transfer of thermal energy through a liquid or gas

NOCTECVONI

☐☐☐☐☐☐☐☐☐☐
8

7. Transfer of thermal energy in waves without matter

TAANOIDIR

☐☐☐☐☐☐☐☐☐
3

8. Energy produced and stored under Earth's crust

LOTHEGRAEM REGNEY

☐☐☐☐☐☐☐☐☐☐☐ ☐☐☐☐☐
6　　10　　　13　17 18

9. Rapid combining of a fuel with oxygen

NOUMISTOCB

☐☐☐☐☐☐☐☐☐☐
1

Place the numbered letters in order to find out what you are doing when you cook food over a campfire.

☐☐☐☐☐ ☐☐☐☐☐☐☐ ☐☐☐☐☐☐
1 2 3 4 5　6 7 8 9 10 11 12　13 14 15 16 17 18

Apply Concepts

2 A student says that four cups of boiling water have the same thermal energy as two cups of boiling water. Critique the student's explanation. Is she correct?

_____

_____

_____

_____

3 Explain how energy is transferred from the cup. Draw arrows showing the movement of energy.

_____

_____

_____

4 5. Name one way in which thermal energy from each of the following sources is used. If thermal energy is changed into another form of energy, describe the changes.

a. solar radiation _____

_____

b. combustion of fuels _____

_____

c. geothermal energy _____

_____

Take It Home! Work with an adult to identify examples of conduction, convection, and radiation around your home. Explain how energy moves from one location to another.

Inquiry Flipchart page 37

Name _____

Essential Question

What Changes Can Energy Cause?

OHIO 5.PS.2 Light and sound are forms of energy that behave in predictable ways. **5.SIA.1** Identify questions that can be answered through scientific investigations. **5.SIA.2** Design and conduct a scientific investigation. **5.SIA.3** Use appropriate mathematics, tools and techniques to gather data and information. **5.SIA.4** Analyze and interpret data. **5.SIA.5** Develop descriptions, models, explanations and predictions. **5.SIA.6** Think critically and logically to connect evidence and explanations. **5.SIA.8** Communicate scientific procedures and explanations.

Set a Purpose

How will this investigation help you observe changes in matter?

_____

_____

State Your Hypothesis

Write your hypothesis.

_____

_____

_____

Think About the Procedure

How hot do you predict the solar cookers will become?

_____

_____

What is the purpose of the aluminum foil?

_____

_____

What variable will you change in this experiment?

_____

_____

What outdoor safety steps should you practice?

_____

_____

Record Your Data

Use technology to draw a data table to record your temperature measurements in degrees Celsius. Attach the table below.

315

Draw Conclusions

Was your hypothesis supported? Why or why not?

_____

_____

_____

_____

Analyze and Extend

1. **Analyze and interpret results to make an inference. How would your results differ if you had made the cooker just from the poster board? Explain.**

_____

_____

_____

_____

2. **How might a solar cooker be useful in places where there is no electricity?**

_____

_____

_____

3. **How could you improve your solar cooker to make it heat faster?**

_____

_____

_____

4. **Using the setup shown below, Dwayne concludes that the solar cooker on the left is the best because it heats up the fastest. Based on the result of your own experiment, analyze, evaluate, and critique Dwayne's conclusion.**

_____

_____

_____

_____

_____

5. **What other questions would you like to ask about using solar energy? What investigations could you do to answer the questions?**

_____

_____

_____

_____

_____

OHIO **5.PS.2** Light and sound are forms of energy that behave in predictable ways.

Lesson **4**

Essential Question

What Is Electricity?

Engage Your Brain!

Find the answer to the following question in this lesson and record it here.

What causes the girl's hair to stand out from her head?

_____

_____

_____

_____

Active Reading

Lesson Vocabulary

List the terms. As you learn about each one, make notes in the Interactive Glossary.

_____

_____

Main Ideas

The main idea of a paragraph is the most important idea. The main idea may be stated in the first sentence, or it may be stated elsewhere. Active readers look for the main idea by asking themselves, What is this section mostly about?

All Charged UP

You can charge a battery. A football player can charge downfield. How is an electric charge different?

Active Reading As you read these two pages, underline the main idea on each page.

What do you, this book, and your desk all have in common? You are all made of atoms. *Atoms* are the building blocks of all matter. Atoms are so small that you cannot even see them without a special microscope. Atoms are made up of even smaller particles called protons, neutrons, and electrons.

The main difference between protons, electrons, and neutrons is their electric charge. *Electric charge* is a property of a particle that affects how it behaves around other particles.

- Protons have a positive charge (+1).

- Electrons have a negative charge (–1).

- Neutrons are neutral. They have no charge.

When an atom has equal numbers of protons and electrons, the positive charges and negative charges cancel each other. The atom itself has no charge.

Protons and neutrons are found in a region of the atom called the nucleus. Electrons are found in a region of mostly empty space called the electron cloud.

Legend

 = neutron = proton ● = electron

318

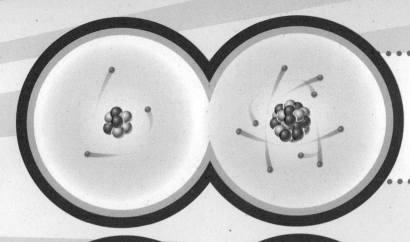

Each of these atoms has the same number of protons and electrons. Both atoms are neutral.

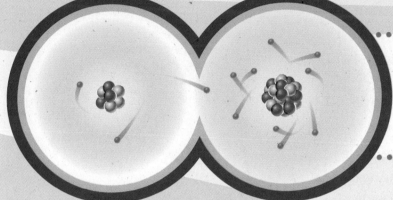

An electron from the atom on the left moves to the atom on the right.

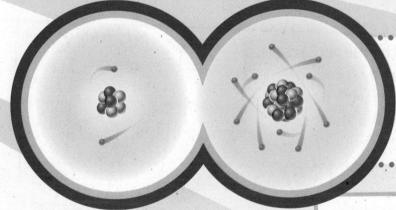

The atom on the left now has a charge of +1. The atom on the right has a charge of –1.

Atoms sometimes gain or lose electrons. This gain or loss causes an atom to have an unequal number of positive and negative charges. For example, if an atom with nine protons and nine electrons gains an electron, the atom will have a charge of –1.

If a neutral atom loses an electron, the number of protons will no longer balance the number of electrons. The atom will have a charge of +1.

▶ Draw an atom with three protons, four neutrons, and two electrons.

What is the charge of this atom?

Opposites Attract

Have you ever had a "bad hair day"? Your hair sticks out in every direction and won't lie flat. What causes that?

Active Reading As you read this page, circle the definitions of *repel* and *attract*. On the next page, draw a box around the sentence with the main idea.

Particles with the same charge repel, or push away from, one another. Particles with opposite charges attract one another, or pull together.

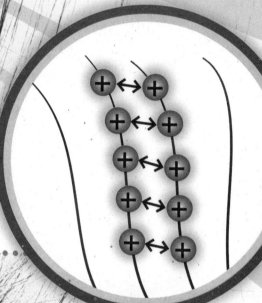

Do the Math!
Positive and Negative Numbers

Fill in the missing squares in the table.

Original charge on an object	Electrons gained or lost	Final charge on the object
+300	Gains 270	
−300	Loses 525	
−270		−500

In the dryer, atoms in clothing gain and lose electrons. Each piece of clothing becomes charged. The positively charged surfaces attract the negatively charged surfaces. As a result, the clothes stick together.

Electric charges can build up on objects. This buildup is **static electricity**. *Static* means "not moving." Objects with opposite electric charges attract each other. Objects with the same charge repel each other.

When you brush your hair, electrons move from each strand of hair to the brush. Soon, all the strands are positively charged. All the strands having the same charge causes them to repel one another and stick out.

A charged object can attract a neutral object. If you rub a balloon on your hair, the balloon picks up extra electrons that give it a negative charge. When you bring the balloon near a wall, electrons in a small part of the wall are repelled and move away, leaving a positive charge at the wall surface. As a result, the balloon sticks to the wall.

Lightning Strikes

Thunderstorms can be scary. Lightning can be dangerous. What is lightning? How can you stay safe during a thunderstorm?

Active Reading As you read these two pages, underline the main idea on each page.

Static electricity is a buildup of charges on an object. Charges stay on an object until it comes close to an object that has a different charge.

As you walk across a carpet, electrons move from the carpet to you. Because electrons repel each other, they spread out all over your body. When you touch something, the electrons jump from your finger to the object. This jumping is called an electrostatic discharge. You feel it as a tiny shock.

Zap! Electrons jump from a person with a negative charge.

▶ Complete this cause-and-effect graphic organizer.

Cause: An object with a negative charge is placed near an object with a positive charge.	Effect: _____ _____ _____

Not all electrostatic discharges cause small shocks. Some result in huge shocks. During a thunderstorm, tiny raindrops or ice particles bump into each other. These collisions cause an electric charge to build in the clouds. Positive charges form at the top of a cloud and on the ground. Negative charges form near the bottom of a cloud.

When the difference in charge between a cloud and the ground is great enough, there is a huge electrostatic discharge that we call lightning. A lightning spark can jump between two clouds, between a cloud and the air, or between a cloud and the ground. The temperature inside a lightning bolt can reach 27,760 °C (50,000 °F), which is hotter than the surface of the sun!

Lightning Safety

- Stay inside during thunderstorms.
- Turn off electrical appliances and stay away from windows.
- If you can't get inside a safe structure, wait in a car with a metal top for the storm to pass.
- Know the weather forecast. If you will be outside, have a plan in case a thunderstorm develops.

When lightning strikes, it can catch objects on fire. A tree struck by lightning may split.

▶ Draw a cloud in the sky. Then, draw positive and negative charges to show what causes lightning to form.

Current Events

Electrostatic discharges may be exciting to watch, but flowing charges are more useful.

Active Reading As you read these two pages, draw a box around the sentence that contains the main idea.

When electric charges have a path to follow, as they do in the wire below, they move in a steady flow. This flow of charges is called an **electric current**.

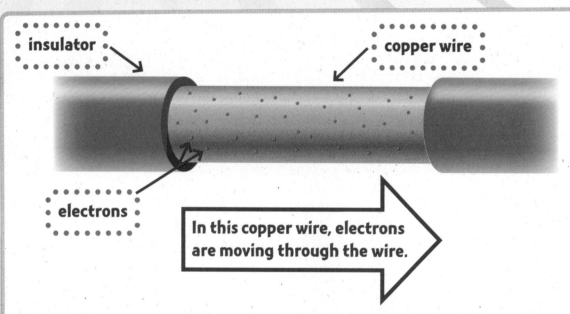

insulator

copper wire

electrons

In this copper wire, electrons are moving through the wire.

An insulator is a material that resists the flow of electrons. Electric currents can flow easily through conductors, such as a copper wire.

▶ What do the blue dots on this wire represent? What is the flow of these blue dots called?

_____

_____

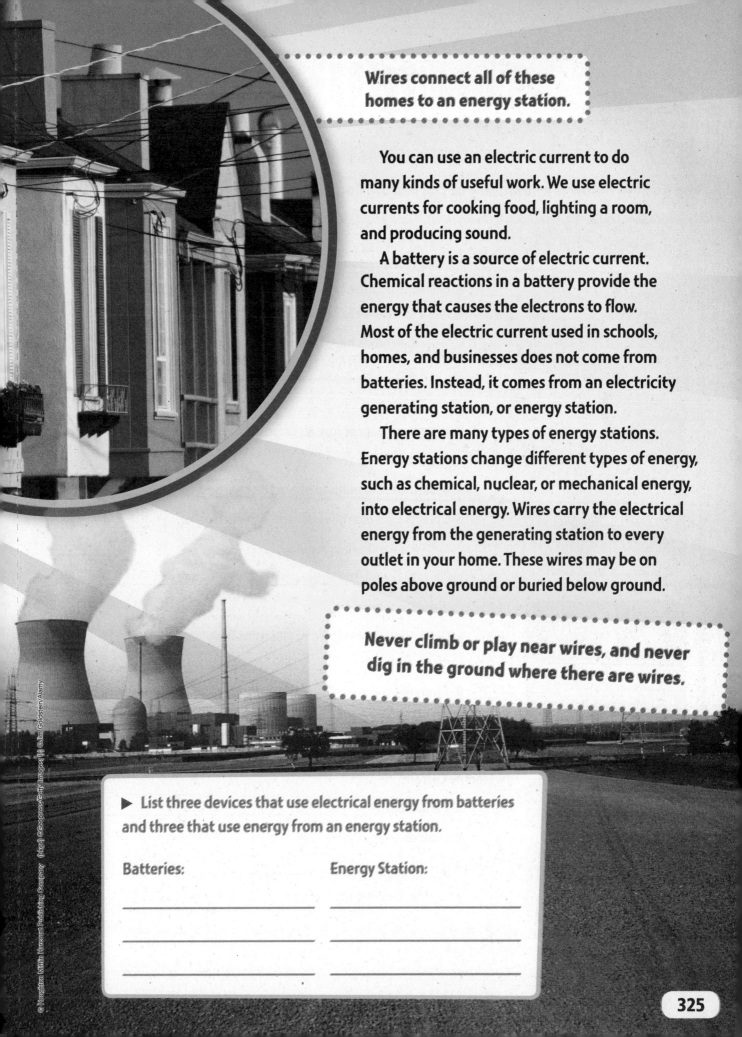

Wires connect all of these homes to an energy station.

You can use an electric current to do many kinds of useful work. We use electric currents for cooking food, lighting a room, and producing sound.

A battery is a source of electric current. Chemical reactions in a battery provide the energy that causes the electrons to flow. Most of the electric current used in schools, homes, and businesses does not come from batteries. Instead, it comes from an electricity generating station, or energy station.

There are many types of energy stations. Energy stations change different types of energy, such as chemical, nuclear, or mechanical energy, into electrical energy. Wires carry the electrical energy from the generating station to every outlet in your home. These wires may be on poles above ground or buried below ground.

Never climb or play near wires, and never dig in the ground where there are wires.

▶ List three devices that use electrical energy from batteries and three that use energy from an energy station.

Batteries: Energy Station:

_____   _____

_____   _____

_____   _____

When you're done, use the answer key to check and revise your work.

The outline below is a summary of the lesson. Complete the outline.

I. Electric Charges

    A. Each of the three types of particles that make up atoms has a different charge.

        1. Protons have a positive charge.

        2. _____

        3. _____

    B. Atoms can gain or lose electrons.

II. Static Electricity

    A. Definition: the buildup of electric charge on an object.

    B. Objects with charges interact with each other.

        1. Like charges repel.

        2. _____

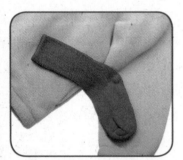

III. Electrostatic Discharge

    A. Definition: the jumping of electrons from one object to another.

    B. Examples

        1. Getting shocked after walking across a rug

        2. _____

IV. Electric Current

    A. Definition: _____

    B. Sources

        1. _____

        2. Generating stations

© Houghton Mifflin Harcourt Publishing Company (b) ©Jim Goldstein/Alamy; (lightning) ©Getty Images Royalty Free

Name _____

Word Play

1 Fill in the blank in each sentence. Then, find the words in the blanks in the word search below.

a. Two positive charges _____ each other.

b. A positive charge and a negative charge _____ each other.

c. The buildup of electric charge on an object is _____ electricity.

d. The flow of electric charges along a path is electric _____.

e. A proton has a _____ charge.

f. A neutron is _____ because it has no charge.

g. An electron has a _____ charge.

h. Electricity is produced at a generating _____.

```
C  N  E  G  A  T  I  V  E
U  F  R  E  P  E  L  R  V
R  I  G  H  T  E  N  I  I
R  N  A  T  T  R  A  C  T
E  G  C  I  T  A  T  S  I
N  E  U  T  R  A  L  L  S
T  I  G  H  T  N  I  N  O
S  T  A  T  I  O  N  G  P
```

Find the letters you didn't circle in the word search. Write them in order from left to right in the blanks below.

Riddle: What do you call a very scary electrostatic discharge?

_ _ _ _ _ _ _ _ _ _   _ _ _ _ _ _ _ _

Apply Concepts

2 List the three particles that make up an atom. Describe the charge of each particle.

Parts of an Atom	
Particle	Charge

Where are these particles found in an atom?

_____

_____

3 Explain why the balloons are sticking to this cat.

_____

_____

_____

_____

_____

4 List three ways you can use an electric current. Describe the energy change that takes place.

_____

_____

_____

_____

_____

Name ___________________________

5 Fill in the blanks to complete the sequence graphic organizer.

A wool sock and a cotton shirt ______________ against each other in a dryer.

↓

Electrons move from the wool to the ______________.

↓

The two pieces of clothing have ______________ charges and they ______________ each other.

6 Explain why the event in the picture takes place.

____

____

____

____

____

____

____

____

____

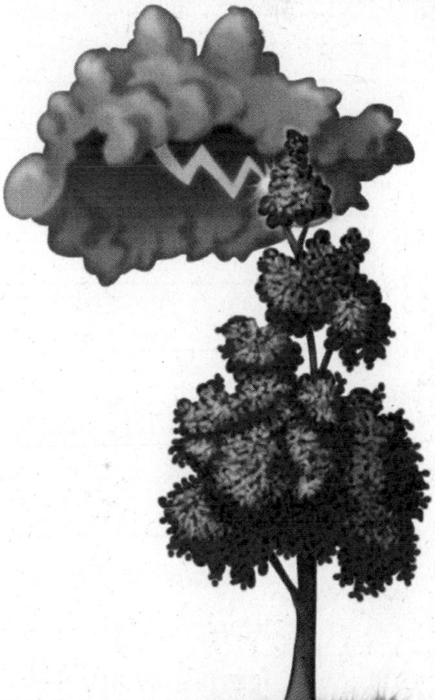

7 Draw a line from each picture to its description. Circle the pictures that show sources of current used by people every day.

electric current	static electricity	electrostatic discharge	battery

 **8** Suppose you are playing soccer at a park, and you hear thunder that sounds far away. Describe some things you should and should not do to stay safe.

_____

_____

_____

_____

_____

_____

 **Take It Home!** Do your clothes stick together when they come out of the dryer? If so, how could you prevent this from happening? Use Internet resources to learn how dryer sheets work to reduce static electricity in your clothes.

OHIO **5.PS.2** Light and sound are forms of energy that behave in predictable ways.

Lesson **5**

Essential Question

How Do Electric Circuits, Conductors, and Insulators Work?

Engage Your Brain!

Find the answer to the following question and record it here.

From this electrical energy control center, workers can shut off electrical energy to parts of their city while leaving others on. How can they do that?

_____

_____

_____

_____

Active Reading

Lesson Vocabulary

List each term. As you learn about each one, make notes in the Interactive Glossary.

_____ _____

_____ _____

_____

Cause and Effect

Some ideas in this lesson are connected by a cause-and-effect relationship. Why something happens is a cause. What happens as a result of something else is an effect. Active readers look for effects by asking themselves, What happened? They look for causes by asking, Why did it happen?

Some Go with the Flow

Would you be surprised to see the prongs on an electrical plug made of plastic? You should be! There's a very good reason why plugs and electrical cords are made of certain materials.

Active Reading As you read these two pages, underline the definitions of key words.

When it comes to working with electricity, knowing the properties of materials is important. Some materials allow electricity to pass through them freely. Others block its flow.

Conductors and Insulators

You would do well to stay away from electrical poles. They're safe enough when they're in good working order. But if one of the wires they carry were to get free, you'd be in trouble! These wires are made of metals, such as copper, which conduct electrical energy. **Conductors** allow electricity to easily travel through them. Some materials prevent the flow of electricity. These materials are called **insulators.** Materials such as plastics, rubber, concrete, glass, and wood insulate electrical energy. Their low cost and flexibility make plastics and rubber great for covering electrical plugs and cords.

Identify Conductors and Insulators

In each box, write *conductor* or *insulator*.

Copper Wire

_____

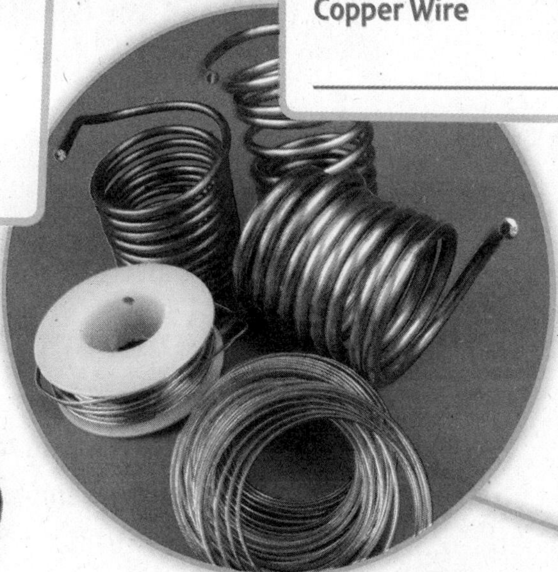

Electrical Gloves

_____

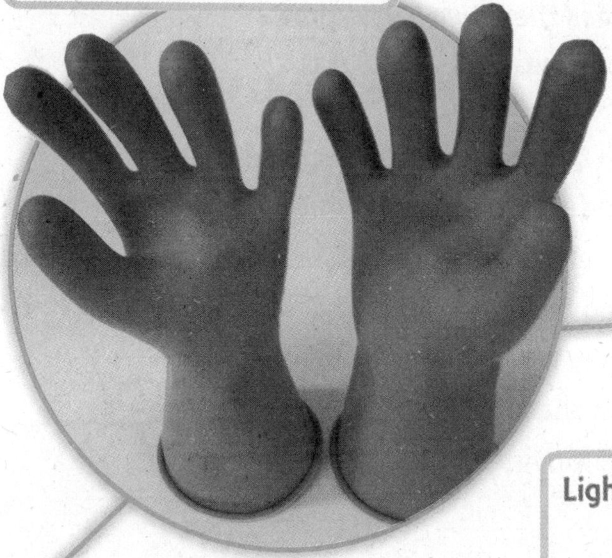

Lightning Rod

_____

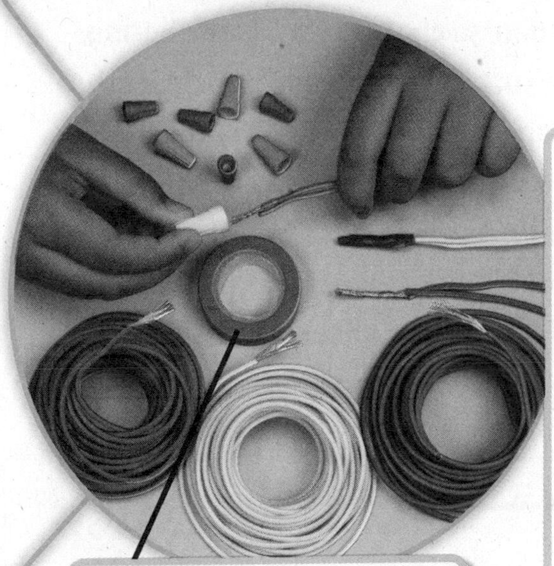

Electrical Tape

_____

▶ The brightly-colored "caps" are twist-on connectors. They are used to hold two or more wires together. These connectors are made of a conductor and an insulator. Where do you think the insulator is? The conductor? Explain.

_____

_____

_____

_____

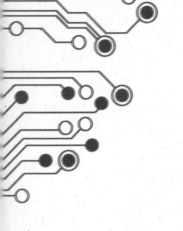

A Path to Charge

Suppose you flip on a light switch
and nothing happens. What's wrong?

Active Reading As you read these two pages, draw
one line under a cause and two lines under an effect

Electricity requires a closed path to flow. An electric **circuit** is a
complete pathway made of conductors through which electric
current can flow. A battery or other electrical energy source makes
electric charges in wires begin to move. When the charges reach
a device like a light bulb or a fan, they provide energy to make the
device work. The path must go from the energy source to the device
and back again to keep the charges moving. This is a complete circuit.

Parts of a Circuit

Opening a switch in a circuit causes
a gap, so charges can't flow. Closing,
or turning the switch "on," closes the
gap. Devices in a circuit such as lamps,
buzzers, or appliances are called
resistances or *loads*. You can draw a
circuit diagram using the symbols in
the key. Notice how each device in the
circuit matches a symbol in the circuit.

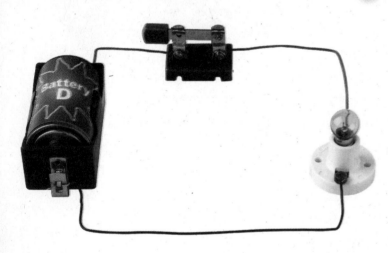

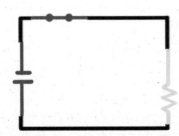

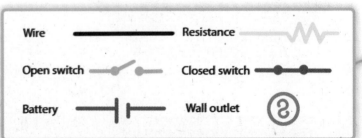

Wire	————	Resistance	⌇
Open switch	⚊⚊/⚊•	Closed switch	⚊●⚊●⚊
Battery	⊣⊢	Wall outlet	⊚

Electricity Changes in Circuits

Electric circuits convert electricity to other forms of energy. For example, circuits in this train change electricity into mechanical energy (motion), light energy, and sound energy. Thermal energy is also produced from electricity to heat the interior of the train cars on cold days.

The hair dryer changes electrical energy into heat and motion as it heats and blows hot air.

Draw a Circuit

Use the key on the previous page to draw a circuit diagram for a complete circuit containing a battery, a switch, and a resistance. Then explain what energy changes take place when the resistance is a light bulb.

_____

_____

_____

_____

_____

_____

_____

Which Path to Take?

One path or many? How do electric charges flow through circuits?

Active Reading As you read these two pages, draw boxes around the names of the two things that are being compared.

There are many electric circuits in your home. The lights and sockets in one room might be on one circuit. An electric oven uses a lot of electricity, so it might be on its own circuit. There are two main types of circuits.

Series Circuit

Can you identify the parts of this circuit? Look at the key at the bottom of this page for help. In a **series circuit**, electric current has only one path to follow to and from the energy source. In this circuit, current passes through both light bulbs, so they both light up. What happens if one light bulb burns out? The other light goes out, too, because the circuit is broken.

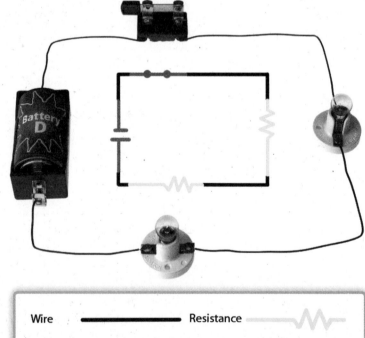

Wire	▬▬▬▬▬	Resistance	∿∿∿
Open switch	•⁄•	Closed switch	•—•
Battery	⊣⊢	Wall outlet	Ⓢ

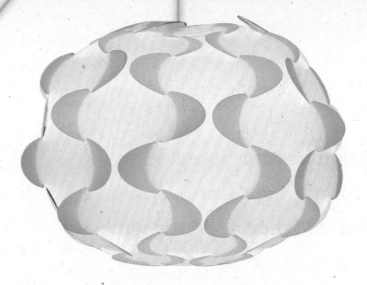

Circuits at Home

At home, you need to turn lights on and off individually. The same is true for other electrical devices. A series circuit only works if all of the devices in the circuit are on. So, which type of circuit do you think is mostly used in homes?

Parallel Circuit

How can you keep the other devices in a circuit working if one stops working? A **parallel circuit** contains two or more paths for electric charges to follow. This emergency flashlight has a light, a radio, and a small siren. Each device is connected to the battery through its own parallel circuit. Three separate switches are used to turn the devices on and off, so that they can work independently of one another.

Where's That Load?

Redraw the emergency flashlight circuit. Include the missing load that represents the siren.

Emergency Flashlight Radio and Siren

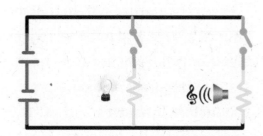

Home Circuits

Look around a room in your house. How many electrical outlets, light fixtures, and switches are there? Are they all in the same circuit? How can you find out?

Active Reading As you read these two pages, draw a line under the main idea.

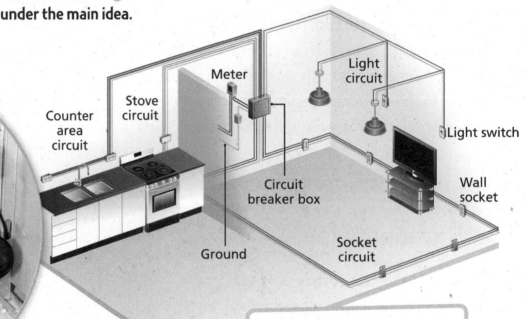

Counter area circuit — Stove circuit — Meter — Light circuit — Light switch — Circuit breaker box — Ground — Socket circuit — Wall socket

▶ Examine the circuits in the diagram. Circle two resistances wired in the same circuit. Box a resistance that is on its own circuit.

Your home electrical system is a small part of a larger system that includes your city, state, and national region. The electricity that you use at home might come from generating stations hundreds of kilometers away. At home, a network of conductors, insulators, and switches are arranged into circuits. It carries electricity into every room. Many meters of wiring make up your home electrical system. However, this is a small fraction of the amount of wiring it takes to bring electricity into your home.

Changing Electrical Energy

Many of the forms of energy you see around your house begin as electricity. Television sets and karaoke machines can convert electricity into light, sound, and thermal energy. Fans, blenders, and can openers change electrical energy into energy of motion. These machines also waste electrical energy as heat and sound. Look at the picture. Can you tell where electrical energy is being changed?

Do the Math!
Interpret a Simple Graph

The symbol % means *percent*, or "out of a hundred." For example, *8%* means "8 out of a hundred." Examine the information in the graph. Then answer the questions below.

1. Which activity consumed the most energy in the home?

_____

2. Which two activities combine to consume 29 out of 100 units of energy?

_____

_____

Home Energy Use

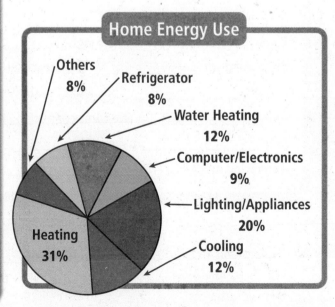

Others 8%

Refrigerator 8%

Water Heating 12%

Computer/Electronics 9%

Lighting/Appliances 20%

Cooling 12%

Heating 31%

When you're done, use the answer key to check and revise your work.

Label the parts of the circuit.

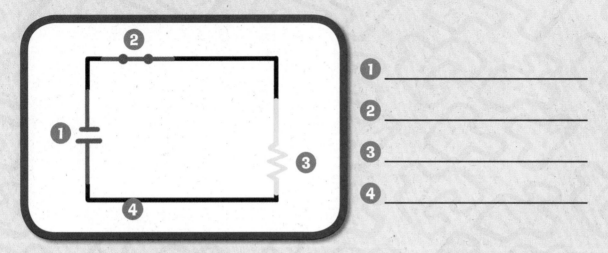

1 _____

2 _____

3 _____

4 _____

5 Assume that the load in the circuit above is a light bulb. Explain what would happen if you open the switch. What is the cause?

_____

_____

Summarize

Fill in the missing words to describe conductors, insulators, and electric circuits.

Electric current easily passes through (6) _____ , such as silver and copper. All metals are good (7) _____ of electricity. Non-metal materials such as wood, glass, plastic, and (8) _____ block the flow of (9) _____ . These materials are called (10) _____ . The wires connecting the battery, switch, and resistance in a (11) _____ have a (12) _____ at their center to conduct electricity and a covering made of a (13) _____ to make the wires safe to handle.

Answer Key: 1. battery **2.** switch **3.** resistance or load **4.** wire **5.** The light bulb would go out because the electric charges no longer have a complete path to flow through **6.** metals **7.** conductors **8.** rubber **9.** electricity **10.** insulators **11.** circuit **12.** metal/conductor **13.** non-metal/insulator

Brain Check

Name _____

Word Play

1 Use the clues to complete the puzzle.

Across

3. Complete path for electric charge
5. Circuit with one path for electric charges
6. Circuit with two or more paths for electric charges
7. Material that allows electrical charges to flow easily
8. Device that changes electricity to other forms of energy

Down

1. Used to open and close a circuit
2. Source of power for a circuit
4. Material that blocks the flow of electric charges

Apply Concepts

2 Select and circle the appropriate equipment that would be safe to use when working with electric current. Explain why some are safer than others.

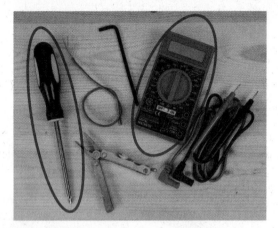

_____

_____

_____

_____

_____

_____

_____

3 A wall switch is connected to a wall outlet. A lamp with a switch is plugged into the outlet. You turn the wall switch on, but the lamp stays off. Give three reasons why this might happen.

_____

_____

_____

4 Analyze the circuit. On the lines below, explain why the circuit isn't complete. Then draw in whatever you need to complete the circuit.

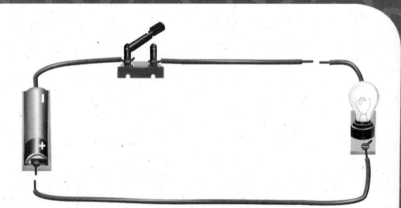

_____

_____

5 Convert this circuit to a parallel circuit that has a light bulb and a buzzer. Show in your circuit a picture of the resistances in each part of the circuit.

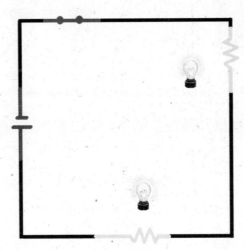

6 In each circuit, electrical energy is being transformed into other forms of energy. Identify the forms of energy produced in each circuit.

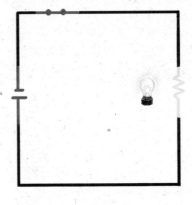  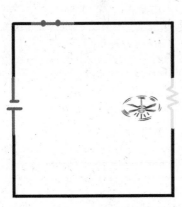

_____ _____ _____

_____ _____ _____

_____ _____ _____

_____ _____ _____

Apply Concepts

7 Analyze the circuit. Name two possible reasons why one light bulb is not lit.

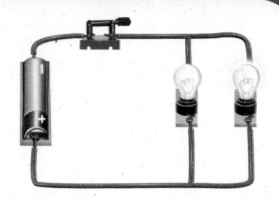

_____

_____

_____

_____

8 Circuits convert electrical energy into other forms of energy. Analyze and evaluate the brightness of the light bulbs in the diagrams. Use logical reasoning and empirical evidence to explain the differences in brightness.

❶

_____

_____

_____

_____

_____

_____

❷

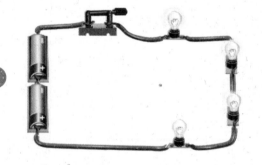

_____

_____

Take It Home! With an adult, find your home's circuit breakers. A circuit breaker is like a switch. Have the adult open one of the breakers. Look around to find which lights are in that circuit. Explain why the lights won't work.

OHIO **5.PS.2** Light and sound are forms of energy that behave in predictable ways. **5.SIA.1** Identify questions that can be answered through scientific investigations. **5.SIA.2** Design and conduct a scientific investigation. **5.SIA.4** Analyze and interpret data. **5.SIA.5** Develop descriptions, models, explanations and predictions. **5.SIA.6** Think critically and logically to connect evidence and explanations. **5.SIA.8** Communicate scientific procedures and explanations.

Name _____

Essential Question

How Does an Electric Circuit Work?

Set a Purpose

What will you learn from this investigation?

_____

_____

_____

Think About the Procedure

Look at the circuit diagram you drew in Step 2. Where in the circuit is the switch?

_____

_____

_____

Switches turn on and off loads in circuits. Does it matter where you put the switch in your circuit? Explain.

_____

_____

_____

_____

_____

Record Your Data

Use the space to draw a circuit diagram. Revise your drawing based on your classmates' feedback and your final working circuit.

Draw Conclusions

A complete path is needed for electricity to flow in a circuit. What empirical evidence did you gather to conclude that the circuit you built was a complete circuit?

_____

_____

_____

_____

Examine your final circuit. Can you improve it? Describe a design for an alternative circuit that could produce the same results.

_____

_____

_____

_____

Analyze and Extend

1. Electricity can be transformed into other forms of energy. Use the evidence you gathered during experimental testing to explain how electricity changed in your circuit.

_____

_____

_____

_____

2. Look at your circuit. Observe how it works. Use this information to explain how you could change your circuit so that the buzzer could be turned off and on separately from the light bulbs. Draw a circuit diagram to show how you would do it.

_____

_____

_____

_____

3. Infer. Do you think there is a limit to the number of devices you can put in a circuit? Explain.

_____

_____

_____

_____

4. Think of other questions you would like to ask about how electrical energy flows in circuits.

_____

_____

_____

_____

OHIO **5.SIA.4** Analyze and interpret data. **5.SIA.6** Think critically and logically to connect evidence and explanations.

How It Works:
Electric Clothes Dryer

You turn the dials on the front of the dryer to open and close circuits. The circuits regulate temperature and how long the dryer will run.

You press the start switch to start the dryer. The switch closes a circuit that turns on an electric motor, an electric heating coil, and a fan. The motor turns the drum.

A thermostat connected to the heating circuit turns the heating elements off and on to keep the temperature you have chosen.

When you open the door, the door switch opens the circuit and stops the drum from spinning.

The motor in the dryer changes electrical energy into energy of motion, thermal energy, and sound energy.

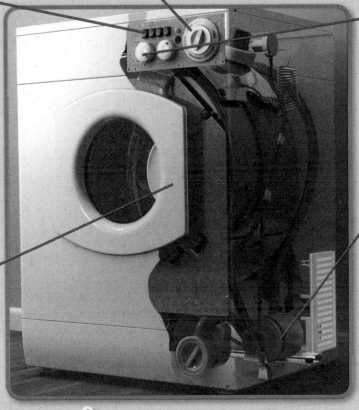

Troubleshooting

The dryer won't start. Put an *X* on two parts that could be broken. Why did you choose those parts?

_____

_____

S.T.E.M.
continued

Show How It Works:

Draw a circuit diagram to show how the door switch might work. Label all the parts of your diagram to show what parts of the dryer they correspond to. Use your circuit to explain why opening the door stops the drum from turning.

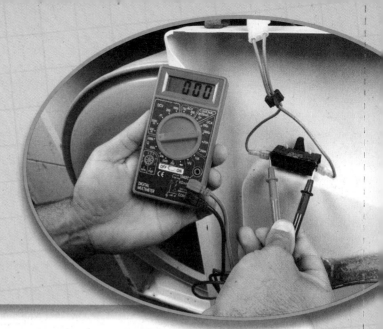

Saving Energy!

Think of a device you could invent to make the dryer stop when the clothes are dry rather than after a fixed length of time. What would be the triggers or inputs for this device? Which of the dryer's systems would be connected to the new device? Draw a circuit diagram and explain how the device would work.

Draw Here

_____

_____

_____

_____

Build On It!

Rise to the engineering design challenge—**Build in Some Science: Circuit Tester** on the Inquiry Flipchart.

Name _____

Vocabulary Review

Use the terms in the box to complete the sentences.

> chemical energy
> electrical energy
> electric current
> mechanical energy
> sound energy
> thermal energy

1. The flow of electrons through a wire is

   a(n) _____.

2. When the string of a guitar vibrates, it

   produces _____.

3. When the sun increases the total kinetic energy of the

   particles in your skin, your _____
   increases.

4. The type of energy released when a match burns

   is _____.

5. Energy that allows a lightbulb to glow

   is _____.

6. The total amount of potential and kinetic energy in a moving

   car is its _____.

Science Concepts

Fill in the letter of the choice that best answers the question.

7. Which of these appliances is **designed** to convert electrical energy into sound energy?

   (A) printer

   (B) refrigerator

   (C) electric heater

   (D) music amplifier

8. The water in a swimming pool tends to be warmer in the daytime and cooler at night. What natural source of energy causes this difference?

   (A) chemical energy

   (B) solar energy

   (C) mechanical energy

   (D) sound energy

Use the diagram to answer questions 9, 10, and 11. It shows thermometers in four cups of water.

1   2   3   4

9. Which is the best explanation for the differences in the temperatures?

Ⓐ The water in each cup came from a different source.

Ⓑ The average kinetic energy of the particles in each cup is different.

Ⓒ There are different numbers of particles in each cup.

Ⓓ There are different types of particles in each cup.

10. Which of the following shows the correct order of the amount of thermal energy in the cups from greatest to least?

Ⓐ 1, 2, 3, 4

Ⓑ 1, 4, 3, 2

Ⓒ 3, 2, 4, 1

Ⓓ 2, 4, 3, 1

11. If the containers in the diagram were touching, which of these describes the flow of heat between them?

Ⓐ from container 2 to container 1

Ⓑ from container 1 to container 2

Ⓒ from container 3 to container 2

Ⓓ from container 3 to container 4

12. Which statement best describes the difference between an electrical insulator and conductor?

Ⓐ A conductor is a metal, and an insulator is a nonmetal.

Ⓑ A conductor contains more electrons than an insulator.

Ⓒ An insulator has a static charge, and a conductor does not.

Ⓓ An insulator does not contain electrons, and a conductor does.

13. The diagram shows a circuit containing a battery and two doorbells. Which statement about the circuit is TRUE?

Ⓐ The bells will ring because it is a series circuit.

Ⓑ The bells will ring because they are attached to the battery.

Ⓒ The bells won't ring because the circuit isn't complete.

Ⓓ The bells won't ring because the battery isn't big enough.

14. Ariel wants to build an electric circuit with a device that can be turned on and off. Which list contains all of the materials she will need for her circuit?

Ⓐ battery, wire, lightbulb, switch

Ⓑ string, buzzer, battery, switch

Ⓒ buzzer, wire, switch, lightbulb

Ⓓ wire, ruler, switch, battery

15. The diagrams show four different electric circuits.

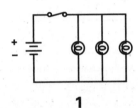
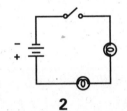

1   **2**

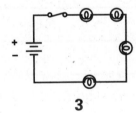
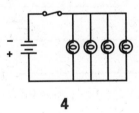

3   **4**

In which of the circuits will other bulbs remain lit when one burns out?

Ⓐ only circuit 1

Ⓑ only circuits 1, 3, and 4

Ⓒ only circuits 2 and 3

Ⓓ only circuits 1 and 4

16. You rub two balloons on your hair on a dry day. Your hair is attracted to both balloons. Then, you bring the balloons near each other. What would you observe?

Ⓐ They repel each other.

Ⓑ They attract each other.

Ⓒ They neither attract nor repel each other.

Ⓓ Opposite charges make one balloon become larger and one become smaller.

17. The diagram shows what happens in a pot of water heated on a stove. Which of the following types of heat transfer is shown by the arrows?

Ⓐ conduction

Ⓑ convection

Ⓒ radiation

Ⓓ evaporation

Apply Inquiry and Review the Big Idea

Write the answers to these questions.

18. Draw and label a diagram that shows how energy changes form in a television.

19. Raul claims that thicker wire will carry more electrons to a lightbulb in an electric circuit, so the bulb will look brighter than when a thin wire is used. Plan and describe an investigation that will provide data to help you analyze and evaluate Raul's explanation.

a. Formulate a testable hypothesis.

_____

_____

b. How will you test your hypothesis? What equipment will you use?

_____

_____

_____

_____

c. How would you use your data to analyze, evaluate, and critique Raul's explanation?

_____

_____

_____

20. Energy is measured in units called *joules* (J). Suppose a roller coaster car starts with 78,000 J of potential energy. In a few seconds, it converts two-thirds of this energy into kinetic energy. As it takes a curve, the car doubles its kinetic energy. How much mechanical energy does the car now have?

_____

Light and Sound

Big Idea

Light and sound are forms of energy that behave in predictable ways.

OHIO 5.PS.2, 5.SIA.1, 5.SIA.2, 5.SIA.3, 5.SIA.4, 5.SIA.5, 5.SIA.6, 5.SIA.8

I Wonder Why

Why does the shape of the bandshell help concertgoers hear the orchestra's music? *Turn the page to find out.*

Here's why Sound energy can reflect, or bounce off, surfaces. The curved, hard surface of the bandshell helps to reflect sound toward the audience. A well-designed bandshell enables concertgoers far from the stage to hear the music just as well as those who are close to it.

In this unit, you will explore the Big Idea, the Essential Questions, and the Investigations on the Inquiry Flipchart.

Levels of Inquiry Key ■ DIRECTED ■ GUIDED ■ INDEPENDENT

Big Idea Light and sound are forms of energy that behave in predictable ways.

Essential Questions

Now I Get the Big Idea!

Science Notebook

Before you begin each lesson, be sure to write your thoughts about the Essential Question.

OHIO **5.PS.2** Light and sound are forms of energy that behave in predictable ways.

Lesson **1**

Essential Question

What Is Sound?

Engage Your Brain!

Find the answer to the following question in this lesson and record it here.

How does a drummer make music?

_____

_____

_____

Active Reading

Lesson Vocabulary

List the terms. As you learn about each one, make notes in the Interactive Glossary.

_____   _____

_____   _____

Compare and Contrast

In this lesson, you'll read about how characteristics of sound are alike and different from one another. Active readers stay focused on comparisons and contrasts when they ask themselves, How are these things alike? How are they different?

Inquiry Flipchart p. 42—Good Vibrations/Thick or Thin

You may have seen water waves that look like this. Water waves move in an up-and-down motion as shown here. No matter how a wave is shaped, it carries energy.

Waves of SOUND

Some waves are long and flat. Other waves are tight and tall. But all waves move from place to place in a regular way.

Active Reading As you read these pages, underline the effect of plucking a guitar string.

Water waves carry energy as they move, one after another, across a lake. A **wave** is a disturbance that transmits energy. There are other kinds of waves that you can't see. Sound energy is a series of vibrations traveling in waves. *Vibrations* are the back-and-forth movements of an object. When you pluck a guitar string, the string vibrates, causing sound waves. The vibrating body of the guitar makes the sound louder.

Musical Vibrations
Use arrows to indicate the parts of the guitar that vibrate.

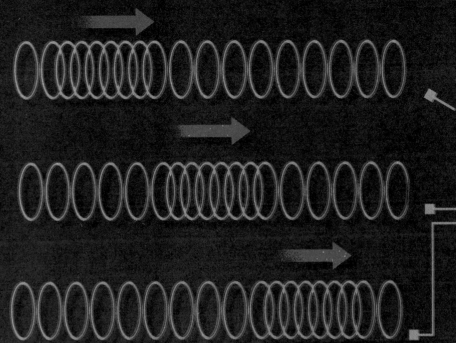

Thinking of a spring toy can help you understand compression waves.

1 The coils in one area become bunched up, or compressed. They then stretch out, or separate.

2 and 3 These compressions and separations occur along the length of the spring as the wave moves away from its starting point.

Musical instruments aren't the only things that make sound. Striking the head of a nail with a hammer causes sound vibrations, too. Many animals make sounds by moving a column of air up through the throat and mouth.

All sound vibrations travel in compression waves. As a compression wave moves, particles of air or other matter are pushed together, or compressed. Then the particles spread apart. Sound energy moves away from its source as this bunching and spreading of particles is repeated over and over. Your ears detect sound waves when the waves make parts of your ears vibrate. Your brain interprets these vibrations as sound.

▶ Tell how a compression wave and a water wave are alike and different.

_____

_____

_____

_____

_____

_____

_____

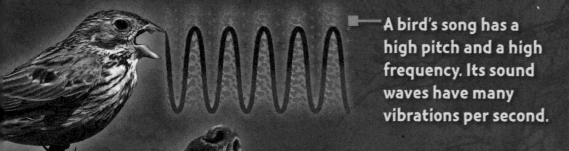

A bird's song has a high pitch and a high frequency. Its sound waves have many vibrations per second.

This dog's bark has fewer vibrations per second. It has a low pitch and a low frequency.

It Sounds LIKE ...

Our world is full of sounds—many of them pleasant, others harsh or annoying.

Active Reading As you read these two pages, underline the definitions of *pitch, frequency,* and *volume.*

People measure characteristics of sound in order to understand, describe, and control how sounds affect our ears. Pitch and volume are two useful ways to measure sound. The highness or lowness of a sound is its **pitch.** A flute produces high-pitched sounds. A tuba produces low-pitched sounds. **Frequency** is the number of vibrations that occur during a unit of time. A sound with a high pitch has a high frequency. Low-pitched sounds have lower frequencies.

The loudness of a sound is its **volume.** Volume is measured in units called *decibels* [DES•uh•buhlz], abbreviated *dB.* The softest sounds that humans can hear are near 0 dB. The humming of a refrigerator is 40 dB. Heavy city traffic is about 85 dB. Any noise at this level can cause hearing loss if a person listens for a long period of time. It's wise to wear earplugs if your ears will be exposed to 15 minutes or more of noise at 100 decibels. No more than one minute of noise at 110 decibels is safe without ear protection.

120 dB — If you are close to a lightning strike, the resulting thunder can be loud enough to cause pain.

100 dB — Sounds that are 85 dB or louder can damage your ears.

80 dB

20 dB

Turn That Down!

Analyze the chart. Then order the sounds from 1, the quietest, to 6, the loudest. Put a star next to any sound that could damage your ears.

Decibel Scale of Common Sounds

Source of Sound	Decibel Level
_____ normal conversation	60 dB
_____ firecracker	150 dB
_____ whispered voices	20 dB
_____ ambulance siren	120 dB
_____ power lawn mower	90 dB
_____ personal stereo system at highest volume	105 dB

The TRAVELS of Sound

Sound can travel through walls, windows, and floors, as well as air and water. Does sound travel at the same speed through solids, gases, and liquids?

Active Reading As you read these two pages, underline places where solids, liquids, and gases are compared or contrasted.

The sound of this boy's voice moves through a gas (air) and a liquid (water) before reaching the other boy's ears underwater.

Sound travels in waves. But sound can only travel if there are particles that the waves can cause to vibrate. Most of the sounds you hear move through the air. Air and other gases have particles that vibrate as sound energy hits them. Liquids and solids are also made of particles, so sound waves can move through these materials, too. However, if there are no particles to move, then sound cannot travel. What would happen if an astronaut dropped a heavy rock on the moon? Would it produce a sound? Since the moon doesn't have an atmosphere, sound waves wouldn't be carried to the astronaut's ears. She might feel vibrations at her feet, but she wouldn't hear a sound.

Do the Math!
Multiply Whole Numbers

Use a calculator and the information in the table to calculate how long it will take a sound to travel 4,575 m through each type of matter.

Type of Matter	Approximate Speed of Sound (m/s)
Pure water	1,525
Dry air	300
Cast iron	4,575

Pure water: _____

Dry air: _____

Cast iron: _____

Sound waves travel through different kinds of matter at different rates. The speed at which sound waves pass through solids, liquids, and gases has to do with how their particles are arranged. Particles in a solid are packed closely together. The particles in gases are far apart. Liquids are in between. For this reason, sound travels through gases more slowly than it travels through liquids and solids.

When you knock on a door, the sound moves through a solid (wood) and through a gas (air) on the other side of the door.

SOUND Off!

Imagine a world without sound! What kinds of things wouldn't you be able to do? Wait—I can't hear you!

Active Reading As you read these two pages, draw one line under an example of sound traveling through a gas, two lines through a liquid, and three lines through a solid.

Talking on the phone or listening to music would be things you wouldn't be able to do. You wouldn't even be able to hear the grumbling of your own stomach! Let's take a look at how many different ways people use sound energy.

Everyday Uses

Sound energy plays a major part in communication and entertainment. You know that sound energy must travel through matter. In many devices, such as cell phones, sound waves from your voice travel through air to a microphone. The sound waves are changed to other forms of energy. When the energy reaches the receiving phone, a speaker changes it back to sound waves that you can hear.

Exploration

When sound energy strikes matter, some of it bounces back toward the source. Materials reflect sound in different ways. Geologists use sound waves to locate underwater resources such as oil. Tools called *sonar* help researchers map the ocean floor or locate sunken ships.

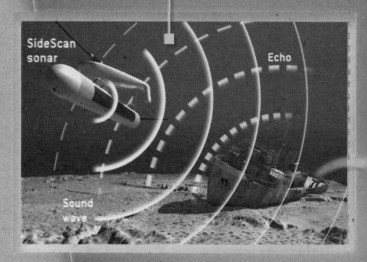

SideScan sonar

Echo

Sound wave

Medicine

Doctors use a simple tool called a stethoscope to listen to your heart. They also use high-frequency sound waves called *ultrasound* to produce images of structures inside the body. This picture shows a heart. Ultrasound can also be used to treat some medical problems. For example, the vibrations from ultrasound can break up hard deposits in the kidneys. As a result, a doctor doesn't have to operate to remove them.

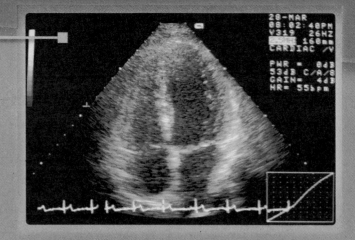

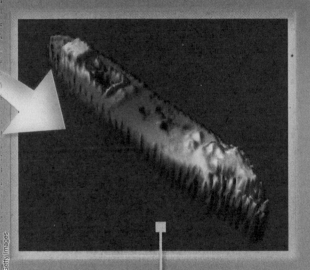

As the waves from a sonar bounce back from a submerged ship, they arrive at different times back to listening devices. A computer changes the collected signals to form a picture of the ship (above).

Fun Sound Facts

Submarines use sonar to locate the position of other ships. Sound moves about five times faster in water than it does through air. Sound travels about 300 m/s in air.

Suppose a sonar signal sent by a submarine takes 2 s to travel from the ship and back again. How far is the submarine from the bottom? Show your work.

_____

_____

_____

_____

Sound All Around

Understanding the properties of sound energy allows people to use and control sound.

Sometimes people want sounds to be softer or to not be heard at all. At other times, people want sounds to be louder or clearer. Engineers design rooms and buildings to reduce outside noise and to make indoor sounds more pleasant.

Sound insulation contains tiny air cells. Sound is absorbed as the cells trap sound waves. This keeps the sound inside the room. Similar technology is used in apartment buildings to help limit the amount of noise you hear from your neighbors!

Engineers use knowledge of sound's properties as they record music, voices, and other sounds in studios. Sound engineers also combine the singer's voice with the background music.

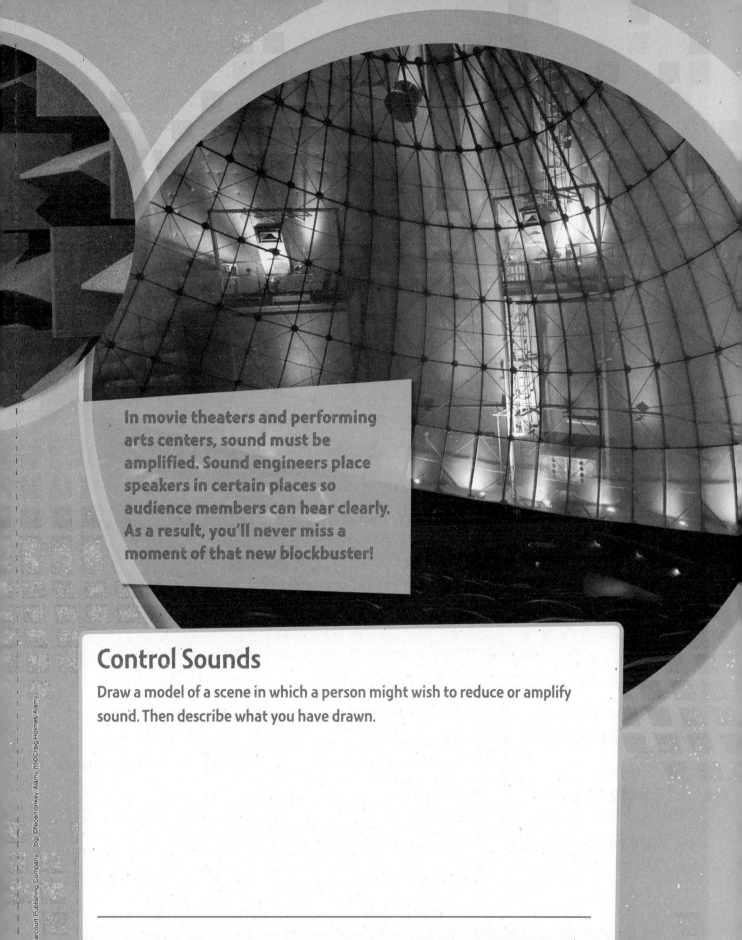

In movie theaters and performing arts centers, sound must be amplified. Sound engineers place speakers in certain places so audience members can hear clearly. As a result, you'll never miss a moment of that new blockbuster!

Control Sounds

Draw a model of a scene in which a person might wish to reduce or amplify sound. Then describe what you have drawn.

When you're done, use the answer key to check and revise your work.

Fill in the blanks to complete the statements that describe the characteristics and uses of sound energy.

Characteristics of Sound

The loudness of a sound is its 1. _____.
It is measured in
2. _____.

The highness or lowness of a sound is called
3. _____.

The number of vibrations in a unit of time is
4. _____.
A sound with a high frequency has a
5. _____.

Uses of Sound Energy

Barking, singing, and sirens, are all uses of sound energy to 6. _____.
Sound energy moves through air by 7. _____.

Ultrasound waves are useful in 8. _____, because they can travel through 9. _____, _____.

Sonar technology uses sound waves for 10. _____.

Name _____

Word Play

1 Match each picture to a term, and each term to its definition.

  decibel   the loudness of a sound

  frequency   disturbances of particles in matter as a sound wave travels forward

  pitch   the number of vibrations that occur in a given unit of time

  vibrations   a disturbance that carries energy

  volume   the highness or lowness of a sound

  wave   the unit of measure for the volume of sound

Apply Concepts

2 Define *wave*. Then explain how vibrations, waves, and energy are related to sound.

_____

_____

3 Label the pictures *1*, *2*, and *3* to indicate the speed at which sound waves travel through each kind of matter. Let *1* be fastest and *3* be slowest.

_____  _____  _____

4 Explain how a sound's pitch and frequency are related.

_____

_____

_____

5 Examine the picture. Which properties of sound are used?

_____

_____

_____

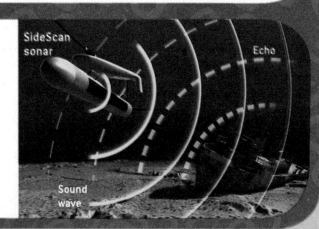

SideScan sonar

Echo

Sound wave

Take It Home!

Spend time walking slowly from room to room. List and classify the sounds you hear with a family member. For example, you might classify them as *loud* and *soft*, or *electronic, mechanical, human,* or *natural.*

OHIO 5.PS.2 Light and sound are forms of energy that behave in predictable ways.

Careers *in* Science

Ask a Sound Designer

Q. What does a sound designer do?

A. The sound designer plans and provides the sounds you hear in a play or movie. They are in charge of making noises and sound effects. They make every sound from the slam of a car door to the roar of a lion.

Q. How do designers come up with the sounds?

A. They study the script, and gather information about the settings of the play or movie, and what sounds a person might hear in those places. They also think about the mood. An audience might not even notice some sounds that provide mood and feelings. Music can give information about a character or a story. It can also help the viewer know when something in a play or movie is about to happen.

Q. What do sound designers need to know about sound?

A. They need to know a lot about the quality of sounds and how they are made. Sound designers have to understand pitch, volume, and how sound travels and lasts.

Did You Hear That?

Can you figure out the sound each object makes?
Read the description of each sound. Write the number
of the sound next to the picture that matches it.

1. This object makes a warning
   sound with a very high volume
   and a high pitch so people are
   sure to hear it.
2. This makes a low-pitched sound
   when you strike it.
3. This makes sounds when you
   strum it.
4. This can make high- or low-
   pitched sounds when you blow
   into it.
5. This object makes a sound with a
   low pitch and a high volume.
6. This organism can make a high-
   volume sound with a high pitch.

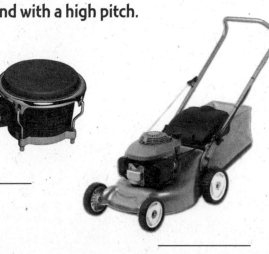

Inquiry Flipchart page 43

OHIO **5.PS.2** Light and sound are forms of energy that behave in predictable ways. **5.SIA.1** Identify questions that can be answered through scientific investigations. **5.SIA.2** Design and conduct a scientific investigation. **5.SIA.4** Analyze and interpret data. **5.SIA.5** Develop... predictions. **5.SIA.6** Think... to connect... explanations. **5.SIA.8** Communicate...explanations.

Name _____

Essential Question

How Does Sound Travel Through Solids, Liquids, and Gases?

Set a Purpose

At the end of this experiment, what will you understand better about sound energy?

_____

_____

Think About the Procedure

What stays the same in all of the trials?

_____

_____

What variable will you change in each trial?

_____

_____

_____

Why will you start by listening to the sound without pressing your ear against any surface?

_____

_____

Record Your Data

Record your observations in the table below.

How do sound waves travel to your ear?	Describe each sound.
Step 1 From the drum through air (gas)	
Step 2	
Step 3	
Step 4	
Step 5	
Step 6	

Draw Conclusions

Why did you place a hand over your free ear in Steps 2–5?

_____

_____

_____

Did the sound change from Step 1 to Step 2? Explain.

_____

_____

_____

_____

_____

Were your descriptions of the sounds in Step 1 and Step 4 different? Why?

_____

_____

_____

_____

_____

Why do you think the sounds produced in Steps 5 and 6 were different?

_____

_____

_____

_____

Analyze and Extend

1. Based on your empirical evidence, construct a scientific explanation about how gases, liquids, and solids can change the way we hear a sound.

    _____

    _____

    _____

2. Analyze, evaluate, and critique the explanations offered by other groups. Why might the results you got differ from theirs?

    _____

    _____

    _____

    _____

3. Most of the sounds you hear travel through air. If you could, how would you change the procedure to better hear sounds transmitted through solids and liquids?

    _____

    _____

    _____

    _____

4. What other questions would you like to ask about how sound travels in different types of matter?

    _____

    _____

    _____

OHIO **5.PS.2** Light and sound are forms of energy that behave in predictable ways.

Lesson **3**

Essential Question

What Are Some Properties of Light?

Engage Your Brain!

Find the answer to the following question in this lesson and record it here.

Why do lighthouses use lenses?

_____

_____

_____

Active Reading

Lesson Vocabulary

List the terms. As you learn about each one, make notes in the Interactive Glossary.

_____   _____

_____   _____

_____

Compare and Contrast

Many ideas in this lesson are connected because they explain comparisons and contrasts—how things are alike and different. Active readers stay focused on comparisons and contrasts when they ask themselves, How are these things alike? How are these things different?

Just Passing Through

Light acts differently when it strikes windows, thin curtains, or brick walls. How does each material affect the light that strikes it?

As you read these two pages, underline sentences that provide details about how light acts when it strikes different materials.

Light is a form of energy that can move through space. Light travels outward, in all directions, in straight lines from its source until it strikes something. Light behaves in different ways depending on the kind of matter it meets. Most objects absorb some of the light that hits them. The amount of light absorbed depends on the material the object is made of.

Opaque materials do not let light pass through them. Instead, the material absorbs light—light enters the material but doesn't leave it. When a material absorbs light, the energy from the light is transferred to the material. Many solid objects are opaque because they are made of materials such as metal, wood, and stone that do not allow light to pass through. Objects that are opaque cause shadows to occur because the objects absorb or reflect all of the light that hits them.

Glass Bulb

> ▶ Write a caption for each picture. Tell whether the object is opaque, translucent, or transparent. Explain how light interacts with each material.

_____
_____
_____
_____

_____
_____
_____

Metal Lampshade

Paper Lampshade

Materials that let light pass through them are **transparent**. Transparent materials absorb very little of the light that hits them. This makes it easy to see objects through transparent materials. Clear glass, air, and pure liquid water are transparent.

A third kind of material both transmits some light and absorbs some light. These materials are **translucent**. Ice, wax paper, and frosted glass are translucent. You can see through a translucent material, but the image is fuzzy or unclear.

Mirror, Mirror

Did you look at yourself in a mirror as you got ready for school? The properties of light enabled you to see your image.

Active Reading As you read these two pages, draw boxes around the words or phrases that signal when things are being contrasted.

The bouncing of light off an object is known as **reflection**. When light traveling from an object strikes a smooth, shiny surface, such as a mirror, all of the light striking the surface from one direction is reflected in a single new direction. Your eyes detect the reflected light, and you see a clear, reversed image of the object—a reflection. In contrast, you can't see an image in something with a rough surface, such as cloth or wood, because the roughness causes light to reflect in many directions.

The smooth surface of the water acts like a mirror. Light rays are reflected back in a way that enables you to see a clear, reversed image.

The backpack appears yellow because its material reflects yellow light and absorbs all other colors of light.

► Compare the surfaces of the metal container and the paper bag. The smooth surface reflects light in a single direction back to your eyes. The rough surface reflects light in all directions. Identify the material that would produce the better reflection.

_____

_____

How an object reflects light also determines what colors you see. As light strikes the surface of an object, the object absorbs certain colors of light and reflects others. A ripe strawberry absorbs nearly all colors of light, but it reflects red light. So, your eyes see the strawberry as red. Grass reflects green light while absorbing all other colors.

Black objects absorb all colors of light. They also absorb more of the energy in light. White objects, though, reflect all colors of light and absorb less energy. Because white clothes don't absorb as much energy, wearing white rather than dark clothes on a bright, hot day will keep your body cooler.

► When we look at these fruits and vegetables, we see a variety of colors.

Choose one fruit or vegetable. Explain why it's the color it is.

_____

_____

_____

_____

_____

_____

Light Bends

What happened to the straw in the glass? Did someone break it? No! What you are observing is another property of light—refraction.

Active Reading As you read these pages, underline words that identify the cause of refraction. Circle words that identify an effect of refraction.

The bending of light as it passes at an angle from one type of matter into another is called **refraction**. Refraction occurs because the speed of light varies depending on the material through which the light travels. As the light changes speed, it bends. Look at the straw at the top of this page. Light from the top of the straw passes through the air and the glass to your eyes. But light from the bottom part starts out in the water and passes into the glass and then into the air. Each time the light enters a new material, it bends slightly because it changes speed. By the time this light reaches your eyes, it is coming from a different angle than the light from the top of the straw. As a result, the straw appears to be bent or broken.

Refraction produced the illusion that this polar bear's head is separate from its body.

A **prism** is a transparent material that separates white light into its component colors by refraction. When white light enters a prism, the different colors of light bend at different angles. The light moves through the prism and exits it as a rainbow.

Light bends in other ways. *Diffraction* is the bending of light around barriers or through openings. If you look at the edges of a shadow cast in bright sunlight, you may notice that the edges of the shadow are blurry. This blurriness is caused by light bending around the edge of the object. The colors of the sunset are a result of diffraction as sunlight bends around particles in the air.

Do the Math!
Angles of Refraction

The diagram shows how light bends as it enters and then exits a transparent material. Use a protractor to measure the angles formed as the light is refracted.

_____

_____

_____

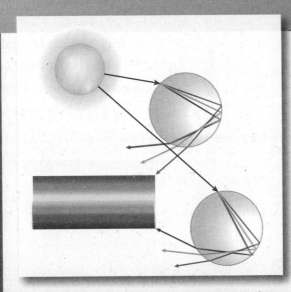

Rainbows are a product of refraction and reflection. Sunlight separates into colors as it passes from the air into a water droplet. The colored light is reflected off the back of the drop, and it is refracted again as it passes into the air. Light from many droplets forms the arcs of color in a rainbow. Red light comes from droplets higher in the air, and violet light comes from lower droplets.

Lenses

Cameras, telescopes, and eyeglasses all contain lenses. Even your eyes have a lens inside each of them! What do lenses do?

Active Reading As you read the next page, put brackets [ ] around the details that describe convex and concave lenses. Draw a line under the main idea that the details help explain.

Lenses are curved transparent objects that refract light. You can find lenses in DVD players, photocopiers, and binoculars. Even the microscope you use in many science activities has a lens. Most lenses are circular and are made of clear glass or plastic. Many devices use a series of lenses to make images clearer. Lenses vary greatly in size. Microscopes use several tiny lenses to magnify small objects. The Yerkes Observatory in Wisconsin has a reflecting telescope with a lens that is over a meter in diameter!

Telescopes use lenses to magnify objects. Incoming light moves through a convex lens, which bends light toward the center of the tube and brings it into focus. The concave eyepiece lens magnifies the image.

© Houghton Mifflin Harcourt Publishing Company (bg) ©AP Worldwide/Alamy

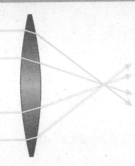

Convex lenses have an outward curve on at least one side. The other side may be curved or flat. These lenses refract light toward a focus, or focal point.

Most concave lenses have an inward curve on both sides. These lenses spread light waves apart.

A *convex lens* is a lens that is thicker at the center and thinner at the edges. Convex lenses are sometimes called positive lenses because they bring light waves together. In other words, a convex lens focuses light. This bending allows an image to form at a point called the focal point.

A *concave lens* is a lens that is thicker at the edges and thinner at the center. Sometimes called negative lenses, concave lenses spread light waves apart from a focal point.

Eyeglasses may have concave or convex lenses, depending on the type of vision correction needed.

Concave, Convex, or Both?

Fill in the Venn diagram to compare and contrast concave and convex lenses.

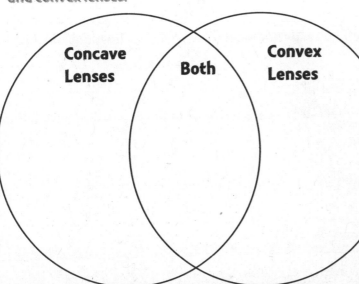

Sum It Up!

When you're done, use the answer key to check and revise your work.

Use the terms below to fill in the graphic organizers about some properties of light.

> reflection   translucent   diffraction
>
> opaque   refraction   transparent

Descriptions of Ways Different Materials Absorb Light

1. _____

2. _____

3. _____

The Bouncing or Bending of Light

4. _____

5. _____

6. _____

Word Play

1 Use the clues to help you write the correct word in each row.
Some boxes have already been filled in for you.

a. | | | | F | R | | | | I | | |
b. | | | | F | R | | | | I | | |
c. | | | | F | | | | | I | | |
d. | | | | | | | | R | I | | |
e. | | | A | | | | | R | | | |
f. | | | A | | | | | | | | |
g. | | | A | | | | | | | |

Clues

a. This makes the edges of a shadow look blurred.

b. It's another way of saying "the bending of light."

c. This is the word for the bouncing of light off an object.

d. This object will separate light into the colors of the spectrum.

e. This word describes objects that let light pass through them.

f. This word describes objects that let only some light pass through them.

g. This word describes objects that let little or no light pass through them.

transparent*   reflection*   prism*   diffraction

translucent*   opaque*   refraction*

* Key Lesson Vocabulary

Bonus

The prefix *con-* means "with." What words with this prefix
can you find in the lesson?

_____

Apply Concepts

2 Which is better: checking your appearance in a regular mirror or checking it in a sheet of crumpled aluminum foil? Explain why one reflective surface is better than the other.

_____

_____

_____

3 Construct an explanation. Why is the fisherman having a hard time catching the fish?

_____

_____

_____

_____

4 Circle the image that shows an opaque material.

Take It Home!

With a family member, walk through the rooms of your home and identify opaque, transparent, and translucent objects. See how many surfaces you can find in which you can see a reflection.

S.T.E.M.
Engineering & Technology

Play It Again

The hand-cranked Victrola was one of the first machines to play back recorded sound. The grooves on a flat disk send a sound vibration through a needle.

A record player makes sound the same way a Victrola did, but it is powered by electricity.

Instead of coming from physical grooves, the sound on a reel-to-reel player comes from signals recorded on magnetic tape.

An MP3 is a type of computer file. It contains the digital code for recorded sounds. Many devices, from computers to phones to pocket-sized music players, can play back MP3 files.

Cassette tapes are magnetic like reel-to-reels, but they are small and portable. So are cassette players.

Compact discs have grooves like records. But a CD player reads the grooves with a laser beam instead of a needle.

Circle the sound devices that use discs. How are the players alike? How are they different?

_____

_____

S.T.E.M.
continued

Devices that play back recorded sound have improved over time.

	How is an electric record player an improvement over a hand-cranked Victrola?
	How is a cassette tape an improvement over a reel-to-reel tape?
	You have to rewind a cassette tape to get back to the beginning after it plays. How is a CD easier to play?
	What makes MP3 files the most convenient way to play back recorded sound?
	Draw a sound playback device that would be even better. What features might it have?

Build On It!

Rise to the engineering design challenge—complete **Design It: Looking Around a Corner** on the Inquiry Flipchart.

Inquiry Flipchart page 46

Name _____

Essential Question

What Happens When Light Is Reflected and Refracted?

OHIO **5.PS.2** Light and sound are forms of energy that behave in predictable ways. **5.SIA.1** Identify questions that can be answered through scientific investigations. **5.SIA.2** Design and conduct a scientific investigation. **5.SIA.3** Use appropriate mathematics, tools and techniques to gather data and information. **5.SIA.4** Analyze and interpret data. **5.SIA.5** Develop descriptions, models, explanations and predictions. **5.SIA.6** Think critically and logically to connect evidence and explanations. **5.SIA.8** Communicate scientific procedures and explanations.

Set a Purpose

What do you expect to understand about light after you complete this investigation?

_____

_____

_____

Think About the Procedure

What is the purpose of the mirror in the investigation?

_____

_____

_____

What is the purpose of the prism in the investigation?

_____

_____

_____

Record Your Data

Draw a diagram of the setup showing the path of the light beam. Record the angles you measured on the diagram.

Draw Conclusions

You have learned that light travels in straight lines. How does the investigation support that statement? Use empirical evidence to support your answer.

_____

_____

_____

_____

_____

How do the angles you measured in Step 6 compare?

_____

_____

_____

_____

_____

Analyze and Extend

1. Suppose the angle at which the light strikes the mirror is 50°. Infer the angle at which the light will reflect.

_____

_____

_____

_____

2. The speed of light changes as it enters and leaves a substance. Use empirical evidence from this investigation to explain how this was observed.

_____

_____

_____

_____

3. Why would a mirror be less useful to people if it scattered light?

_____

_____

_____

_____

4. What other questions would you like to explore about how light travels when it strikes a mirror or passes through a transparent medium such as water or glass.

_____

_____

_____

_____

_____

Unit 8 Review

Vocabulary Review

Use the terms in the box to complete the sentences.

> light
> opaque
> reflection
> refraction
> translucent
> volume

1. Materials that do not let light pass through them

   are _____.

2. A form of energy that can travel through space

   is _____.

3. The loudness or softness of a sound is

   its _____.

4. The bending of light as it passes at an angle from one type

   of matter to another is called _____.

5. Materials, such as wax paper, that absorb some
   light and allow some light to pass through them

   are _____.

6. When light strikes a smooth, shiny surface, it bounces back

   in a process called _____.

Science Concepts

Fill in the letter of the choice that best answers the question.

7. Which term best describes the form
   sound takes as it travels away from
   a drum?

   Ⓐ gas

   Ⓑ music

   Ⓒ waves

   Ⓓ particles

8. Which of the following uses light energy
   and can be found in binoculars, cameras,
   and eyeglasses?

   Ⓐ a lens

   Ⓑ a laser

   Ⓒ a prism

   Ⓓ a CD

9. Julio wants to know what happens when light strikes a prism. The diagram shows his investigation.

Which statement best describes what Julio observes?

(A) a prism focusing light

(B) a prism diffracting light

(C) a prism reflecting light in straight lines

(D) a prism refracting light into its component wavelengths

10. Kwan says that Julio's investigation proves that light doesn't travel in straight lines. Which statement best analyzes and interprets the diagram to evaluate Kwan's claim and produce an alternative explanation?

(A) The prism causes the light to curve around it.

(B) The prism reflects the light back to its source.

(C) The light scatters in straight lines as it strikes the prism.

(D) The light changes direction but always travels in straight lines.

11. People often use sounds to identify objects they can't see. What properties of sound help you identify a referee's whistle?

(A) low frequency, high volume

(B) high frequency, high volume

(C) low frequency, low volume

(D) high frequency, low volume

12. Which diagram shows what will happen to the light when Alain shines a flashlight at a mirror?

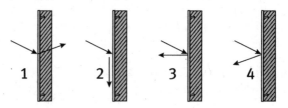

(A) Diagram 1

(B) Diagram 2

(C) Diagram 3

(D) Diagram 4

13. What happens to white light when it strikes a red shirt?

(A) Red light is reflected and all other colors are absorbed.

(B) Red light is absorbed and all other colors are reflected.

(C) White light breaks into different wavelengths as it is reflected.

(D) White light breaks into different wavelengths as it is absorbed.

14. Look at the illustration below.

Which sentence best summarizes what is happening to light that is hitting the surface of the mirror?

Ⓐ It is reflected in many new directions.

Ⓑ It passes through the surface of the mirror.

Ⓒ It is reflected back in the same direction from which it came.

Ⓓ It changes speed and bends slightly as it moves in a single new direction.

15. Giorgio connects the bottom of two cans with a string. Giorgio and a friend each take one of the cans and stand apart until the string is taut. Placing the can to his ear, Giorgio can hear what his friend whispers into his can. How is the string being used in this activity?

Ⓐ The string produces sound waves.

Ⓑ Sound waves move along the string.

Ⓒ Thermal energy is absorbed by the string.

Ⓓ Light waves travel along the string between the cans.

16. While swimming underwater in a pool, Hamid hears the honking of a truck's horn. What happened as the sound waves traveled from the horn to Hamid's ears?

Ⓐ The waves stopped as they reached the water.

Ⓑ The waves did not change speed as they passed from the air to the water.

Ⓒ The waves slowed down as they passed from the air to the water.

Ⓓ The waves sped up as they passed from the air to the water.

17. Beth wants to know more about rainbows. Which of the following is a question Beth might answer with an investigation?

Ⓐ Do all animals see rainbows?

Ⓑ What is the order of colors in a rainbow?

Ⓒ Why can't you reach the end of a rainbow?

Ⓓ How many rainbows appear in a year?

18. Which tools might you use to collect and record observations in an investigation on sound?

Ⓐ a microphone, a notebook, and a computer

Ⓑ test tubes, water, and a magnet

Ⓒ mirrors, prisms, and a notebook

Ⓓ a drum, a calculator, and a flashlight

Apply Inquiry and Review the Big Idea

Write the answers to these questions.

19. Curt wants to know more about how the shape of a mirror affects the angle at which the mirror reflects light.

    a. What is a testable hypothesis that Curt might use for his investigation?

    _____

    _____

    _____

    b. What tools and equipment should Curt select for his investigation? What procedure will he use? What data will he collect? How will he decide if his hypothesis is correct?

    _____

    _____

    _____

    _____

    _____

    _____

    _____

20. In a movie, Hua saw a man put his ear on a railroad track and announce that a train was coming. No one else could see or hear the train. Based on what you have learned, how would you evaluate the man's claim?

    _____

    _____

21. The speed of sound in air at 20 °C is 343 m/s. Its speed in water at 20 °C is 1,483 m/s. How much longer would it take for sound in air to travel 10 km than in water? Round your answer to the nearest second.

    _____

Don't Wait

Tick...tick...tick. Time is wasting. Don't wait until the last minute. Start your research and planning now!

What kind of project is it?

What is the goal of the project? Is it an experiment, an engineering challenge, or something entirely different? Find out about the rules and expectations.

Projects in
Science

by Michael DiSpezio

Since you're reading this section, there's probably a science project in your future. Right?

Don't worry, we're here to guide you along. Whether you were given specific steps to follow or want to create your own totally awesome project, you've come to the right place. We'll show you how to put it together.

What topic should I pick?

You'll be spending quite a bit of time on this undertaking, so select a topic that you're interested in.

What's the plan?

When you know your goals, formulate a plan. Make a calendar that shows completion dates for various steps. Try to stick to that schedule, but update it as needed.

What materials do I need?

Make sure you use materials that are safe, available, and affordable.

Gathering
Information

The first step in any project is to learn as much as you can about the subject.

You'll need to fine-tune your research skills to help you complete your project. As you learn more about your topic, you'll be able to design a better project. You may even change your topic based on what you uncover.

A Search Engine for Kids

These days, it's easy to access a global library of information. All it takes is an Internet connection and the ability to use a search engine. A search engine is a tool that scours the Internet and locates web pages containing documents, images, and videos. All you have to do is enter keywords or phrases that relate to your subject. The search engine does the rest and generates a list of relevant links. Click on a link, and a new web page opens that contains information related to your search.

▶ Suppose the subject of your project is hurricane damage. Write down five keywords or phrases that you would enter into a search engine to learn more about this subject.

_____

_____

_____

_____

_____

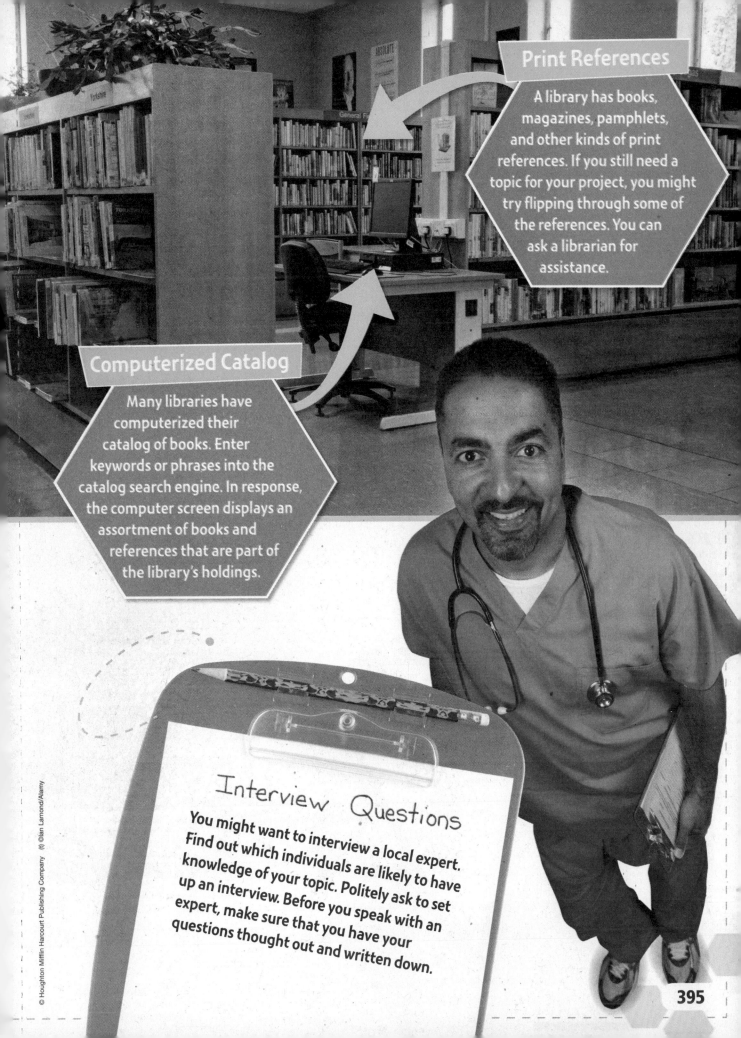

Print References

A library has books, magazines, pamphlets, and other kinds of print references. If you still need a topic for your project, you might try flipping through some of the references. You can ask a librarian for assistance.

Computerized Catalog

Many libraries have computerized their catalog of books. Enter keywords or phrases into the catalog search engine. In response, the computer screen displays an assortment of books and references that are part of the library's holdings.

Interview Questions

You might want to interview a local expert. Find out which individuals are likely to have knowledge of your topic. Politely ask to set up an interview. Before you speak with an expert, make sure that you have your questions thought out and written down.

Tell It or Type It...
Transmit Information!

The world is at your fingertips! Communication is important at every step of a science project, from working with members of a team to sharing your results with others. Technology makes sending and receiving information easier than ever before.

▲ Scientists used to communicate by writing books and journal articles. This process could take several months or even years. Today, you can communicate instantly using the Internet.

Friends might use cell phones to communicate, but text messages aren't always clear. Are there better ways to communicate scientific information? ▶

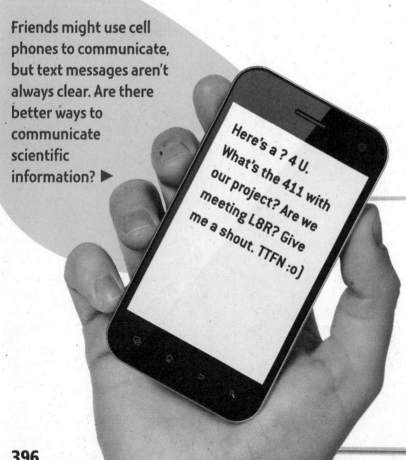

Here's a ? 4 U. What's the 411 with our project? Are we meeting L8R? Give me a shout. TTFN :o)

Say What?

What message was sent on the cell phone?

_____

_____

_____

_____

SCIENCE BLOG SITES

Search [ ]

Home | About | Video

Blogs and Websites

The Internet is a great tool for communicating with others. You can send e-mails about a project to team members. You can make a website to post your results and share them with others. You can read blogs to find out what projects others are doing. Computers keep records, so it's easy to track the progress of your project.

Internet Safety Tips

▶ Your parents or teacher should know when you are using the Internet.

▶ Never enter personal information on websites.

▶ If something makes you uncomfortable, tell your parents or teacher immediately.

▶ Just like you shouldn't talk to strangers on the street, you shouldn't communicate with strangers on the Internet.

Share Your Results

Tell Your Story

Field Reports

Internet a global system of computers that are connected together

Website a collection of online pages that a person, an organization, or a company puts on the Internet for others to view

Blog an online diary where people post information about hobbies or experiences

Science Fair Projects

Is your school going to stage a science fair? You'll have several weeks to prepare an award-winning project. But where should you start? The answer is easy—right here!

Experimental Design

Design an investigation to answer your question. Keep it simple and to the point. Most questions will lead to an investigation that explores how one factor affects a subject. For example, "How does temperature affect seed germination?"

Begin with a Question

Most science fair projects answer a question. A good question can be solved by an investigation. To come up with a good question, you may need to do some research about your topic.

Scientific Methods

Write a hypothesis about how you think things will turn out. During your investigation, make sure you are using scientific methods.

Keeping Notes

Keep a notebook that describes everything about the project. Make sure that it stays up-to-date with descriptions of your materials, experimental setup, steps, and collected data. You can transfer this information to a computer so it can be printed out later.

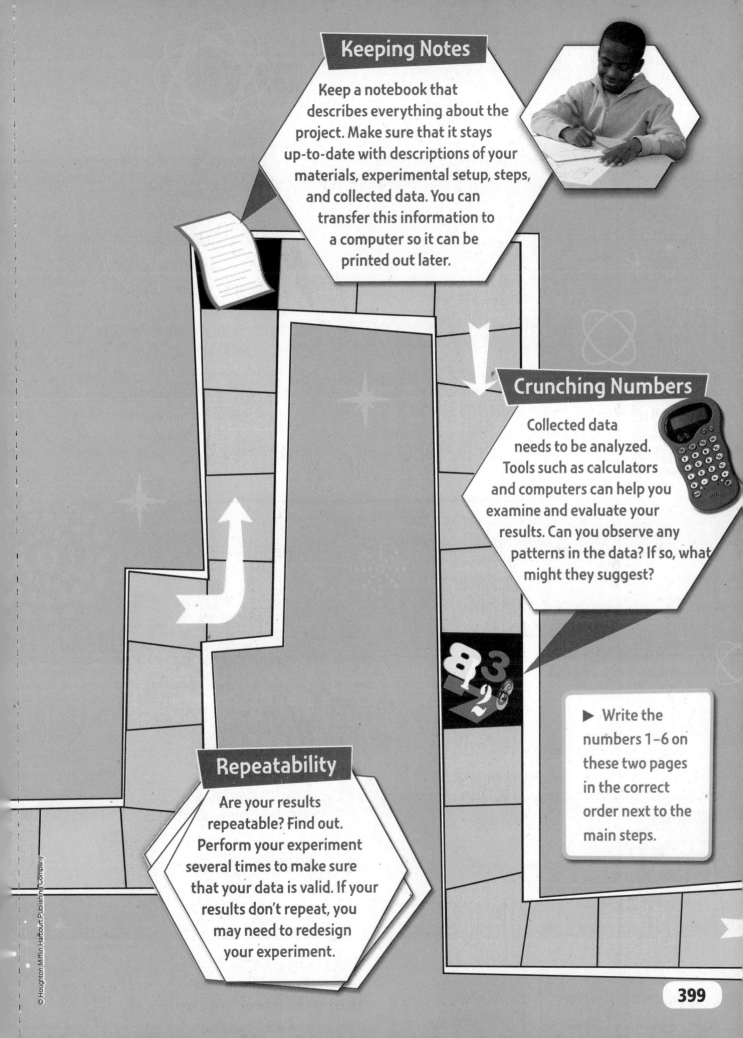

Crunching Numbers

Collected data needs to be analyzed. Tools such as calculators and computers can help you examine and evaluate your results. Can you observe any patterns in the data? If so, what might they suggest?

► Write the numbers 1–6 on these two pages in the correct order next to the main steps.

Repeatability

Are your results repeatable? Find out. Perform your experiment several times to make sure that your data is valid. If your results don't repeat, you may need to redesign your experiment.

Communicate What You've Learned

When you're finished with your project, it's time to communicate your findings at a science fair. Chances are the event will be held in a cafeteria, gym or other large space. Here, you'll have the opportunity to present your project to other students, teachers, parents, and judges.

Drawing Conclusions

Once you've analyzed your data, it's time to evaluate your hypothesis. Do the collected measurements agree with your educated guess? If so, describe this relationship and how it is supported by your data. If not, describe how your hypothesis is disproved by your findings.

Show It Off

You may want to take pictures to document your project.

FINISH

Before you talk about your project, know what to say. Have your key points written down or memorized. Practice in front of a mirror or before friends and family.

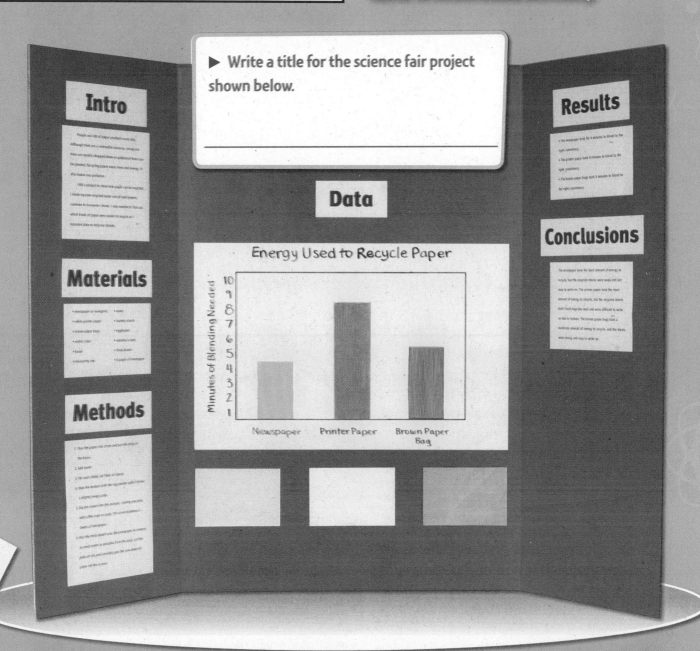

▶ Write a title for the science fair project shown below.

Intro

Materials

Methods

Data

Energy Used to Recycle Paper

Minutes of Blending Needed

Newspaper   Printer Paper   Brown Paper Bag

Results

Conclusions

For display and judging, you'll probably set up an exhibit on a tabletop. Most often, science fair projects are communicated using a self-standing display made of cardboard. You can buy a tri-fold display or make your own. If a single sheet is too small, try taping three large pieces together. Each section of the display shows a different part of the project. In addition to a poster, you might want to exhibit materials, parts of the setup, or models of what you investigated.

Citizen Science:
Get Involved

In a citizen science project, you can collect data that can be used by scientists.

Hey, Robin. I've been having this strange feeling that someone's been watching us. It started a few days ago when those students first appeared with binoculars. Be honest. Am I just being paranoid, or do they keep staring at us?

Listen, bird brain, of course they're looking at us. They're doing a bird count. It's part of a citizen science project. That's when ordinary folks collect data and share it with scientists. Using all the collected data, scientists can perform more extensive research.

When people participate in citizen science, scientists can quickly gather a lot of data.

Did you know that there are other citizen science projects? One involves analyzing local water samples to help monitor pollution. Another project has volunteers making local weather observations. To find out more, do a web search.

I see six crows and one robin. We'll e-mail the data to the local bird preserve. They'll post it online and share it with scientists and other bird watchers.

Field Guide to Humans

▶ Make a list of materials you'd need to participate in a local bird count.

_____

_____

_____

_____

_____

Engineering a Challenge

Classroom engineering challenges are like real-world construction projects. Are you up for the challenge?

Engineering challenges offer the opportunity to plan, test, and improve original designs. To start, learn as much as you can about the challenge and its associated science. Be familiar with the rules before you begin to brainstorm ideas.

Creativity

Be creative! Have fun! At this point, don't worry if your ideas are perfect. Brainstorm and generate a list of all design options. Later on, you'll select and test your best ideas.

Materials

Consider what sort of materials would be best to use. Make sure that you are aware of the guidelines for the challenge. There may be limits to kinds of materials or to the cost of supplies used to assemble your entry.

Blueprints

As you start to think up a design, draw simple diagrams or blueprints on paper. It's much easier to change a drawing than an assembled project, so this is the perfect time to update your plans.

Teamwork

If you're working with others, make sure that each person has a specific responsibility. Share what you know. Work together to engineer a design based on the entire team's understanding and experience.

Test and Redesign

Once you have a model assembled, test it. Does it perform as you imagined? Test it again. From what you observe, can you improve your design? Continue making improvements until it's time to show off your completed project.

A Better Design?

How would you change one element in this wacky design?

_____

_____

Try These
Challenges

Would you like to challenge your classmates
to a friendly design competition?
Here are some suggestions.

Bridge Building

When it comes to engineering, bridges
offer an "inside" view of design. Unlike
buildings, whose beams are concealed
by outer walls, the structural framework
of bridges is often exposed. How would
you build a bridge using craft sticks and
white glue? How much weight could
you add to the bridge before the
structure collapsed?

Solar-Powered Racers

Fill 'er up—with sunshine, that is!
Here's your chance to build a solar-
powered vehicle. The energy to run
the car's motor comes from a solar
cell. Beyond the motor and cell, the
design is up to you! Should it have
four wheels or three? Where
should you place the motor and
cells? What style of car body will
you design?

Towering Towers

How high can you build a tower using only 20 straws and modeling clay? Draw a blueprint to show how you would design your tower.

Parachute Drop

3...2...1... Release! Can you design a soft lander that will prevent a dropped egg from cracking? To meet this challenge, you might use a parachute or bumpers that cushion impact.

Robotic Challenges

Robot competitions offer a more difficult challenge. To assemble a robotic device, you'll need construction materials that include motors and other electronic parts. Your entry's design will be guided by the contest's specific task. Perhaps, it will compete in some sort of robotic basketball game? Score!

My Project Plan

Title of project: _____

Type of project: _____

Teammates (if any): _____

Describe the project.

_____

_____

List the goals of the project.

_____

_____

What materials are needed for the project?

_____

_____

The safety issues (if any) are:

_____

What are some sources of background research?

_____

_____

How will you communicate or display your project?

_____

How will you evaluate the project?

_____

_____

Interactive Glossary

As you learn about each term, add notes, drawings, or sentences in the extra space. This will help you remember what the terms mean. Here are some examples.

Fungi [FUHN•jeye] A kingdom of organisms that have a nucleus and get nutrients by decomposing other organisms

A mushroom is from the kingdom Fungi.

physical change [FIZ•i•kuhl CHAYNJ] Change in the size, shape, or state of matter with no new substance being formed

When I cut paper, the paper has a physical change.

Glossary Pronunciation Key

With every glossary term, there is also a phonetic respelling. A phonetic respelling writes the word the way it sounds, which can help you pronounce new or unfamiliar words. Use this key to help you understand the respellings.

Sound	As in	Phonetic Respelling	Sound	As in	Phonetic Respelling
a	bat	(BAT)	oh	over	(OH•ver)
ah	lock	(LAHK)	oo	pool	(POOL)
air	rare	(RAIR)	ow	out	(OWT)
ar	argue	(AR•gyoo)	oy	foil	(FOYL)
aw	law	(LAW)	s	cell	(SEL)
ay	face	(FAYS)		sit	(SIT)
ch	chapel	(CHAP•uhl)	sh	sheep	(SHEEP)
e	test	(TEST)	th	that	(THAT)
	metric	(MEH•trik)		thin	(THIN)
ee	eat	(EET)	u	pull	(PUL)
	feet	(FEET)	uh	medal	(MED•uhl)
	ski	(SKEE)		talent	(TAL•uhnt)
er	paper	(PAY•per)		pencil	(PEN•suhl)
	fern	(FERN)		onion	(UHN•yuhn)
eye	idea	(eye•DEE•uh)		playful	(PLAY•fuhl)
i	bit	(BIT)		dull	(DUHL)
ing	going	(GOH•ing)	y	yes	(YES)
k	card	(KARD)		ripe	(RYP)
	kite	(KYT)	z	bags	(BAGZ)
ngk	bank	(BANGK)	zh	treasure	(TREZH•er)

Interactive Glossary

acceleration [ak•sel•er•AY•shuhn] Any change in the speed or direction of an object's motion (p. 246)

accurate [AK•yuh•ruht] In measurements, very close to the actual size or value (p. 51)

adaptation [ad•uhp•TAY•shuhn] A trait or characteristic that helps an organism survive (p. 178)

asteroid [AS•tuh•royd] A chunk of rock or iron less than 1,000 km (621 mi) in diameter that revolves around the sun (p. 130)

astronomy [uh•STRAHN•uh•mee] The study of objects in space and their properties (p. 144)

axis [AK•sis] The imaginary line around which Earth rotates (p. 112)

balance [BAL•uhns] A tool used to measure the amount of matter in an object, which is the object's mass (p. 48)

balanced forces [BAL•uhnst FAWRS•iz] Forces that cancel each other out because they are equal in size and opposite in direction (p. 258)

bioengineering [by•oh•en•juh•NEHR•ing] The application of the engineering design process to living things (p. 92)

circuit [SER•kuht] A path along which electric charges can flow (p. 334)

biotechnology [by•oh•TEK•nahl•uh•jee] A product of technology used to benefit organisms and the environment (p. 93)

comet [KAHM•it] A chunk of frozen gases, rock, and dust that revolves around the sun (p. 131)

C

chemical energy [KEM•ih•kuhl EN•er•jee] Energy that can be released by a chemical reaction (p. 295)

community [kuh•MYOO•ni•tee] A group of organisms that live in the same area and interact with each other (p. 164)

conductor [kuhn•DUK•ter] A material that lets heat or electricity travel through it easily (p. 332)

chlorophyll [KLAWR•uh•fil] A green pigment in plants that allows a plant cell to use light to make food (p. 203)

Interactive Glossary

consumer [kuhn•soom•er] A living thing that cannot make its own food and must eat other living things (p. 205)

dwarf planet [DWORF PLAN•it] A nearly round body, slightly smaller than a planet, whose orbit crosses the orbit of another body (p. 130)

control [kuhn•TROHL] The experimental setup to which you will compare all other setups (p. 31)

E

ecosystem [EE•koh•sis•tuhm] A community of organisms and the environment in which they live (p. 163)

criteria [kry•TEER•ee•uh] The standards for measuring success (p. 72)

electric current [ee•LEK•trik KER•uhnt] The flow of electric charges along a path (p. 324)

D

decomposer [dee•kuhm•POH•ser] A living thing that gets energy by breaking down dead organisms and animal wastes into simpler substances (p. 209)

electrical energy [ee•LEK•tri•kuhl EN•er•jee] Energy that comes from electric current (p. 293) energy [EN•er•jee] The ability to cause changes in matter (p. 286)

evidence [EV•uh•duhns] Information collected during a scientific investigation (p. 6)

energy pyramid [EN•er•jee PIR•uh•mid] A diagram that shows how much energy is passed from one organism to the next at each level in a food chain (p. 222)

experiment [ek•SPAIR•uh•muhnt] An investigation in which all the conditions are controlled to test a hypothesis (pp. 25, 30)

engineering [en•juh•NEER•ing] The use of science and math for practical uses, such as the design of structures, machines, and systems (p. 67)

F

food chain [FOOD CHAYN] The transfer of food energy between organisms in an ecosystem (p. 219)

environment [en•VY•ruhn•muhnt] All the living and nonliving things that surround and affect an organism (p. 162)

food web [FOOD WEB] A group of food chains that overlap (p. 220)

Interactive Glossary

force [FAWRS] A push or pull, which may cause a change in an object's motion (p. 254)

gravity [GRAV•ih•tee] The force of attraction between objects, such as the attraction between Earth and objects on it (p. 256)

frequency [FREE•kwuhn•see] A measure of the number of waves that pass a point in a second (p. 358)

H

habitat [HAB•i•tat] The place where an organism lives and can find everything it needs to survive (p. 166)

friction [FRIK•shuhn] A force that acts between two touching objects and that opposes motion (p. 257)

heat [HEET] The energy that moves between objects of different temperatures (p. 306)

G

galaxy [gal•UHK•SEE] A group containing billions of stars, objects that revolve around those stars, gas, and dust (p. 147)

I

instincts [IN•stinkts] Behaviors that an organism inherits and knows how to do without being taught (p. 184)

insulator [IN•suh•layt•er] A material that does not let heat or electricity move through it easily (p. 332)

investigation [in•ves•tuh•GAY•shuhn] A procedure carried out to carefully observe, study, or test something in order to learn more about it (p. 4)

K

kinetic energy [ki•NET•ik EN•er•jee] The energy an object has because of motion (p. 288)

L

light [LYT] A form of energy that can travel through space (p. 374)

M

mechanical energy [muh•KAN•ih•kuhl EN•er•jee] The total potential and kinetic energy of an object (p. 294)

microscopic [my•kruh•SKAHP•ik] Too small to be seen without using a microscope (p. 45)

motion [MOH•shuhn] A change in position of an object (p. 241)

N

niche [NICH] The role a plant or an animal plays in its habitat (p. 166)

Interactive Glossary

opaque [oh•PAYK] Not allowing light to pass through (p. 374)

opinion [uh•PIN•yuhn] A personal belief or judgment based on what a person thinks or feels, but not necessarily based on evidence (p. 9)

orbit [AWR•bit] The path of one object in space around another object (p. 110)

parallel circuit [PAIR•uh•lel SER•kit] An electric circuit that has more than one path for the electric charges to follow (p. 337)

photosynthesis [foh•toh•SIN•thuh•sis] The process that plants use to make their own food (p. 203)

pitch [PICH] The highness or lowness of a sound (p. 358)

planet [PLAN•it] A large, round body that revolves around a star in a clear orbit. (p. 122)

population [pahp•yuh•LAY•shuhn] All the organisms of the same kind that live together in an ecosystem (p. 164)

position [puh•ZISH•uhn] The location of an object in relation to a nearby object or place (p. 241)

prototype [PROH•tuh•typ] The original or test model on which a product is based (p. 70)

R

potential energy [poh•TEN•shuhl EN•er•jee] Energy that an object has because of its position or its condition (p. 288)

reflection [RI•flehk•shuhn] The bouncing of light waves when they encounter an obstacle (p. 376)

prism [PRIZ•uhm] A transparent object that bends and separates white light into the colors of the rainbow (p. 379)

refraction [RI•frak•shuhn] The bending of light waves as they pass from one material to another (p. 378)

producer [pruh•DOOS•er] A living thing, such as a plant, that can make its own food (p. 204)

revolve [ri•VAWLV] To go around another object (p. 110)

Interactive Glossary

rotate [ROH•tayt] To spin on an axis (p. 112)

solar system [SOL•ler SIS•tem] A star and all the planets and other bodies that revolve around it (p. 122)

S

science [SY•uhns] The study of the natural world through observation and investigation (p. 5)

speed [SPEED] The measure of an object's change in position during a certain amount of time (p. 244)

scientific methods [sy•uhn•TIF•ik METH•uhds] The different ways that scientists perform investigations and collect reliable data (p. 24)

spring scale [SPRING SKAYL] A tool used to measure force (p. 49)

stars [STARZ] Huge balls of very hot, glowing gases in space that produce their own light and heat (p. 144)

series circuit [SIR•eez SER•kit] An electric circuit in which the electrical charges have only one path to follow (p. 336)

static electricity [STAT•ik ee•lek•TRIS•uh•tee] The buildup of electric charges on an object (p. 321)

translucent [trahns•LOO•suhnt] Allows only some light to pass through (p. 375)

T

technology [tek•NAHL•uh•jee] The use of science knowledge to solve practical problems (p. 68)

transparent [trahns•PAIR•uhnt] Allows light to pass through (p. 375)

U

temperature [TEM•per•uh•cher] The measure of the average energy of motion of particles of matter, which we feel as how hot or cold something is (p. 305)

unbalanced forces [uhn•BAL•uhnst FAWRS•iz] Forces that cause a change in an object's motion because they don't cancel each other out (p. 258)

thermal energy [THUR•muhl EN•er•jee] The total amount of kinetic energy of the particles in a substance (p. 304)

universe [YOO•nuh•vers] Everything that exists, including galaxies and everything in them (p. 146)

Interactive Glossary

variable [VAIR•ee•uh•buhl] Any condition that can be changed in an experiment (p. 31)

velocity [vuh•LAHS•uh•tee] The speed of an object in a particular direction (p. 244)

volume [VAHL•yoom] The loudness of a sound (p. 358)

wave [WAYV] A disturbance that carries energy, such as sound or light, through matter or space (p. 356)

Index

circuits, 334–339, 347
conductors and insulators, 324, 332–333
current, 324–325
electrical energy, 293, 311
generation of, 325, 338
in homes, 336, 337, 338–339, 347–348
lightning, 322–323
solar generation of, 283–284
static electricity, 320–323
uses of, 325
electron cloud, 318
electron microscopes, 45
electrons, 318–319, 321, 322
electrostatic discharge, 322–323
elliptical galaxies, 148
elliptical orbits, 123
empirical evidence, 6
energy, 285–297, **286.** *See also* electricity; light; sound; thermal energy
change of form, 286–289, 293, 294–295, 308–311, 325, 335, 338, 347
chemical energy, 295, 296
combustion of fuels, 309
conductors and insulators, 324, 332–333
electrical energy, 293, 318–325
flow of, in ecosystems, 218–222
geothermal energy, 309, 311
kinetic energy, 188–291, 294–295, 304–305
light energy, 292–293
mechanical energy, 294–296, 335, 339, 347
photosynthesis, 203
potential energy, 288–289,

294–296
solar radiation, 283–284, 308, 310
sources of, 283, 308–309
transfer of, 306–307
uses of, 310–311, 325
in waves, 356
energy pyramid, 222–223
energy stations, 325, 338
engineering, 67
bioengineering, 92–93
designing a new dog, 229–230
design process, 65–75
Engineering and Technology. *See also* STEM (Science, Technology, Engineering, and Mathematics)
aquariums and terrariums, 193–194
artificial environments, 193–194
dog design, 229–230
electric clothes dryers, 347–348
sound recording, 385–386
space tools, 153–154
sports safety gear, 271–272
environment, 162. *See also* ecosystems
adaptations to, 187, 188–189
artificial, 193–194
biotechnology, 93
biotic and abiotic parts of, 162–163
changes in, 187, 189, 223
humans and, 169, 210
enzymes, 209
equator, 169
equinox, 114, 115
Europa, 130
evaluate, in critical thinking, 5
evidence, 6, 6–7

experiments, 25, 30
ask questions, 30
design the experiment, 31
draw conclusions, 33
hypothesize, 30, 31, 33
in investigations, 30–33
procedures, 32
record and analyze data, 33
variable and control, 31
eyeglasses, 381
eyes, 293

Fahrenheit scale, 47
fall equinox, 114
fall season, 114–115
fans, 294
field trip tools, 42–43
find a problem, in design process, 70
fish and ocean animals
clam, 222
coral reefs, 168, 169
crab, 208
herring, 222
kelp forests, 210, 211
krill, 222
leopard seal, 222
life cycles, 186
moray eel, 164
octopus, 184, 222
phytoplankton, 204, 222
salmon, 186, 222, 223
sea turtle, 159–160, 211
sea urchin, 211
shark, 167, 208
whale, 27
flashlights, 293
flow charts, as models, 28
food
energy from, 286, 295

persistence in making, 74–75
push and pull, 254–255, 260–261

Q

Quaoar, 130
questions, in investigations, 4–5, 24, 30

R

radiation, 307
rain, 187
rainbows, 379
rain forests, 168, 169
Reading Skills
    Cause and Effect, 83, 107, 253, 331
    Compare and Contrast, 40, 121, 285, 303, 355, 373
    Main Idea and Details, 239
    Main Ideas, 23, 161, 317
    Problem-Solution, 65
    Signal Words, 143, 177, 201
    Using Diagrams, 217
    Using Headings, 3
record data, 33, 34
Record Your Data, 19, 39, 57, 81, 99, 141, 175, 231, 273, 275, 315, 371, 387
redesign, in design process, 72–73
red giant stars, 145
Redi, Francesco, 6–7
reference point, 241, 243
reflection, 376
    of light, 292, 376–377, 379
    of sound, 353–354, 362
refraction, 378–379
reproduction, in plants, 182
reptiles
    chameleon, 183

corn snake, 221
lizard, 182
salamander, 210, 221
snake, 188, 189, 206, 220, 221
tiger salamander, 210
turtle, 207, 244
repulsion, 320–321
resistance, 334
revolution
    of planets, 124, 128
    in sun-Earth-moon system, 110–111
revolve, 110
ring systems, of planets, 126, 127
risks, 88
    of technology, 88–89
robotic arms, 153
rockets, 264–265
roller coasters, 288–289
roller skates, 70–73
rotate, 112
rotation
    of planets, 127, 128
    in sun-Earth-moon system, 112–117
rotting food, 6–7
rowing a boat, 255
rubber, 332
rubber bands, 289

S

safety
    on the Internet, 397
    in lightning storms, 323
    in science, xxiii–xxiv
    in sports, 271–272
safety engineers, 277–278
sand dunes, 125
sandpaper, 257
satellite, 110
Saturn, 126, 128, 129

savannas, 164
scanning electron microscope (SEM), 45
scavengers, 208, 219
science, 3–13, **5.** *See also* **inquiry**
    classify and order, 13
    critical thinking, 5
    data, recording and anlyzing, 33
    data display, 34–35
    drawing conclusions, 8, 9, 25, 33
    evidence, 6–7
    experimentation, 25, 30–33
    investigations, 23–35
    logical reasoning, 9
    models, 25, 28–29
    observation, inference, and opinion, 8–9
    observations, 8–9, 25, 26–27
    predict, 26, 27
    process for investigation, 24–25
    questions and investigations, 4–5
    safety in, xxiii–xxiv
    scientific methods, 24, 25
    testing, experimental, 25
science tools, 41–53
    calculators, 52
    computers, 52–53
    for field trips, 42–43
    in the laboratory, 44–45
    to measure, 46–51
scientific methods, 24, 25
scientists
    role of, 4–5
    types of, 12–13
seasons
    on Earth, 114–115
    on Uranus, 127
seed plants, 182
seeds, 182
sequence (order), 13
series circuit, 336